Oregon's

BEST WILDFLOWER HIKES

Northwest Region

D1603013

TEXT AND PHOTOGRAPHY BY
George Wuerthner

WESTCLIFFE PUBLISHERS
www.westcliffepublishers.com

ISBN: 1-56579-391-9

TEXT AND PHOTOGRAPHY: George Wuerthner, © 2001. All rights reserved.
MAP ILLUSTRATIONS: Rebecca Finkel, © 2001. All rights reserved.

EDITORS: Kelly Kordes Anton, Martha Ripley
DESIGN AND PRODUCTION: Rebecca Finkel, F + P Graphic Design, Inc.; Fort Collins, CO
PRODUCTION MANAGER: Craig Keyzer

PUBLISHER: Westcliffe Publishers, Inc.
P.O. Box 1261
Englewood, Colorado 80150-1261
WWW.WESTCLIFFEPUBLISHERS.COM

Printed in China by H & Y Printing, Ltd.

*For more information about other fine books and calendars from
Westcliffe Publishers, please call your local bookstore, contact us
at 1-800-523-3692, write for our free color catalog, or visit us on
the Web at www.westcliffepublishers.com.*

LIBRARY OF CONGRESS CATALOGING-IN-PUBLICATION DATA:

Wuerthner, George
    Oregon's best wildflower hikes, northwest region / text and
photography by George Wuerthner.
        p. cm.
    Includes index.
    ISBN: 1-56579-391-9
    1. Hiking—Oregon—Guidebooks. 2. Wild flowers—
Oregon—Guidebooks 3.Oregon—Guidebooks. I. Title.
GV199.42.07W84   2001
582.13'09795—dc21   2001022521

COVER PHOTO:
*Penstemon and paintbrush
on Mary's Peak, Siuslaw
National Forest, Coast Range.*

PREVIOUS PAGE:
*Lupine and balsamroot,
Tom McCall Preserve,
Columbia River Gorge.*

OPPOSITE:
*Wildflowers below Cone Peak,
Cascade Range, Willamette
National Forest.*

PLEASE NOTE:
Risk is always a factor in backcountry and high-mountain travel. Many
of the activities described in this book can be dangerous, especially when
weather is adverse or unpredictable, and when unforeseen events or
conditions create a hazardous situation. The author has done his best to
provide the reader with accurate information about backcountry travel, as
well as to point out some of its potential hazards. It is the responsibility of
the users of this guide to learn the necessary skills for safe backcountry
travel, and to exercise caution in potentially hazardous areas, especially on
glaciers and avalanche-prone terrain. The author and publisher disclaim
any liability for injury or other damage caused by backcountry traveling,
mountain biking, or performing any other activity described in this book.

Dedication

This book is dedicated to Roger Rosentreter,
BLM state botanist in Idaho, long-time friend, and
botanist extraordinaire. Roger never met a plant he
didn't find interesting. Through his exuberance and
enthusiasm for plants, Roger helped me to better
appreciate the natural world.

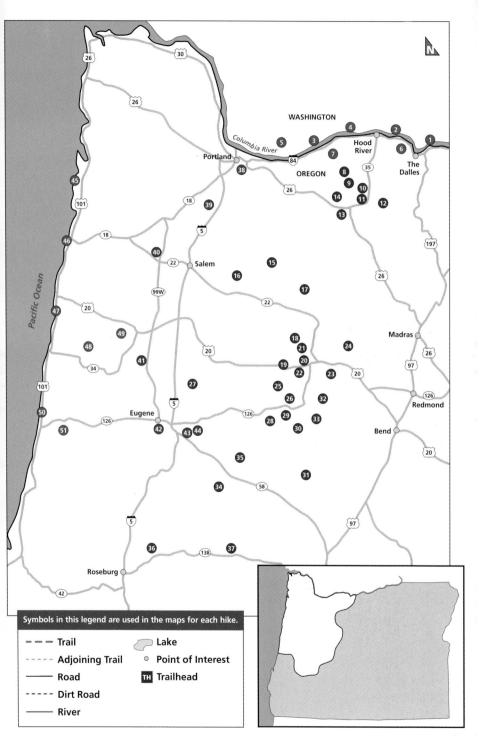

WASHINGTON

Columbia River

OREGON

Portland

Hood River

The Dalles

Salem

Madras

Redmond

Eugene

Bend

Roseburg

Pacific Ocean

Symbols in this legend are used in the maps for each hike.

- – – Trail
- – – Adjoining Trail
- ——— Road
- – – – Dirt Road
- ——— River

Lake
○ Point of Interest
TH Trailhead

OPPOSITE: *Lupine, balsamroot, and ponderosa pine, Mayer State Park, Columbia River Gorge.*

Contents

Wildflower Profiles

Introduction

Western Oregon's varied landscape provides a host of different habitats, ranging from low-elevation Sitka spruce forests along the coast to alpine tundra on the slopes of Mount Hood. Each habitat sports its own diverse array of wildflowers. Not only is there a wide variety of species, but given the elevation range encountered—from sea level to well over 11,000 feet—something is blooming somewhere in the region almost continuously from January through September. Indeed, the prolonged wildflower blooming season makes Oregon one of the most attractive places to live in the entire country.

Selecting Hikes

I selected the hikes in this book based on several criteria: distance from western Oregon's major urban centers in the Willamette Valley, diversity of ecosystem types, season of bloom, and hike length.

You can reach all the hikes in this volume from Portland or Eugene in three hours or less (most are closer). Because the majority of the hikes lie south of Portland, most are also easily reached within three hours from any other major Willamette Valley community, including Salem and Corvallis. Unless otherwise stated, you can drive to all the hikes in a normal two-wheel-drive vehicle.

The diversity of flowering plants you'll see is related to the time of year you hike as well as the diversity of the habitat along the path. I have included hikes that feature a diversity of plant species or an outstanding bloom of a few spectacular plants.

Some hikes will have flowers as early as March, while others see flowers blooming as late as August and even into early September in some years. Most of this difference in flower phenology stems from elevation, but slope, aspect, and proximity to the ocean all influence the peak blooming season. Because of the generally mild climate, the blooming season in Oregon is quite long compared to a place such as the Rockies, where the flowering season is compressed into the summer months. The species you find blooming will vary depending on when you hike the trail. In all likelihood, you'll see some of the species mentioned in the text, especially if you learn to identify them by vegetative features.

Oregon has a strong diversity of habitats. Even within a three-hour drive of Portland, you can potentially explore coastal Sitka spruce forest, oak savanna woodlands, ponderosa pine forest, old-growth Douglas fir, and alpine meadows, just to name a few habitats. You'll find all these ecosystems and many of their associated floras in this book.

This guide includes low-, mid-, and high-elevation hikes. The low-elevation hikes range in elevation from sea level to approximately 1,500 feet, mid-elevation hikes range from 1,500 to 4,000 feet, and high-elevation hikes range from 4,000 feet up to timberline near 7,000 feet.

As a general guideline, you can count on finding blooming flowers at lower elevations beginning in March and continuing through June. Mid-elevation blooms begin in May and continue into July. Most of the high-elevation hikes are not really accessible until mid-July because of snow. Although some look to elevation as an indicator of the fitness level required for a hike, it better signifies when flowers will be blooming. Keep in mind that flowering times can vary as much as a month one way or the other from year to year depending on snowfall, temperatures, and other factors. For a general guide to the peak bloom season for a particular hike, see Appendix A: Hikes by Elevation.

The final criterion I used in selecting hikes was length. All hikes in this book are day hikes; most are less than 8 miles round-trip, and many are shorter. I selected shorter hikes for two reasons: fitness level and time. Many people can't hike a dozen miles in a day—even those in reasonable health. You need to slow down and look at the landscape if you're planning to identify plants. Shorter hikes are more conducive to meeting these goals.

Because of distance considerations, I left out some really fine wildflower viewing, particularly in many of the subalpine and alpine areas. Jefferson Park in the Mount Jefferson Wilderness, for example, is well-known as a spectacular spot for wildflowers. However, the shortest hike there is more than 10 miles round-trip, so I didn't include it in this book. The same goes for Paradise Park on the slopes of Mount Hood, another hike of more than 10 miles.

How to Use This Guide

At the beginning of each hike you will find the following information:

1. **NEAREST TOWN:** Gives the name of the closest large community.

2. **HIGHLIGHTS:** Details the best features of the hike.

3. **TRAIL RATING:** Notes my sense of whether this is an easy, moderate, or difficult hike. Please bear in mind that these are subjective ratings— one person's easy stroll may be another person's wilderness trek. See Appendix B: Hikes by Difficulty to easily find hikes of each difficulty level.

4. **TRAIL LENGTH:** Lists the distance in miles of the described hike. You can use this as a relative measure of difficulty. (As most hikes are less than 8 miles round-trip, I rate most of them as easy or moderate hikes.)

5. **LOCATION:** Gives a designated place name, such as Three Sisters Wilderness or South Beach State Park.

6. **ELEVATION:** Provides the elevation range you will encounter on the hike.

7. **CONTACT:** Tells whom to contact for more information—typically a state or federal land-management agency. I tried my best to provide accurate directions and detailed descriptions of the trails. However, nothing in nature or of human creation is forever. Trails wash out. More

likely, roads wash out. New logging roads are created, wiping out old trails or making previous directions inaccurate. If you prefer to be absolutely certain about everything, call the managing agencies or authorities listed in Appendix C: Contact Phone Numbers to get the most up-to-date information about road or trail conditions and directions.

8. **BLOOM SEASON**: Offers my best guess for the length of the bloom season, from beginning to end. Although this will vary considerably from year to year, it nevertheless provides some relative time frame for trip planning.

9. **PEAK BLOOM**: Offers my best guess for when flowers will be in their prime—but of course this depends on the species under consideration.

10. **DIRECTIONS**: Provides directions, including the major road junctions, highway and road numbers, and distances. Getting to the trailhead is often the most difficult aspect of any hiking adventure.

TRAIL DESCRIPTIONS

While describing the hikes, I tell you to look "by the boulder by the river" or "on the other side of the bridge by the Douglas fir" to locate specific flowers or groups of blooms. Such features—both human and natural—are markers to help you locate your position on the hike. If you note the bridge or the big boulder and look around at the plants I've listed in the book, you should be able to identify at least some of the species you encounter. Flowering trees, bushes, and plants are set off in bold type for easy identification.

It's important that you read the description for each hike before you set out so you know which markers are critical. Some hikes have numerous switchbacks, and I may note special features at certain switchbacks, so it's helpful to know which one you're at as you wind your way up a mountain.

READING MAPS

The maps in this book are designed to get you to the trailhead and show you the general route. They are not, however, detailed enough for off-trail hiking. In addition to the maps provided in the book, I recommend various other maps to help you find your way to the trailhead and aid your exploration of the trails. There isn't, unfortunately, one set of maps that will serve you for all the different hikes described in this book.

One of the maps I recommend is the free Oregon Department of Transportation highway map. This map is essential for getting an overview of the route to the trailhead. The map is available free at visitor centers, gas stations, and chamber of commerce offices.

I also recommend two good atlases that cover Oregon: the *Oregon Road & Recreation Atlas* and the *Oregon Atlas & Gazetteer*. The *Oregon Road & Recreation Atlas,* produced by Benchmark Maps of Medford, has eight recreation maps that show major landowners (Bureau of Land Management, State of Oregon, U.S. Forest Service, etc.) at a scale of 1:750,000. The atlas also contains

37 landscape maps at a scale of 1:250,000. These more detailed maps are useful for finding one's way on back roads.

The competing atlas is DeLorme's *Oregon Atlas & Gazetteer*. The atlas has 72 topographic maps of the state at larger and smaller scales, depending on which part of the state you are viewing. Western Oregon, the Cascades, and west-central Oregon are at a very detailed 1:150,000 scale.

Depending on the land-management agency, you may find maps for a specific area's hikes. For example, most state parks have maps that show all the trails in the park.

The U.S. Forest Service has maps for each of its national forests. These maps are crucial for route-finding given the bewildering number of logging roads that lace most non-wilderness national forest lands. If you're trying to find a trailhead off a major highway, I highly recommend that you obtain the appropriate national forest map that covers the area you are seeking. Although these forest maps do not contain topographical information, they do show most trails. For topographical information, you can usually find Forest Service topo maps of some of the designated wildernesses under agency management. Check with Forest Service offices, local bookstores, sporting goods stores, and even gas stations for maps.

If you are seeking maps that show trails, roads, mountains, lakes, streams, and other geographical features, then the U.S. Geological Survey 1:24,000 maps are the answer. You can usually find USGS maps at sporting goods stores. You can also order maps and obtain a key to topographical maps by contacting the Map Distribution Center directly at USGS Map Sales, P.O. Box 25286, Federal Center, Building 810, Denver, CO 80225, or visiting their website, http://mapping.usgs.gov.

The problem with individual topo maps is their expense. However, a number of CD compilations have all the topo maps for an entire region or even the whole United States on one CD. From the CD, you can print maps that cover the specific area you intend to hike. If you hike often, these CDs are considerably less costly than buying individual maps from the USGS or your local sporting goods or map stores.

Understanding Plant Names

Throughout this book, when I mention a flowering species by its common name, I also include the Latin genus and species names. (Note that I did not include Latin names for non-flowering trees.) In a few instances, with particularly difficult groups such as lupines, some asters, and others, I include only the genus name (*Lupinus sp.*) rather than the genus name and the species name. Nevertheless, knowing the genus name should help you identify the species.

I include Latin names with the common names for several reasons. Common names, particularly for plants, vary enormously. Some species have several commonly used names—for example, serviceberry is variously known as Saskatoon berry, shadberry, and juneberry, depending on the part of the country you're from. The Latin name, on the other hand, is the same no matter where you call home.

Bear in mind, though, that the Latin names and species relationships are under continual revision. Some plants once considered to be different species may now be lumped together under a single genus name, while others that were considered a single species may be divided into two new species. Furthermore, new genetic techniques are changing the entire evolutionary understanding of plant relationships, and in the near future, some major revisions of the entire plant genus and family organization will likely occur. For example, shrubby cinquefoil used to bear the Latin name *Potentilla floribunda*, but it is now referred to as *Dasiphora floribunda*. Some names used in this book may be outdated or no longer valid within a few years. Nevertheless, with Latin names as a guidepost, you can usually determine what the species used to be.

In most cases, I simply name the plants you're likely to see rather than providing detailed descriptions. Hikers interested in learning more about Oregon's flora should have at least one of the major field guides with them to help identify the plants they encounter. There are two varieties of guides—pictorial and taxonomic keys. The best pictorial guides for Oregon include:

- *Plants of the Pacific Northwest Coast* by Jim Pojar and Andy MacKinnon
- *Wildflowers of the Western Cascades* by Robert A. Ross and Henrietta L. Chambers
- *Wildflowers of the Columbia Gorge* by Russ Jolley
- *Wayside Wildflowers of the Pacific Northwest* by Dr. Dee Strickler
- *Trees & Shrubs of Washington* by C.P. Lyons

If you're motivated to learn about every species you see, invest in a good taxonomic key. Unfortunately, no good flora resource exists that covers all of Oregon. M.L. Peck's *Oregon Flora,* published in 1961, is outdated and hard to find. *Flora of the Pacific Northwest* by C. Leo Hitchcock and Arthur Cronquist covers most of Oregon well but hasn't been updated since the 1970s. Since these books appeared, new plants have been discovered and other plants and families have been assigned new names. An updated *Flora of Oregon* book is under way at Oregon State University, but it is years away from completion.

A helpful on-line resource to explore is Flora ID Northwest's CD series featuring the flora of various states. This company provides a color key for all of the flowering plants of the Columbia Gorge, as well as other statewide keys. You can reach Flora ID Northwest via e-mail at flora@ucinet.com, or at their website, www.xidservices.com/FID.

Learning About Plants

If you're buying this book, I presume you want to learn the local wildflowers and flowering shrubs you encounter while hiking in the woods and meadows. Learning the local flora is one way to increase your enjoyment of nature. The ability to name the plants you see adds immeasurably to any hiking experience.

Furthermore, once you learn to distinguish one plant from another, you can begin to see patterns in the locations where different species grow. This heightened awareness leads to ecological appreciation—and with awareness and appreciation comes a desire to protect and preserve.

Protecting Oregon's Native Flora

Oregon has an estimated 4,400 plant species. Botanists, native flora enthusiasts, and government agencies are concerned about the future of 15 percent of these 4,400 species. Some plants are rare simply because they are at the edge of their natural range. Cottongrass, for instance, a species common in the north, reaches its southern limits in Oregon. Other plants are rare because they have unique or special habitat requirements or simply exist in small populations. Certain parts of Oregon have an unusual number of rare or unique species, including three regions covered by this book: the Willamette Valley, the Columbia Gorge, and the Mount Hood vicinity.

The great majority of rare and threatened plants owe their status to human activities, including logging, livestock grazing, fire suppression, farming, and the spread of exotic weeds. The changes in forest structure that come with logging are obvious. Timber cutting has shifted the proportion of older to younger trees toward the younger age classes. Loss of old-growth forests results in less downed woody debris, snags, and larger wood. Large boles and trunks take longer to decompose and provide far more wildlife habitat than do smaller-diameter trees. Heavy equipment compacts soil, which affects seedling and plant establishment. Timber cutting often brings roads, which carry vehicles and are vehicles themselves for the spread of invasive animal and plant life. For instance, a root rot that attacks Port Orford cedar, a species unique to southwest Oregon, is spread in the mud carried by logging trucks.

Fire suppression is another human activity that threatens plants. Most of the justification for putting out fires is to "save" forests. In truth, all of Oregon's major plant communities are adapted to periodic fire. Even the wet west-side old-growth forests tend to burn on occasion. Fires help recycle nutrients, cleanse the forest of pathogens, reduce competition between species, and create snags, downed logs, and other structural features critical to ecosystem stability.

Farming has probably obliterated more of Oregon's native flora than any other human impact. Approximately 15 percent of the state has been plowed and cleared for agriculture. Farming requires removing the native vegetation and favoring one or only a few domesticated species on the site. This obviously simplifies and destroys native ecosystems.

Farming impacts are not, however, evenly distributed across the state. In the Willamette Valley, despite having the highest human population in the state, it is farming, not cities or sprawl, that has destroyed the majority of native plant communities. Where farming hasn't directly plowed over native plant communities, it has fragmented them, affecting genetic exchange, species migration, and ecological maintenance processes such as fire. Though the Willamette Valley produces a wide variety of crops and orchard products, grass seed and pasture vegetation are the two largest crops produced by acreage.

Statewide, livestock grazing has had the greatest impact on native flora, although its impact in western Oregon's dense forest is significantly less than east of the Cascades. Livestock eat the more desirable species, leaving behind unpalatable "weedy" species. They eat the blooms on flowers, thereby reducing seed production and affecting pollinators. Without blooms, pollinators may not have sufficient food resources, thus leading to the decline or even local extinction

of some species of butterflies and other insects. Livestock also reduce fine fuels such as dried grasses, thus reducing fires and significantly altering natural fire regimes. Further, trampling livestock have destroyed stream-bank vegetation and increased the entrenchment of streams, degrading riparian ecosystems.

Exotic weed invasion is also a widespread problem, particularly in more open land-scapes. Indeed, exotic weeds make up 10 to 25 percent of the plant species typically found even in protected landscapes. The spread of exotic weeds is usually favored by human disturbances, including logging, farming, and live-stock production. When nutrients, water, and space are going to an alien species, there is that much less available for native species. Some exotic weeds, such as Himalayan blackberry, are very aggressive invaders, crowding out native species. The best control over exotic weeds is to limit the human factors that assist their spread and growth.

All lovers of the natural world should be concerned about the long-term, global biological impoverishment occurring with the decline in biodiversity. The loss of one or two species may not cause a disruption in ecosystem function, but if you remove enough species, at some point you may reach a threshold where the ecosystem will collapse.

To learn more about Oregon's rich flora and how to help preserve it, contact the Native Plant Society of Oregon at NPSOregon.org.

ABOVE: *Paintbrush and serviceberry on Hamilton Mountain, Beacon Rock State Park.*

Wildflower
Hike 1 ## Dalles Mountain Ranch

Balsamroot in a meadow below the Columbia Hills, Dalles Mountain Ranch State Park.

Located in the Columbia Hills flanking the Columbia River, Dalles Mountain Ranch anchors the eastern edge of the Columbia Gorge National Scenic Area. Congress created the 300,000-acre Columbia River Gorge National Scenic Area in 1986 to protect the scenic qualities of the 80-mile-long canyon carved by the Columbia River. The gorge is the only low-elevation route across the entire Cascade Range and has for centuries been a major corridor for the movement of wildlife and people. As it traverses the Cascades, the scenic area offers a diversity of habitats, from lush rainforest in the west to dry, bunchgrass hills in the east. More than 800 plant species call this area home.

Nearest Town	The Dalles
Highlights	Spacious hills flanking the Columbia River, bursting with the color of spring wildflowers
Trail Rating	moderate
Trail Length	More than 1.0 mile each way
Location	In Washington, just across the Columbia River from The Dalles, Oregon
Elevation	1,000–3,200 feet
Contact	Horsethief Lake State Park, Washington, 509-767-1159
Bloom Season	April to June
Peak Bloom	late April
Directions	From The Dalles, take US 197 north across the Columbia River. Turn right onto WA 14, drive east about a mile, and turn left onto The Dalles Mountain Road. (If you reach Horsethief Lake State Park, you've gone too far on WA 14.) Drive 2.7 miles up the dirt road to the park boundary (not well-marked). Watch for a hilltop house: When the house appears for the second time, the park boundary, marked by a fence, is up ahead. Another 0.7 mile beyond the park boundary (about 3.5 miles from the pavement) you reach a road junction where barns and other ranch buildings stand. Turn left (north). After 1.4 miles on this steep dirt road, you reach a locked gate and turnaround area with parking for the Columbia Hills Natural Area Preserve.

In 1992 the State of Washington purchased Dalles Mountain Ranch, which lies within the boundaries of the national scenic area. The 3,100-acre southern section of the ranch is now part of The Dalles Mountain Ranch State Park; the northern section is managed by the Washington Department of Natural Resources as the 2,997-acre Columbia Hills Natural Area Preserve. Together, these areas provide infinite opportunities for wildflower explorations and offer a visually spectacular experience. On a clear day you can catch great views of Mount Hood. Visitors are free to wander at will about The Dalles Mountain Ranch State Park, but access to the natural preserve is limited to hiking the roadway within the preserve. Both park and preserve have only minimal development—no official trails, nor any other facilities. Even so,

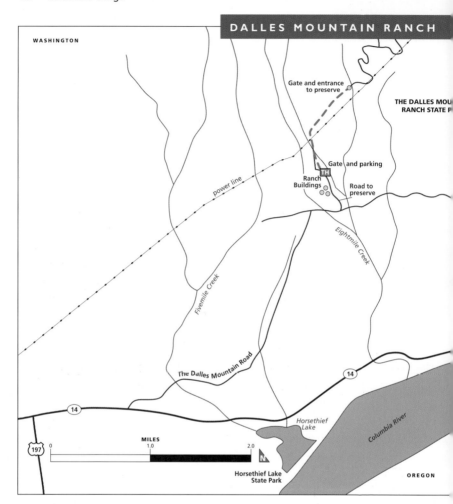

as a hiking destination the area is superb. If you wish to explore for several days, you can find camping facilities at Horsethief Lake State Park.

You have several hiking options in the park; I discuss another easy hike at the end of this chapter. Here I describe a walk along an old road from one gate, at the junction by the ranch headquarters, to another gate at the entrance of the preserve, and beyond. Just past the private house on your left, you cross the first gate and enter the ranch's spacious, open grasslands on a south-facing slope. Since you don't find a lot of topographical variety here, the flowers are fairly well distributed throughout the entire hillside.

The south-facing slope here greens up early in spring and can turn yellow with **arrowleaf balsamroot** *(Balsamorhiza sagittata)* blooms. Three rare plants— **obscure buttercup** *(Ranunculus triternatus)*, **Douglas' draba** *(Draba douglasii)* and **hot-rock penstemon** *(Penstemon deustus)* can be found here. The park and preserve also protect outstanding representatives of the Idaho fescue/ houndstongue/hawkweed vegetation types and the **Douglas' buckwheat** *(Eriogonum douglasii)*/Sandberg bluegrass vegetation types.

The open grasslands that make up the park are mostly Idaho fescue, a densely tufted bunchgrass. Native to the Columbia Basin, bunchgrasses grow in clumps, hence their name. Since most of the interior West did not support large, grazing herds of animals such as bison, most native grasses are relatively intolerant of heavy grazing pressure. In much of the region, the native bunch-grasses have suffered severely from heavy livestock grazing in modern times.

Clumps of the yellow, sunflowerlike blooms of **arrowleaf balsamroot** are almost everywhere. American Indians used to consume the large taproot. Elk and deer graze the young shoots, while bighorn sheep are very fond of the flower head and leaves. The plants are extremely tolerant of heavy grazing, which may account for their abundance despite years of livestock herbivory.

Mixed in among the **balsamroot** are the purple-blue, pealike spikes of **broadleaf lupine** *(Lupinus latifolius)*. The **lupine** may get so thick that they actually color the hills blue. **Lupine** can be fatal to livestock if consumed in large quantities, but other wildlife, including elk, deer, and bear, feed upon the plants. A legume, **lupine** has nodules with bacteria on the roots that fix nitrogen from the air and make it available for plant growth, thereby enriching the soil.

About 0.75 mile from the entrance, the road pulls close to a creek drainage where you find a fair amount of Oregon white oak growing on the northeast- and east-facing slopes. Under the oaks grow **chokecherry** *(Prunus virginiana)*, a shrub with clusters of white flowers in spring and blue-black berries in August. The fruit is edible if not altogether tasty. Animals including birds and black bears seek out the fruit; deer and elk graze on the twigs.

Growing beneath the oaks are lovely clusters of white blooming **Howell's brodiaea** *(Brodiaea howellii)*, also known as **Triteleia howellii**. It is particularly common at the top of The Dalles Mountain Road. **Small-flowered prairiestar** *(Lithophragma*

BARESTEM DESERT-PARSLEY
Lomatium nudicaule

Barestem desert-parsley is common on open grassy slopes throughout the Columbia River Gorge and along The Dalles Mountain Road. It has a bluish stem arising from a stout taproot. The leaves are egg-shaped, and the yellow flowers grow in a compact head. The young leaves of this plant taste a bit like celery and were eaten by American Indians as a cure for tuberculosis. This accounts for the other common name for the plant—the **consumption plant.**

parviflora) also grow among the oaks. This delicate white flower is a type of saxifrage. Near the trees are patches of **orange ridge fiddleneck** *(Amsinckia retrorsa)*. This member of the borage *(Boraginaceae)* family looks something like the **forget-me-not** *(Mysotis sp.)* to which it's related.

As you continue up the slope, the road gradually turns to the northeast and traverses the slope toward the gate near the Columbia Hills Natural Area Preserve entrance.

There are more **balsamroot** and **lupine** all along this stretch, but also **barestem desert-parsley** *(Lomatium nudicaule)*. A variety of different **lomatiums** live in the Columbia Gorge, but this one is rather distinctive with a thick central stalk rising from oval basal leaves. Another **lomatium** found along the road is **slender-fruited desert-parsley** *(Lomatium leptocarpum)*, which has thin, narrow, highly dissected leaves. **Lomatiums** are high in vitamin C and were consumed in quantity by the American Indians.

A real highlight of the open grasslands toward the top of the preserve is the endemic **Dalles Mountain buttercup** *(Ranunculus reconditus)*. You may also see **Gairdner's penstemon** *(Penstemon gairdneri)*, **Douglas' buckwheat, Douglas' draba** *(Draba douglasii)*, and the beautiful pink **bitterroot** *(Lewisia rediviva)*.

Another relatively rare species is the **Yakima milk-vetch** *(Astragalus reventiformis)*. This species can easily be confused with another **white milk-vetch** growing on the ranch, known as the **Hood River milk-vetch** *(Astragalus hoodianus)*. You can tell them apart by the leaves. **Hood River milk-vetch** leaves are less robust than those of the **Yakima milk-vetch**. More than 50 kinds of **milk-vetch** exist in Washington, making identification somewhat problematic. This member of the pea family, like all legumes, captures free nitrogen from the atmosphere and fixes it, making it available in a form usable by plants.

When you reach the fence and gate for the Columbia Hills Natural Area Preserve, you can continue—as long as you remain on the road—to the top of 3,200-foot Stacker Butte, which provides a fine view of the surrounding region.

Another hiking option at the ranch is an easy mile-or-so hike that takes off just 0.4 mile past the park boundary you looked for in the approach to the hike just described. Watch for a locked metal gate on your left where the road makes a 90-degree turn to the east. If you reach the road junction leading to the Columbia Hills Natural Area Preserve, you've gone too far. Parking for several vehicles is available here. An old, relatively level ranch track, suitable for small children, leads across the hill to an old homestead with fine views of Mount Hood.

Catherine Creek

Oak trees along the Catherine Creek Trail,
Gifford Pinchot National Forest.

White Salmon, Washington	***Nearest Town***
A grassy ponderosa pine/oak savanna with great views of the Columbia River	***Highlights***
easy	***Trail Rating***
2.0 miles round-trip	***Trail Length***
Gifford Pinchot National Forest	***Location***
270–500 feet	***Elevation***
Wind River Ranger District, Gifford Pinchot NF, 360-891-5000	***Contact***
March to May	***Bloom Season***
April	***Peak Bloom***
From Portland, drive east on I-84 to Hood River. Cross the Columbia toward White Salmon, then turn right onto WA 14 and drive east 5.8 miles. At Rowland Lake, turn left onto the old highway, now a county road, and drive 1.2 miles around the lake and up a hill to parking and the trailhead on the left.	***Directions***

Most of the lower-elevation terrain in the Columbia River Gorge is in private hands. Catherine Creek is one of the few areas where the Gifford Pinchot National Forest nearly reaches the river. The area offers a very scenic landscape dominated by an open meadow with gentle terrain for hiking. Although you find a fair amount of **poison oak** *(Rhus diversiloba)* throughout the area, it's still possible to wander off-trail here for hours of exploration. The trail dries out early in the season, reaching its prime bloom in early to mid-April.

When I hiked it in mid-May, many flowers had already gone to seed.

From the parking lot, go through the gate and follow the old road to the right. As the road goes across slabs of rock, you immediately see **tapertip onion** *(Allium acuminatum)*. These pretty flowers grow from an edible, spicy root. Also on these shallow soil sites are found the edible **bitterroot** *(Lewisia rediviva)*, named for explorer Meriwether Lewis (see sidebar at left). **Common centaury** *(Centaurium erythraea)* and **northern buckwheat** *(Eriogonum compositum)* thrive on rocky outcrops as well.

The trail descends down to Catherine Creek, a small flow no more than 5 or 6 feet wide. **Yarrow** *(Achillea millefolium)* grows near the creek. As you descend down the old road toward the creek, there is more **northern buckwheat** on the left slope. The lovely **ball head cluster lily** *(Brodiaea congesta)*, a type of onion, also grows here. Less obvious to the casual visitor are the tiny, bicolored **true baby stars** *(Linanthus bicolor)*, also

BITTERROOT
Lewisia rediviva

Bitterroot is a conspicuous flower that seems leafless. The leaves sprout early in the spring but usually wither before the lovely pink blossoms appear. The plant typically appears in April, growing on rocky outcrops and dry soils.

Bitterroot was named for Meriwether Lewis of the Lewis and Clark expedition. Lewis and Clark first described the plant in journals from their historic trip across the country from 1804 to 1806. Lewis collected the plant in the Bitterroot Valley of Montana (it is the state flower of Montana). American Indians collected the bulbs in the spring and ate them; the white inner core was baked, boiled, or eaten raw. **Bitterroot**, though, is not likely to be a favorite food unless you're desperately hungry. As its name indicates, the taste is rather harsh.

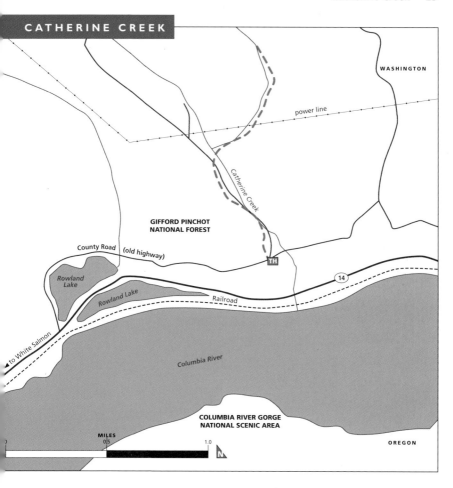

CATHERINE CREEK

WASHINGTON

power line

Catherine Creek

GIFFORD PINCHOT
NATIONAL FOREST

County Road (old highway)

Rowland
Lake

Rowland Lake

Railroad

14

to White Salmon

Columbia River

COLUMBIA RIVER GORGE
NATIONAL SCENIC AREA

MILES
0.5

1.0

OREGON

known as **flax flower**. More Oregon white oak are clustered along the creek. Growing under the oak are large-leaved vines of **wild cucumber** *(Marah oreganus)* with tiny, white flowers. Opposite the oaks on the left, you can find the shrub **ocean-spray** *(Holodiscus discolor)*.

The trail continues along the creek, and in one place there is **yellow monkey-flower** *(Mimulus guttatus)*, a plant typical of seep areas. The area is also thick with **Suksdorf's desert-parsley** *(Lomatium suksdorfii)*, a ball of leaves showing large, flat-topped, flowering yellow heads.

You will eventually intersect the creek and cross it. The trail begins to ascend a hill, passing a corral and an old barn en route. Just above the barn site, you'll see several color phases of **deerbrush** *(Ceanothus integerrimus)*. **Deerbrush** look similar to lilac, and are sometimes called **wild lilac** for that reason. Most **ceanothus** species are well-adapted to fire; their seeds tend to sprout after a fire.

About 0.5 mile beyond the creek, you pass under a power line. Look for bicolored **Howell's brodiaea** *(Brodiaea howellii)*, another member of the onion family. If you continue up the road, you'll eventually end up on a plateau. I chose to go left at the fork and ambled farther up the creek drainage through some nice pine. It appears that a fire recently burned the area, killing the smaller trees. Fires are a natural thinning agent for these kinds of ponderosa pine ecosystems; larger trees are adapted to the fire and usually suffer no harm from the blazes.

Growing abundantly beneath the pine is **miner's lettuce** *(Claytonia perfoliata)*. The stem leaves are fused to form a disk just below the small white flowers of this plant. It's called **miner's lettuce** because early settlers used it as a salad ingredient; it's also high in vitamin C. At this point, the trail just fizzles out, and I returned to the trailhead about 1 mile away. Note the column basalt in the canyon walls of Catherine Creek. Column basalt is formed when lava cools and shrinks rapidly.

Hamilton Mountain

A view of the Columbia River Gorge from Hamilton Mountain.

Portland	**Nearest Town**
Cliff-side meadows with great views of the Columbia Gorge	**Highlights**
moderate	**Trail Rating**
8.0 miles round-trip	**Trail Length**
Beacon Rock State Park	**Location**
400–2,436 feet	**Elevation**
Washington State Parks, 360-753-5755	**Contact**
April to July	**Bloom Season**
May to June	**Peak Bloom**
From Portland, drive east on I-84 to the Bridge of the Gods and cross the Columbia. Turn left onto WA 14 and drive west 5.0 miles to Beacon Rock State Park. Take the signed right turn for the campground and drive uphill to the trailhead at its north end. Park here or at the picnic area trailhead, just below the campground, which unites with the other trailhead in less than 0.5 mile.	**Directions**

The hike up Hamilton Mountain takes you through coniferous forests to open steep meadows and cliff-side hanging gardens. The climb is steady but not difficult, with lots of switchbacks en route. Along the way, you pass several fine waterfalls that make for pleasant turnaround points for those not inclined to go all the way to the lower or upper summits. The actual top of the mountain offers little to look at, but a lower ridge just prior to the final summit climb offers grassy, sweeping slopes with unobstructed views up and down the Columbia River.

Hamilton Mountain lies within the 4,482-acre Beacon Rock State Park. Beacon Rock, visible near the riverbank for miles up and down the Columbia River, was aptly named by Lewis and Clark, who camped at its base in 1805. The rock is an andestie plug—the inner neck of an ancient volcano. For American Indians living along the river, the rock signaled the end of rapids and the start of smooth water for the rest of the way west to the ocean. A trail popular with rock climbers now leads to the top of the rock.

The trail up Hamilton Mountain begins at the north end of the campground. At the campground trailhead you will see old-growth Douglas fir. **Vine maple** *(Acer circinatum)* and **red alder** *(Alnus rubra)* dominate understory trees. The ground cover includes **sorrel** *(Oxalis oregana),* **Oregon grape** *(Mahonia nervosa),* **Pacific bleedingheart** *(Dicentra formosa),* **candyflower** *(Claytonia sibirica),* and **vanillaleaf** *(Achlys triphylla).* As you amble up the trail from the first switchback, you'll encounter **cow-parsnip** *(Heracleum lanatum),* **trillium** *(Trillium ovatum),* **palmate**

SERVICEBERRY
Amelanchier alnifolia

Serviceberry is an early-flowering shrub that is covered with white blossoms. The leaves are 1–2 inches long and oval in shape with teeth on all or part of the outer edges. The fruit is dark blue and bears a good resemblance to a blueberry.

Serviceberry thrives across North America and has several common names, including **shadberry, juneberry,** and **Saskatoon berry.** *Alnifolia* means "alder-leaved" after the leaves' resemblance to those of the alder tree. **Serviceberry** was an important food for American Indians, who often mixed the fruit with fat to create pemmican. The shrub is also a favorite of wildlife: Bears and birds eat the berries. Elk, deer, and other browsers feed on the twigs.

coltsfoot *(Petasites palmatus)*, and **bracken fern** *(Pteridium aquilinum)*. On my hike, I even saw one **Pacific rhododendron** *(Rhododendron macrophyllum)*. The trail leaves the forest momentarily, entering a power-line corridor in which the overstory forest has been removed. In this sunny area, you will find lots of **thimbleberry** *(Rubus parviflorus)* with its large maplelike leaves and ample white blossoms. The sun-loving exotic **Scotch broom** *(Cytisus scoparius)*, with their yellow pealike flowers, grow profusely in the power-line corridor. Along the trail in this section you'll also see **wild strawberry** *(Fragaria vesca)*, **false Solomon's seal** *(Smilacina racemosa)*, and **red huckleberry** *(Vaccinium parvifolium)*. A curious flower also found here is the **inside-out flower** *(Vancouveria hexandra)*. The flower looks something like a white shooting star. Its Latin name honors an English sea captain, George Vancouver, for whom the cities in British Columbia and Washington state are named. **Star-flowered false Solomon's seal** *(Smilacina stellata)* and **trailing blackberry** *(Rubus ursinus)* also live here.

The trail joins the forest again, and the flowers change dramatically with the shade. **Hooker fairy-bell** *(Disporum hookeri)*, with its downward-hanging flowers, live here, along with **three-leaved anemone** *(Anemone deltoidea)*, **yellow violet** *(Viola glabella)*, and **striped coral-root** *(Corallorhiza striata)*, an orchid. The **coral-root** has no chlorophyll; instead, it parasitizes the roots of other plants for its food.

In this forest, watch for a huge piece of petrified wood with a plaque honoring Ed Hardy, the first superintendent of Beacon Rock State Park. Scattered around on the ground you can find more **vanillaleaf, candyflower, trillium, thimbleberry, Pacific bleedingheart, sword-fern** *(Polystichum munitum)*, and **Oregon grape**. There is a trail junction—stay left on the larger trail that is fringed by **candyflower**.

The trail comes out under the power-line corridor again and follows it for a ways. Along here you'll see **thimbleberry, Scotch broom**, bigleaf maple, **chokecherry** *(Prunus virginiana)*, **Indian paintbrush** *(Castilleja hispida)*, **fringecup** *(Tellima grandiflora)*, and **lupine** *(Lupinus sp.)*. Back at the forest edge, I spotted a **honeysuckle** *(Lonicera ciliosa)*.

Eventually, the trail begins an uphill switchback under the power line, and you'll end up by a bench adjacent to the power-line tower. From here you have nice views up the river valley and to the face of Hamilton Mountain. Oregon white oak grows just behind the bench. Since it prefers drier terrain, Oregon white oak is more common farther east in the Gorge; it's unusual to see it this far west. Adjacent to the bench is the dainty **broad-leaved starflower** *(Trientalis latifolia)* and **arnica** *(Arnica latifolia)*. The **oval-leaved viburnum** *(Viburnum ellipticum)* shrub grows by the tower.

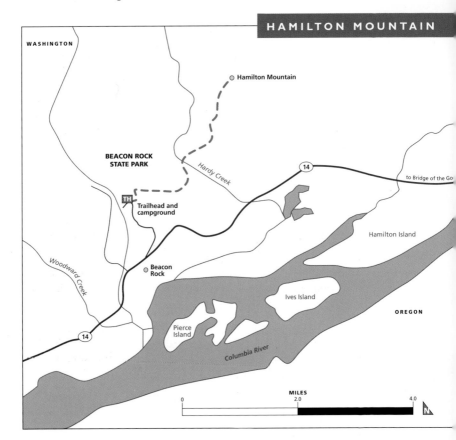

Just beyond the bench is a trail junction. The trail to the right heads back down the mountain to the picnic parking area. The main trail, which lies straight ahead, goes to the waterfalls and Hamilton Mountain.

Just beyond the trail junction, you enter the woods again. **Vanillaleaf** and **Hooker fairy-bell** thrive here. **Pacific waterleaf** (*Hydrophyllum tenuipes*) grow in abundance as well. The trail climbs steadily uphill through a lovely Douglas fir forest, which includes some very large trees. Other plants that live along the trail here include **thimbleberry, starflower, false Solomon's seal,** and plenty of **vine maple**. When you come to a wooden bridge, you'll see **maidenhair fern** (*Adiantum pedatum*), a delicate and lacy plant.

The trail swings around the creek drainage and into the next creek and the site of Hardy Falls. A second trail descends rightward to a platform where once you could probably have viewed the falls. Now trees obscure them. Some **ocean-spray** (*Holodiscus discolor*) grow near the viewing platform.

Continue on the main trail to a junction near Rodney Falls. Go left to see Pool of the Winds and right to continue on this hike. The trail switchbacks down to a bridge over the creek; the bridge provides the best view of Rodney Falls. If you have small children or are pressed for time, you may well wish to turn around at this point. From the falls onward, the trail climbs dozens of switchbacks, all the way to the top of Hamilton Mountain. Although it is 2.6 miles from the creek to the summit, the switchbacks make the elevation gain tolerable —and the best wildflower displays and views are ahead.

As you climb up to the ridge above the falls, you'll pass some more **maidenhair fern**. Once you gain the ridge above the falls, the trail begins a switchback through beautiful Douglas fir forest. Here and there in the understory, you may see some **Pacific dogwood** *(Cornus nuttallii),* a lovely tree with large white blossoms. At the turn for the second switchback, you'll see **wild rose** *(Rosa gymnocarpa),* **ocean-spray,** and **thimbleberry**. Along the fourth switchback, I saw more **striped coral-root**. At the sixth switchback, you gain the ridge where you can again look down into Hardy Creek.

Just beyond is a trail junction without a sign. The left fork goes along the creek. Take the right fork, which leads to more switchbacks. At the fourth switchback you encounter a boulder of breccia (a conglomerate of volcanic rock formed when molten lava mixes with chunks of partially-cooled lava). By the time you reach the thirteenth switchback, the trail begins to get rocky with cliffs adjacent to the path. On the rocky wall, look for pink-flowered **plectritis** *(Plectritis congesta),* a flower that is more common the higher you are up the mountain. **Stonecrop** *(Sedum oregonense),* a succulent species that grows well on dry, rocky sites, also lives here. Also growing on the rock face is **cliff larkspur** *(Delphinium menziesii).*

At the fourteenth switchback, you're granted a fine view of Beacon Rock. **Chocolate lily** *(Fritillaria lanceolata),* along with the **oval-leaved viburnum** and **serviceberry** *(Amelanchier alnifolia)* shrubs, are growing here. You encounter cement stairs, which were designed to help reduce erosion. Go up two more switchbacks to the sixteenth one, and you'll encounter another shrub—**buckbrush** *(Ceanothus sanguineus).* **Paintbrush** and **wild rose** abound along this stretch of trail as well.

As the trail ascends the ridge, there are more openings in the forest and grassy patches on the steep slopes. You'll see some **fern-leaf desert-parsley** *(Lomatium dissectum)* and **meadow death-camas** *(Zigadenus venenosus).* **Death-camas** has narrow, lilylike leaves and white flowers. As its name suggests, the plant is poisonous.

Eventually, you reach a rock ridge with sweeping views and cliffs above. Take a moment to savor the views of the gorge and Mount Hood. If you have small children with you, watch them closely: The cliffs drop hundreds of feet from this ridge. Covering the cliffs are pink **spreading phlox** *(Phlox diffusa),* with lesser amounts of **big head clover** *(Trifolium macrocephalum)* and **field** chickweed *(Cerastium arvense)*. If you are inclined to turn around at this point, consider going a bit farther—the views only get better.

If you go on, the trail climbs three quick switchbacks, then begins a long traversing of the slope. Plenty of **larkspur,** pink **plectritis, chocolate lily, red Indian-paintbrush** *(Castilleja miniata),* and **serviceberry** grow along this stretch of trail. The open, steep slopes offer great views down the gorge and up Hardy Creek.

You eventually reach the base of Hamilton Mountain's final summit. From this rocky ridge, you have views of Bonneville Dam. On the ridge, you'll see lots of **serviceberry** along with **kinnikinnick** *(Arctostaphylos uva-ursi).* Supposedly, American Indians dried **kinnikinnick** and smoked the leaves as a tobacco substitute.

From here, it's another 0.8 mile, with more switchbacks, to the summit. For the best views, take a long look around, and then start back down the trail. At about 100 yards back down, you should notice a path leading off to the left and up the slope. Follow this path as it climbs steadily to the crest of the ridge; when it tops out, you can savor one of the best views in the entire Columbia Gorge. A large, grassy meadow covers the ridge, and the adjacent slopes are dotted with **red Indian-paintbrush, chickweed, chocolate lily,** and other flowers. **Serviceberry** is abundant along the margins of the meadow.

Despite the abundance of flowers in the meadow, it's hard to focus downward with such a spectacular view in all directions. You can look up and down the entire Columbia River, across to Mount Hood, and back along the Hardy Creek drainage. This is as far as most will want to go. After enjoying the view, retrace your steps back to the campground.

Dog Mountain

Wildflower Hike 4

Mollie Matteson and a friend identify plants on Dog Mountain, Gifford Pinchot National Forest.

Carson, Washington	**Nearest Town**
Outstanding views and cliffside flower gardens of lupine and balsamroot	**Highlights**
difficult	**Trail Rating**
0.6 mile to the first trail junction, 3.7 miles to the top of the mountain	**Trail Length**
Columbia River Gorge National Scenic Area	**Location**
200–2,948 feet	**Elevation**
Gifford Pinchot National Forest, 360-891-5000	**Contact**
March to July	**Bloom Season**
May	**Peak Bloom**
From Carson, Washington (about 30 miles east of Washougal), drive 9.0 miles east on WA 14 to the trailhead, just past Grant Lake and adjacent to the highway.	**Directions**

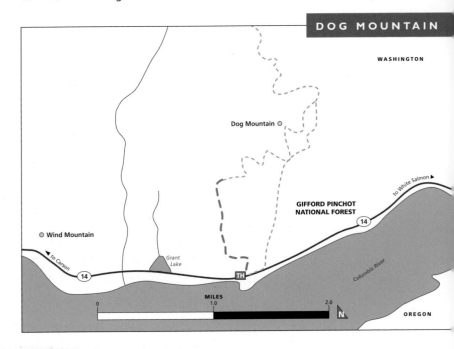

Dog Mountain lies in the middle of the spectacular Columbia River Gorge on the Washington side, about halfway between Stevenson and White Salmon. The mountain rises abruptly from the Columbia River to 2,948 feet and features steep meadows on the west and southwest faces near the top. The elevation gain of nearly 3,000 feet in less than 4 miles, from the river to the top of the mountain, gives a hint about the trail that switchbacks repeatedly up the face of the mountain. The brow of the mountain was the location of an old Forest Service fire lookout, and, indeed, you feel as if you are perched on the edge of an eagle's nest with the entire Columbia River Gorge unfolding below you. You can gain an even more impressive view, including Mount Hood, by climbing to the south peak of Dog Mountain.

Dog Mountain lies in the middle of the gorge at a transition point from the wet west side of the Cascades to the more arid east side in the rain-shadow of the mountains. Ponderosa pine, more common east of the mountains, along with Douglas fir and bigleaf maple trees more common in western Oregon, are mixed in here. Adjacent to the trail sign beneath a towering ponderosa pine grow **broadleaf lupine** (*Lupinus latifolius*). **Poison oak** (*Rhus diversiloba*) also lives here, so keep to the trail. The lovely white blossoms of the **serviceberry** (*Amelanchier alnifolia*) shrub grow in the forest near the outhouse located about 100 yards from the trailhead. **Serviceberry** have an edible bluish fruit, something like a blueberry, that ripens in August. Elk and deer also find the shrub's branches quite tasty.

From the outhouse, the trail begins a steep climb 800 feet up the face of the mountain, switchbacking 10 times before reaching a trail junction in little more than 0.5 mile. The forest near the beginning of the climb consists mostly of Douglas fir with an understory of **tall Oregon grape** *(Mahonia aquifolium),* with its distinctive evergreen, hollylike leaves and yellow cluster of flowers. The plant takes its name from the purple, grapelike fruit that it produces late in the summer.

Just beyond the first switchback, where the trail turns east to traverse the slope, you can find a few **chocolate lily** *(Fritillaria lanceolata)* on the upslope side. The American Indians of the coast used to collect the bulbs of this flower, boil them, and eat them. Reportedly, the bulbs taste something like bitter rice. The rocky slope also harbors nine-leaf **desert-parsley** *(Lomatium triternatum).* American Indians gathered and consumed **desert-parsley** leaves and roots. A "leggy" pealike plant with purple flowers, **American vetch** *(Vicia americana)* sprawl across the slope. Like all legumes, **vetch** can capture free nitrogen from the atmosphere, fix it in its roots, and make it available for plant growth.

As you approach the second switchback, keep an eye out for the white blossoms of **wild strawberry** *(Fragaria vesca)* lying close to the ground. If you've ever tasted a **wild strawberry**, you know we've lost a great deal of the taste by domesticating this plant.

The third switchback is relatively short, continuing up through a Douglas fir forest. At the beginning of the fourth switchback there is a **bitter cherry** *(Prunus emarginata).* **Bitter cherry** is more like a small tree, covered with dense terminal clusters of white flowers in April.

The fourth switchback is very short. You pass a **Pacific dogwood** tree *(Cornus nuttallii).* The tree's Latin name refers to Thomas Nuttall, an early botanist who explored the Columbia River

CHOCOLATE LILY
Fritillaria lanceolata

Chocolate lily has mottled, greenish-yellow flowers that hang down singly or in clusters. The leaves are lance-shaped—hence the Latin name *lanceolata.* **Chocolate lily** are common in grassy meadows and open woods along the coast, but they also thrive inland along major rivers such as the Columbia.

Chocolate lily's bulb has numerous ricelike bulblets, giving rise to its other common name, **rice root**. Coastal peoples of the Pacific Northwest formerly ate the bulbs. The bulbs are said to taste like rice but with a slightly bitter flavor.

region near Fort Vancouver in 1834. Just after the upper turn of the fourth switchback you can also find **common vetch** *(Vicia sativa).*

Along the sixth switchback, a few more ponderosa pine mix with clumps of **serviceberry.** At the turn, pause for good views of the gorge. **Broad-leaved starflower** *(Trientalis latifolia)* grow in the understory of the forest.

At the seventh switchback is a good specimen of bigleaf maple, along with more **serviceberry.**

With the eighth switchback you begin a long traversing of the slope and pass through a windswept Oregon white oak grove. In the open understory you find lots of **lupine** and the showy yellow blossoms of **deltoid balsamroot** *(Balsamorhiza deltoidea).* You can also spot **grand hounds-tongue** *(Cynoglossum grande),* a robust plant with large leaves and blue flowers that identify it as a member of the borage family.

The ninth switchback is relatively short. The forest is a bit denser here, and you can find **striped coral-root orchid** *(Corallorhiza striata).* Some of these orchids are albino specimens and somewhat yellow instead of the usual pink color. **Coral-root orchid** are parasitic, living off the fungi that decay logs and other detritus. In the process of evolution, the plants have lost their chlorophyll, and their roots have shrunk to fleshy fibers.

As you approach the turn for the tenth switchback, watch for the drooping white flowers of **Hooker fairy-bell** *(Disporum hookeri)* with their lance-shaped leaves.

Just beyond the tenth switchback, the trail reaches a major junction about 0.5 mile from the trailhead. The surrounding forest is mostly Douglas fir with an understory of **vine maple** *(Acer circinatum).* This is a good place to turn around and retrace your steps to the trailhead.

For those intent on climbing to the top of the mountain to see more views and flowers, you have two choices. Straight ahead, the left fork of the trail climbs steeply up the northwest flank of the mountain to the summit. The right fork of the trail loops around the mountain to the east before joining the other trail in a bid for the summit. The right fork affords better views as you climb the mountain.

Silver Star Mountain

Wildflower Hike 5

Ridgeline near Silver Star Mountain, Gifford Pinchot National Forest.

ocated not more than an hour or so from Portland in the Gifford Pinchot National Forest, the hike up Washington's Silver Star Mountain offers vast subalpine meadows with fantastic views of the Columbia Gorge and the Cascades volcanoes. The huge Yacolt Fire, one of the largest in Washington's history, burned the area in 1902, leaving behind a legacy of snags and open, flowered ridges. Although much of the lower elevation forest has recovered, more than a third of the area remains treeless meadowlands.

The higher rocky peaks, covered with **beargrass** *(Xerophyllum tenax)* and **serviceberry** *(Amelanchier alnifolia),* have an alpine appearance due to fire. Silver Star Mountain rises 4,380 feet above the surrounding lowlands

Nearest Town	Washougal, Washington
Highlights	Subalpine meadows with extensive views of Cascade volcanoes
Trail Rating	moderate
Trail Length	3–7 miles, depending on turnaround point
Location	Gifford Pinchot National Forest
Elevation	2,400–4,390 feet
Contact	Mt. St. Helens Ranger District, Gifford Pinchot NF, 360-891-5000
Bloom Season	May to July
Peak Bloom	June
Directions	From Portland, take I-205 north across the Columbia to Vancouver, Washington, then turn right (east) onto WA 14 to Washougal. Take the Washougal River Road exit, and follow the road 6.9 miles to Bear Prairie Road and turn left. Take this road 3.2 miles, then turn right onto Skamania Mines Road. After 2.7 miles turn left on gravel Road 200 and drive 5.7 miles to Grouse Creek Vista (no vista here), where a sign on the right and a flat, wide spot in the road mark the Tarbell Trail.

and once supported a fire lookout. As a result of the rich floral displays produced by the fire-burnt landscape, this forestland is a premier botanical preserve and has been proposed for wilderness designation. Old roads that once penetrated the forest have been closed and are now reverting to trails, although illegal ORV use still occurs.

In a direct line to receive Pacific Ocean storms, the area receives between 85–95 inches of precipitation a year but is usually free of snow by late May to early June. Here you find one of the earliest flowering seasons for "subalpine" flowers in the Portland area.

The trail begins as an old abandoned road, which was once barricaded to keep out ORV users (the barricade is no longer functional). As soon as you enter the forest, you're surrounded by Douglas fir forest with a dense under-story of **salal** *(Gaultheria shallon),* an evergreen shrub with small, white, urnlike flowers. Other species in the first 0.25 mile of this trail include **vine maple** *(Acer circinatum),* **red huckleberry** *(Vaccinium parvifolium),* and **wild rose** *(Rosa gymnocarpa).* You'll also see the easy-to-identify **Oregon grape** *(Mahonia nervosa)* with their evergreen hollylike leaves and clusters of yellow flowers that turn into blue, grapelike berries in the fall, and **Hooker fairy-bell** *(Disporum hookeri),* showing two white, hanging flowers with pointed leaves that aid water runoff—an adaptation to the heavy precipitation in the area.

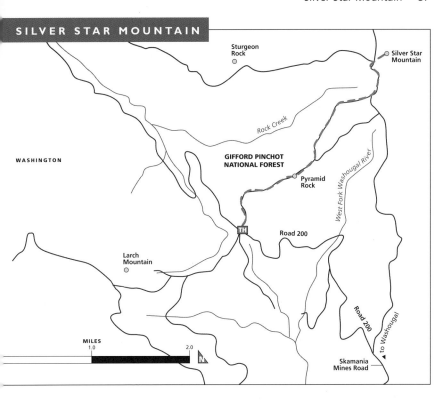

SILVER STAR MOUNTAIN

As you proceed up the trail, you encounter the large maplelike leaves and conspicuous white blossoms of **thimbleberry** *(Rubus parviflorus),* a shrub that produces a sweet, red berry later in the summer. Along with the **thimbleberry,** you'll see a considerable amount of **salmonberry** *(Rubus spectabilis)*, which sports bright pink flowers in the spring and orange berries in early summer. The shrublike **goatsbeard** *(Aruncus dioicus),* with its cluster of small, white flowers, lines the trail. Closer to the forest floor grow **candyflower** *(Claytonia sibirica),* characterized by the heart-shaped leaves surrounding the stem just below the white flowers.

About 200 yards up the road you come to a trail junction. Head right for Silver Star Mountain (a sign on the ground identifies FS Trail #122). **Red alder** *(Alnus rubra),* fast-growing deciduous trees that enrich the soil by adding nitrogen, line the trail. Just beyond another ineffective road barrier, you'll find a few **devil's club** *(Oplopanax horridum).* These tall, tropical-looking plants feature huge leaves and thorn-covered stems, which give rise to the common name. **Devil's club** produce a large cluster of red berries in the fall.

Along this stretch of trail, you'll also see **Pacific bleedingheart** *(Dicentra formosa),* **youth-on-age** *(Tolmiea menziesii),* **inside-out flower** *(Vancouveria hexandra),* and quite a bit of **salmonberry** growing along the trail's edge.

The rocky trail continues steeply up the hill, crossing a small creek that offers a potential drink of water. Growing along the creek are **western buttercup** *(Ranunculus occidentalis)* and **false lily-of-the-valley** *(Maianthemum dilatatum).*

The trail winds through small dense stands of Douglas fir mixed with Pacific silver fir and western hemlock. Along the trail I encountered some black bear scat.

The trail turns northeast and is lined with **small-flowered paintbrush** *(Castilleja parviflora).* **Oval-leaf huckleberry** *(Vaccinium ovalifolium)* thrive here, and a few **Oregon iris** *(Iris tenax)* grow among the **paintbrush**. In shady spots, **queen's cup lily** *(Clintonia uniflora)* and the delicate, white-blossomed **foamflower** *(Tiarella trifoliata)* grow. **False azalea** *(Menziesia ferruginea),* with their small, urnlike flowers, become increasingly common as you climb higher up in elevation.

You reach a patch of particularly large old-growth Pacific silver fir. Beneath these trees you may find **dwarf dogwood** *(Cornus canadensis),* which sport bright red berries in the fall.

Just beyond the cluster of large fir trees, you break out into an open area with views of Silver Star Mountain and the Rock Creek drainage. In this open subalpine terrain, you will find clumps of **golden-pea** *(Thermopsis montana),* a yellow pealike flower common in the subalpine region. Other species here include dense cover of **beargrass** *(Xerophyllum tenax)* with large, showy blooms, **Sitka valerian** *(Valeriana sitchensis),* **red Indian-paintbrush** *(Castilleja miniata),* **broadleaf lupine** *(Lupinus latfiolius),* and the **white poison hemlock** *(Conium maculatum).* **Poison hemlock,** a member of the carrot family is— as its name implies—very poisonous. (Supposedly, a drink made from **poison hemlock** killed Socrates.) In the disturbed, rocky areas along the trail grow scattered patches of

WESTERN COLUMBINE
Aquilegia formosa

Western columbine emerge from taproots. Their red and yellow flowers have reddish spurs, and the leaves are twice divided in groups of three. These plants grow in moist meadows and are very attractive to hummingbirds.

fiveleaved bramble *(Rubus pedatus)*, one of the native **blackberries** found in the Pacific Northwest.

The trail turns northeast and is lined by narrow-leaved **hawkweed** *(Hieracium umbellatum)*, a yellow-flowered plant that looks something like a dandelion. Occasionally, in rocky areas along the trail, you'll see the bluish-flowered **woodland penstemon** *(Nothochelone nemorosa)*. A few orange blossoms of **tiger lily** *(Lilium columbianum)* poke up through the other plants. **Paintbrush, beargrass,** and **valerian** remain common and a few noble fir appear.

The trail reaches a junction just below Pyramid Peak. The route to the top of Silver Star Mountain continues to the left. The peak is another mile or so beyond. For a quick view to the south, take the right fork and ascend quickly to a pass below Pyramid Peak. There, an old two-track leads up the small hill to the southwest. To the northeast rises Pyramid Peak and then Silver Star Mountain. To the south are views of Mount Hood, Mount Jefferson, and the Columbia Gorge. Clear-cuts define the lowland forests.

On top of this mini-summit grow plenty of wind-sheared **serviceberry**, plus **American bistort** *(Polygonum bistortoides)*, **wild rose, golden-pea, poison hemlock, tiger lily,** and **red western columbine** *(Aquilegia formosa)*, all rising up from a dense cover of **beargrass**. This makes a good turnaround point. More motivated hikers can return to the trail junction and continue to the top of Silver Star Mountain, where you can enjoy further views of Mount Adams, Mount St. Helens, and Mount Rainier.

Wildflower
Hike 6 # Plateau Trail

Balsamroot and lupine light up the Tom McCall Preserve along the Columbia River Gorge.

Nearest Town   Hood River

Highlights   Deltoid balsamroot and lupine displays, gorgeous views

Trail Rating   easy

Trail Length   1.0 mile one way

Location   Tom McCall Preserve

Elevation   600 feet

Contact   The Nature Conservancy, 503-228-9561

Bloom Season   March to July

Peak Bloom   mid-April to early May

Directions   From Hood River, take I-84 east 5.0 miles to the Mosier Exit 69; from The Dalles, take I-84 west 8.0 miles to the Rowena Exit 76. From either exit take US 30 (Mosier–The Dalles Highway) to milepost 6 and park at the Rowena Crest overlook.

The Tom McCall Preserve in the Columbia River Gorge is perhaps western Oregon's best wildflower area. From late February through June and beyond in some years, a continual display of wildflowers grace this grassland mesa. From the preserve's trails, you're treated to spectacular views up and down the Columbia River. The preserve, created by land purchases in 1978, was expanded with several additions throughout the 1980s and 1990s. The preserve is named for former Oregon governor Tom McCall, who was instrumental in passing the state's more progressive environmental laws (including its nationally known land-use planning and zoning regulations).

A mix of oaks and grassland thrives upon a plateau that was created by basalt outflows. The preserve lies at the juncture of two major ecosystems—the wet, forested Cascades and the arid, bunchgrass prairies of eastern Oregon.

The preserve houses more than 300 plant species, including four unique to the gorge area: **Thompson's broadleaf lupine** *(Lupinus latifolius thompsonianus),* **Thompson's waterleaf** *(Hydrophyllum thompsonii),* **Columbia desert-parsley** *(Lomatium columbianum),* and **Hood River milk-vetch** *(Astragalus hoodianus).*

You can take one of two trails from here: the 1.0-mile Plateau Trail that starts from the interpretative sign, or the 3.0-mile McCall Point Trail from the south side of the turnaround, which rises 1,000 feet. Hazards along both trails include rattlesnakes and **poison oak** *(Rhus diversiloba).*

The Plateau Trail begins at a sign with parking for only a few vehicles; more parking is across the highway at the Rowena Crest overlook. From the trailhead, robust yellow blossoms of **deltoid balsamroot** *(Balsamorhiza deltoidea)* immediately surround you. Along with the **balsamroot** grow the blue raceme of **broadleaf lupine** *(Lupinus latifolius).* The two flowers together make a lovely foreground for photos of the gorge. Scattered here and there are the large-leaved vines of **wild cucumber** *(Marah oreganus).*

As the trail approaches the western edge of the plateau, look for the white-flowered clusters of **Howell's brodiaea** *(Brodiaea howellii)* or **Howell's triteleia.** It looks something like an onion. The white flowers have pale blue lines on the

DELTOID BALSAMROOT
Balsamorhiza deltoidea

Deltoid balsamroot is a robust plant with large, yellow, sunflowerlike blooms. The large leaves are basal and triangular. The plant grows in great abundance on grassy, low-elevation meadows, sometimes turning entire hillsides yellow.

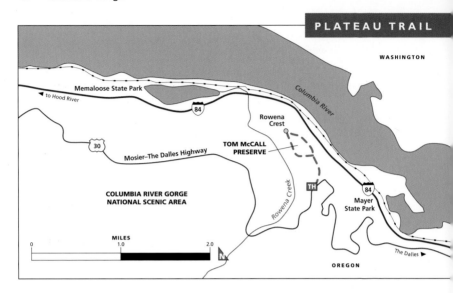

petals. As the trail turns north, a small cluster of **yellow monkey-flower** *(Mimulus guttatus)* lives in a small drainage swale. Mixed in the grasses are the purple blooms of the **upland larkspur** *(Delphinium nuttallianum),* which are poisonous to livestock.

Rounded clumps of **Columbia desert-parsley** have already gone to seed by mid-April. **Desert-parsley,** or **lomatiums,** members of the parsley family, have a distinctive, umbrellalike crown of flowers. The entire plant is edible; Native Americans often consumed the roots.

As the trail winds back toward the narrow isthmus of the plateau, orange **small-flowered fiddleneck** *(Amsinckia menziesii)* along with **common stork's-bill** *(Erodium cicutarium)* both grow on rocky soils. **Common stork's-bill,** an exotic, non-native plant, is now widely distributed in the wild.

About 0.3 mile down the trail is a trail sign. The trail continues northwest toward a small pond surrounded by windswept Oregon white oak and Oregon ash. A short side path leads down to the shore of the pond. **Western buttercup** *(Ranunculus occidentalis)* are scattered among **poison oak.** Directly adjacent to the pond grow dense thickets of **snowberry** *(Symphoricarpos albus)* and **serviceberry** *(Amelanchier alnifolia).*

About 100 feet past the pond a trail takes off to the northeast. This loop trail circles the pond and eventually takes you back to the trailhead. (The sign for this trail is on the ground and difficult to spot.) If you want to short-circuit your journey, you can return on this trail. To continue to the top of the plateau, stay on the main trail heading northwest.

The nearly-level trail passes a second pond with a similar flora of windswept Oregon white oak and Oregon ash. **Snowberry, serviceberry,** and **wild rose** *(Rosa gymnocarpa)* fill in the understory. On the edge of the pond are some **yellow monkey-flower**. On the drier soils away from the pond grow two **buckwheat** *(Eriogonum sp.)* species: the white form of **northern buckwheat** *(Eriogonum compositum),* which David Douglas gathered during his plant-collecting journeys of the 1820s, and Blue Mountain's **strict buckwheat** *(Eriogonum strictum).*

As you continue toward the tip of the plateau, you encounter scattered white slender **popcorn-flower** *(Plagiobothrys tenellus),* along with **slender woodlandstar** *(Lithophragma tenellum).* **Western buttercup** remain abundant in the wetter swales. As the trail descends toward the point, you find a dense thicket of oak to the right (north), with a few dandelion-looking yellow flowers known as **false agoseris** *(Microseris troximoides)* growing along the trail.

The tip of the point affords a fine close-up view of the river. Retrace your steps back to the trailhead.

Awash in the abundant balsamroot at Tom McCall Preserve.

Wildflower
Hike 7 **Eagle Creek**

Forest and flowered meadow along the Eagle Creek Trail, Columbia Wilderness.

Eagle Creek runs within the Columbia River Gorge National Scenic Area, which boasts 77 major waterfalls. Eagle Creek produces 11 of these waterfalls, including Punchbowl Falls at the terminus of this hike. Eagle Creek is one of the most beautiful falls in the entire scenic area, and the Eagle Creek drainage, protected in the Columbia Wilderness, is a salmon spawning ground.

Volcanic flows deposited the Eagle Creek Formation 20 million years ago, and more than 40 tropical forest species are preserved as fossils in this rock record.

The trail, constructed just after the turn of the century, was blasted right out of cliff faces in spots. Although cables provide security in some

Nearest Town	Portland
Highlights	Deep gorge with waterfalls, cliff-side gardens, and old-growth forests
Trail Rating	moderate
Trail Length	4.2 miles round-trip
Location	Columbia Wilderness
Elevation	120–400 feet
Contact	Mount Hood National Forest, 503-666-0700
Bloom Season	April to July
Peak Bloom	May
Directions	From Portland, drive I-84 east toward Hood River and take the Eagle Creek Exit 41. Follow the road past the fish hatchery to the trailhead and parking at its end.

dangerous sections, people who are nervous about drop-offs may not want to hike this trail. The trail ends 13.3 miles uphill at Wahtum Lake.

Beginning at the trailhead, look for **thimbleberry** *(Rubus parviflorus)*, **sword-fern** *(Polystichum munitum)*, **salmonberry** *(Rubus spectabilis)*, **meadowrue** *(Thalictrum occidentale)*, **baneberry** *(Actaea rubra)*, and **hazelnut** *(Corylus cornuta)*. **Bracken fern** *(Pteridium aquilinum)* make up a great deal of the ground cover. Bigleaf maple, a tall subcanopy tree common in western Oregon, dominate the streamside forest.

About 40 or 50 feet beyond the trailhead is a large Douglas fir. The most common conifer along the trail, Douglas fir is distinguished by its gray, corrugated bark and cones with three-pronged bracts on each scale.

As you move farther up the trail, you see **salal** *(Gaultheria shallon)*, a plant with evergreen leaves and white, urn-shaped flowers. Another evergreen species you encounter is **Oregon grape** *(Mahonia nervosa)*, identified by its hollylike leaves. In spring, **Oregon grape** has yellow flowers; in fall, it has bluish, grapelike berries—hence the name.

The trail soon passes a rocky cliff outcrop. **Stonecrop** *(Sedum oregonense)* are conspicuous by their thick, succulent leaves and yellow, featherlike blossoms. Here is the rocky-outcrop species **western saxifrage** *(Saxifraga occidentalis)*, which tends to bloom in mid-April. Small-flowered **alumroot** *(Heuchera micrantha)*, a saxifrage with large heart-shaped but serrated leaves, is common on rock crevices and rocky slopes throughout the lower Eagle Creek drainage.

Another saxifrage growing on the rock face is **Merten's saxifrage** *(Saxifraga mertensiana)*. **Common stork's-bill** *(Erodium cicutarium)*, with pink flowers and much-divided fernlike leaves, are common along the base of this outcrop. Growing from a drippy, mossy slope is **maidenhair fern** *(Adiantum pedatum)*, a fern common in wet areas.

Just beyond this damp site you find a thick growth of **thimbleberry** with **sword-fern. Broad-leaved starflower** *(Trientalis latifolia)*, **false Solomon's seal** *(Smilacina racemosa)*, **meadowrue**, and **Cascade penstemon** *(Penstemon serrulatus)* also grow here.

You reach a second cliff, which has a steep drop-off and a cable strung along the cliff to provide a safety railing. More rock-loving and crevice-loving flowers grace the cliff, including **western saxifrage** and small-flowered **alum-root**. On the cliffs and slopes, note the occurrence of **Scouler's heliotrope** *(Valeriana scouleri)*, characterized by a terminal cluster of pink flowers.

Just beyond the cliff, watch for **ocean-spray** *(Holodiscus discolor)*, a shrub with drooping white clusters of flowers. Below the trail on the open slope you'll see some stunted Oregon white oak. **Chocolate lily** *(Fritillaria lanceolata)* and **cliff larkspur** *(Delphinium menziesii)* also thrive on this slope. Pink **plectritis** *(Plectritis congesta)* grow thickly on the slope and on adjacent cliffs. The white blossoms of **small-flowered prairiestar** *(Lithophragma parviflora)* are mixed with **larkspur** and **plectritis** on open slopes. More **Oregon grape, vine maple** *(Acer circinatum)*, and **sword-fern** live in the shadier parts of the slope up from the trail.

The trail crosses a small creek where you find ample patches of **maidenhair fern**. Just beyond the creek is a bench and a "no camping" sign. As you move beyond this area, you'll see **queen's cup lily** *(Clintonia uniflora)*, **starflower**, and more **Oregon grape**.

PLECTRITIS
Plectritis congesta

In early spring, **plectritis** are so profuse that some hillsides turn pink. An annual, **plectritis** has a thick head of small, pink flowers and opposite leaves. *Plectritis* is Greek for "plaited"; *congesta* is Latin for "congested" or "crowded" (referring to the blooms).

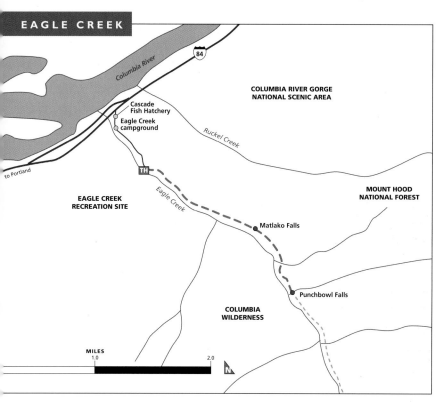

Finally, the trail brings you to a spectacular viewpoint for Punchbowl Falls, which were created by an erosion-resistant layer of lava. More **salal, bracken fern,** and **twinflower** *(Linnaea borealis)* grow in the immediate area.

After enjoying the view and the flowers in this area, the falls makes a good turnaround point for the hike back to the parking lot.

Wildflower Hike 8

Lost Lake
Old-Growth Trail

A boardwalk meanders past old-growth western red cedar along the Lost Lake Old-Growth Trail.

Nearest Town	Hood River
Highlights	Nature trail through old-growth forest
Trail Rating	easy
Trail Length	1.0 mile each way
Location	Lost Lake Campground
Elevation	3,150 feet
Contact	Mount Hood National Forest, 503-666-0700
Bloom Season	June to August
Peak Bloom	July
Directions	From Portland, take US 26 east 42 miles to Zigzag. Turn left (northeast) onto Lolo Pass Road (FR 18). After 7.0 miles, take another left onto FR 13 and drive 6.0 miles to Lost Lake and the trailhead.

Lost Lake offers one of the most perfect picture-postcard views in all of Oregon. To see Mount Hood across the placid waters of Lost Lake is an unforgettable experience. The U.S. Forest Service created a major campground at the popular lake, and a number of trails radiate from this site. The Lost Lake Old-Growth Trail runs from the campground to the group camping area and passes through some exceptionally large stands of western red cedar and Douglas fir.

The trail starts out in the main campground by the D loop, where you find a small pull-out by the trailhead. The trail first descends below the campground, passes just beyond the lower campsites, and eventually snakes through older trees on a boardwalk.

The forest just around the trailhead consists largely of western hemlock. Pink-flowered **Pacific rhododendron** *(Rhododendron macrophyllum),* plus **dwarf dogwood** *(Cornus canadensis),* **broadleaf lupine** *(Lupinus latifolius),* **vanillaleaf** *(Achlys triphylla),* and **oval-leaf huckleberry** *(Vaccinium ovalifolium),* recognizable by their red twigs, also grow here.

At the first switchback you'll see a clump of **devil's club** *(Oplopanax horridum),* an indicator of high precipitation. Large, maplelike leaves give the plant a tropical appearance.

Just beyond the switchback, the trail passes through more **huckleberry.** **Twinflower** *(Linnaea borealis),* a species common in northern forests, lines the trail. Just as you approach the second switchback, watch for the long, grasslike clumps of **beargrass** *(Xerophyllum tenax).* In early July, the white-plume flowers of **beargrass** are typically in full bloom and make for a striking floral display. More **dwarf dogwood, trillium** *(Trillium ovatum),* and **rhododendron** thrive here below the Douglas fir.

After the third switchback, look for **striped coral-root orchid** *(Corallorhiza striata).* A saprophyte, this plant gains its nutrients from other plants.

The trail eventually intersects the main trail that encircles the lake. At this trail junction, you can recognize **vanillaleaf** by its triple wedge-shaped leaflets with the middle wedge shaped somewhat like a goose foot. Another distinctive plant you'll see here is **whiteveined wintergreen** *(Pyrola picta),* which has thick, leathery leaves with white veins—hence its name.

Just after turning left, you encounter the first sign on the nature trail. **Oval-leaf huckleberry** is thick around the sign, along with **foamflower** *(Tiarella trifoliata),* a few **devil's club,** and more **coral-root orchid.** You will soon cross a short bridge. Look here for **star-flowered false Solomon's seal** *(Smilacina stellata),* **bracken fern** *(Pteridium aquilinum),* and **devil's club.**

The trail passes a large, toppled Douglas fir. The root wad and bare soil created here allow new trees to become established. Windfall and fire both create holes in the forest canopy that stimulate new plant growth. Just beyond

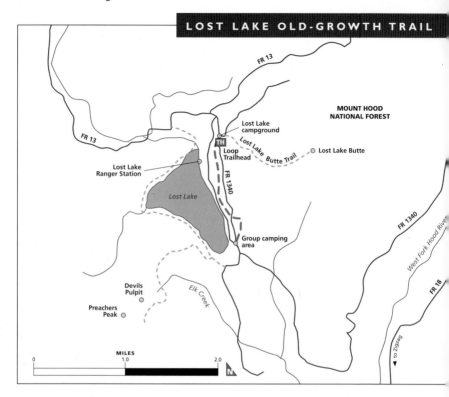

the fallen tree is a small clump of **prince's-pine** *(Chimaphila umbellata).* After you cross another small wooden bridge, look for **red elderberry** *(Sambucus racemosa),* a small shrub-tree that produces beautiful clusters of red berries in the autumn.

When you reach another trail junction, go left to continue on the Lost Lake Old-Growth Trail. If you turn right, the trail leads down to a parking lot and picnic area near the lake. At the trail junction you can spot a significant amount of **fireweed** *(Epilobium angustifolium),* which have tall stems with bright red flowers.

Travel a short way on the Lost Lake Old-Growth Trail to yet another trail junction. The Express Lake Shore trail is to the right. Go left here on the Old-Growth Trail, which passes campsite D8, where you can discover lots of **thimbleberry** *(Rubus parviflorus)* and **huckleberry.**

Quite a few trees have been blown over by the wind here; a sign explains winter storms and the importance of wind-thrown trees to the ecosystem. Slightly down the trail you can read another sign about the importance of dead trees in promoting new life. Indeed, some ecologists believe dead trees may ultimately be more important to the forest ecosystem than live trees.

Dead trees provide long-term nutrient sources, structural components to the forest and stream ecosystems, not to mention homes for many vertebrate and invertebrate animals.

The trail continues southward, passing through more **salmonberry** *(Rubus spectabilis),* **devil's club, vanillaleaf, thimbleberry, huckleberry, foam-flower,** and **dwarf dogwood**. Soon, you reach a wooden platform with **skunk cabbage** *(Lysichitum americanum)* and **devil's club** growing below.

The trail crosses a paved road and continues on a boardwalk through the forest, which is dominated by large western red cedar and more **devil's club, thimbleberry, star-flowered false Solomon's seal, salmonberry,** and some **oak-fern** *(Gymnocarpium dryopteris)*. Winter wren and chickadee flit through the forest here.

As you continue, you'll reach a sign beside a very large tree. Large trees here are primarily western red cedar and Douglas fir, with **devil's club** dominant in the understory. You pass a side platform with a bench, where **oak-fern** and **false lily-of-the-valley** *(Maianthemum dilatatum)* grow. Signs explaining various aspects of the old-growth forest ecology are posted along here. One sign discusses the diversity of insects living in the forest canopy—some 1,500 insects have been recorded. After passing through a number of other signs, the trail ends at group sites 30 and 31.

DEVIL'S CLUB
Oplopanax horridum

Devil's club is aptly named, as the stem and leaves are armed with spines. The sprawling plant may reach heights of 9–10 feet and has huge, maplelike leaves with spines covering the undersides. The white flowers grow in a terminal cluster, and in autumn the plant has bright red berries. Typically, **devil's club** grows only where there is abundant moisture.

Devil's club is related to ginseng. American Indians used the plant to treat many different ailments, including diabetes, arthritis, and ulcers; they also rubbed the berries on their heads as a cure for lice.

Wildflower
Hike 9 ## Vista Ridge

Mount Hood looms above wildflower meadows on the Vista Ridge Trail.

With a hike named Vista Ridge, how can you lose? Although this trail doesn't provide any panoramas for the first 2.5 miles, once you break above timberline the views are some of the finest in Oregon. Ladd Glacier on Mount Hood's north flank is right above you and views of Mount Adams, Mount St. Helens, and Mount Rainier are easily seen to the north. Acres and acres of wildflower meadows laced with tumbling streams evoke a *Sound of Music* feeling.

The first part of the trail follows an overgrown primitive road. **Alder** *(Alnus crispa),* which often colonize disturbed sites, encroach upon the trail. **Alder** is a nitrogen fixer, taking nitrogen from the atmosphere and chemically changing it so other plants can use it. You can also encounter **mountain**

Nearest Town	Zigzag
Highlights	Subalpine meadows below glacier-clad Mount Hood
Trail Rating	difficult
Trail Length	6.0 miles round-trip
Location	Mount Hood Wilderness
Elevation	4,500–6,000 feet
Contact	Mount Hood National Forest, 503-666-0700
Bloom Season	July to September
Peak Bloom	August
Directions	From Portland, take US 26 east 42 miles to Zigzag. Turn left (northeast) onto paved Lolo Pass Road (FR 18), drive 10.5 miles to the pass, then turn right onto gravel McGee Creek Road (FR 1810). Drive 7.7 miles until FR 1810 rejoins FR 18, then another 3.2 miles to FR 16. Turn right and watch for signs to Vista Ridge Trail. It's 9.0 miles on FR 16 and FR 1650 to the trailhead and limited parking.

boxwood *(Pachistima myrsinites),* an evergreen that has opposite leaves and toothed margins.

Another flower growing along the trail is **pearly-everlasting** *(Anaphalis margaritacea).* The white, woolly flowers are often used in dried bouquets.

As you follow the old road farther, watch for the white blossoms of **beargrass** *(Xerophyllum tenax),* a member of the lily family. The plant grows from a tussock of thin, narrow leaves.

You can also find **fireweed** *(Epilobium angustifolium)* scattered here and there. **Fireweed,** like **alder,** is a pioneering plant that colonizes recently disturbed sites—such as burned areas—hence its common name.

Black huckleberry *(Vaccinium membranaceum)* grow in forested areas, but also in open areas such as burned sites. Another berry producer is **pinemat manzanita** *(Arctostaphylos nevadensis),* which features twisted, reddish stems with evergreen leaves.

After 0.2 mile, the old road ends and the trail enters a mountain hemlock forest with a dense understory of **beargrass.** The trail stays in this forest another 0.2 mile before reaching a trail junction. At the junction, a sign describes the Mount Hood Wilderness. The trail to the left heads to Red Hill. To reach Vista Ridge, turn right and follow the long forested ridge upward.

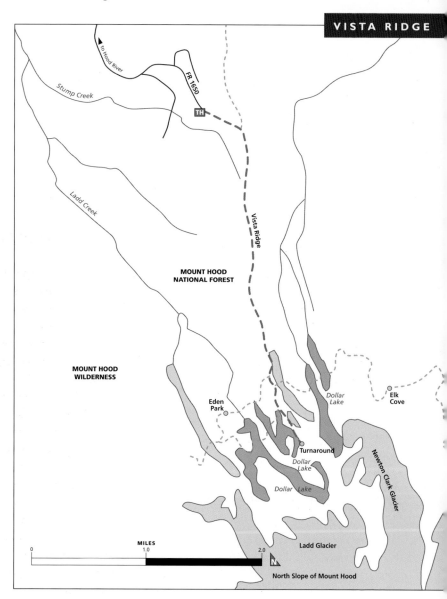

As you climb, the trail passes through patches of **Pacific rhododendron** *(Rhododendron macrophyllum),* with their beautiful pink flowers, and along the edge of a small valley filled with carpets of white **avalanche lily** *(Erythronium montanum).* White **avalanche lily** grow from British Columbia down into northern Oregon, including the Mount Hood area.

You'll see a few **lupine** *(Lupinus sp.)* along the trail as you gradually climb up the ridge, coming to a switchback. Hike up another switchback and come to the sign marking the boundary for Mount Hood Wilderness. The 74-square-mile wilderness, first designated in 1964 and expanded in 1978, encircles Oregon's highest peak, Mount Hood (11,237 feet). The volcano has 11 glaciers. The 38-mile Timberline Trail, accessible via the Vista Ridge Trail, circles the entire mountain, passing through many wildflower meadows.

The trail continues up the ridge passing through lots of **beargrass** and **avalanche lily. White-flowered rhododendron** *(Rhododendron albiflorum),* a species you see more of farther north in Washington, is relatively common here.

The trail cuts across a slope with some **pink mountain-heather** *(Phyllodoce empetriformis),* a spreading evergreen shrub. After a very short switchback, the trail winds toward the southeast, passing through some yellow **arnica** *(Arnica latifolia).* **Arnica**, a member of the sunflower family, tends to grow in shady forested areas.

As you near timberline, the forest begins to thin out with larger patches of flowers. Flowers along this stretch include **Sitka valerian** *(Valeriana sitchensis),* **red Indian-paintbrush** *(Castilleja miniata),* yellow-flowered **fan-leaved cinquefoil** *(Potentilla flabellifolia),* and **false hellebore** *(Veratrum viride).* The trail moves along the edge of the ridge with views of Mount Hood straight ahead. An abundance of **beargrass, red Indian-paintbrush, pink mountain-heather**, and mop-topped **old-man's whiskers** *(Anemone occidentalis)* grows in the meadow patches. You'll also encounter the small tree-shrub **Sitka mountain-ash** *(Sorbus sitchensis).* Views to the north reveal other Cascade volcanoes, including Mount Adams, Mount St. Helens, and Mount Rainier.

The trail reaches a junction with the Timberline Trail. Elk Cove is to the left, Eden Park to the right. You will find an abundance of **Pink mountain-heather, lupine,** and old-man's whiskers in this area, along with **partridgefoot** *(Luetkea pectinata).*

OLD-MAN'S WHISKERS
Anemone occidentalis

Mop-topped **old-man's whiskers** is named for the drooping, long, feathery styles that flow from the flower head after it has gone to seed. The hairy achenes are a distinctive feature of subalpine and alpine meadows in late summer. Another common name for the plant is **western pasqueflower**.

The large, white flowers, often tinged with purple, appear nearly as soon as the snow disappears in spring and often before the leaves are fully developed. The leaves are divided into narrow segments, and the stem leaves generally lack stalks.

The trail veers to the left toward Elk Cove and enters a basin full of **lupine**, which was buzzing with bees the day I visited. The scent fills the air and Mount Hood's north face rises dramatically above the flowers. From this point on, you can explore acres of meadows and ridges filled with **lupine**, **old-man's whiskers**, and **pink mountain-heather**. Plus, the vistas of the Columbia Gorge and the Cascades of Washington are truly extraordinary.

After exploring to your heart's content, take the same path back to the trailhead.

Hiker Mollie Matteson takes in the subalpine beauty of the Mount Hood Wilderness.

Cooper Spur

Paintbrush redden the lower slopes of Mount Hood.

This hike begins at Cloud Cap, where there is an old, historic lodge as well as a campground. The trailhead provides access to the Mount Hood Timberline Trail—in fact, the first portion of this hike is part of the Timberline Trail. Cooper Spur is the highest point on Mount Hood that you can reach by trail. If you wander onto the ridge far enough, you can reach the edge of glaciers.

Although the hike starts out in forest, it soon breaks out of the trees. As you ascend, you're treated to ever-better views of Mount Hood as well as the entire Cascade Range stretching from north to south. Since this hike is so high, the best flower-viewing opportunities are not until late in summer. When I hiked it in late June, however, I still found plenty of flowers peeking out from occasional snowbanks.

Nearest Town	Hood River
Highlights	A climb through subalpine forest above the timberline with terrific views of Mount Hood
Trail Rating	moderate
Trail Length	3.0 miles round-trip
Location	Mount Hood Wilderness
Elevation	5,850–6,500 feet
Contact	Mount Hood National Forest, 503-666-0700
Bloom Season	July to September
Peak Bloom	late July
Directions	From Hood River, take OR 35 south about 23 miles to the turnoff for Cooper Spur and the ski area. Turn right and go 3.3 miles to the junction for Tilly Jane. Turn left onto FR 3512 for the Cloud Cap Saddle campground and the trailhead, some 10.3 miles on a winding gravel road.

Starting from the parking lot, head across the campground and into the woods at the large trailhead bulletin board. Go straight toward Gnarl Ridge. When the trail forks in less than 100 yards, stay left. The dominant tree here is mountain hemlock. In the forest openings, you will find **white marshmarigold** *(Caltha leptosepala)*. A member of the buttercup family, **marshmarigold** is one of the first flowers to bloom after the snow melts.

Another early bloomer is the beautiful, pink-flowered **tall mountain shooting star** *(Dodecatheon jeffreyi)*. The buzzing vibrations of a bee activates **shooting star** to shed pollen from its anthers. You can also see **fan-leaved cinquefoil** *(Potentilla flabellifolia)* here.

Along the trail on rockier substrates you can find **Alaska saxifrage** *(Saxifraga ferruginea),* which have toothed, narrow, wedge-shaped leaves. The whitish petals on the flowers are distinctly spotted with yellow. In deeper, moist soils you find **false hellebore** *(Veratrum viride),* a member of the lily family with large leaves that have parallel veins.

The forest shifts from mountain hemlock to a mixture of silver fir, whitebark pine, lodgepole pine, Engelmann spruce, and subalpine fir. Lodgepole pine is relatively common on the eastern side of the Cascades and through the Blue Mountains to the Rockies. And a smaller, squatter version, known as shore pine, grow along the coast.

COOPER SPUR

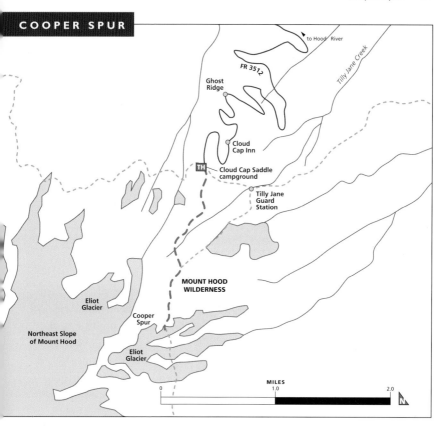

As the trail climbs upwards through the forest, you pass **Brewer's mitrewort** *(Mitella breweri)* and **Jacob's-ladder** *(Polemonium pulcherrimum)*. I observed elk tracks in the forest here, and I also heard a varied thrush.

Grouseberry *(Vaccinium scoparium),* also known as **whortleberry**, is a common understory plant here. **Grouseberry** is a tiny **huckleberry** with edible, if small, berries.

The trail crosses a meadow that a drainage ditch cuts across. The ditch is full of **false hellebore, shooting star,** and **white marshmarigold**. After the meadow, the trail heads back into the forest, which has lots of **grouseberry** beneath the trees. The path continues to curve to the right (west), where you will see more **Jacob's-ladder** and some **Sitka valerian** *(Valeriana sitchensis).*

The path then veers to the left along a side hill through an open forest of whitebark pine. The forest openings are adorned with **broadleaf lupine** *(Lupinus latifolius)* in bloom. Along this stretch of trail you can capture fantastic views of Mount Hood. The trail continues across an open, gravelly slope where **silverleaf phacelia** *(Phacelia hastata),* **Jacob's-ladder**, and **sulfur buckwheat** *(Eriogonum umbellatum)* grow.

The trail passes back into scattered trees with very sandy soils composed of volcanic ash. The droughty soils support **mountain boxwood** *(Pachistima myrsinites)* and **pinemat manzanita** *(Arctostaphylos nevadensis)*. The trail curves to the east, offering outstanding views to the south. Plenty of **manzanita** grow here, along with **Newberry's knotweed** *(Polygonum newberryi)*.

After a short switchback, the trail heads up Cooper Spur to Mount Hood. On this austere, rocky, gravelly ridge grow more **pinemat manzanita** and **mountain boxwood**. An alpine garden boasts colors ranging from the purple blooms of **lupine**, the red flowers of **Indian paintbrush** *(Castilleja hispida)*, and the white blossoms of **cat's-ear lily** *(Calochortus subalpinus)* to the purple flowers of **Davidson's penstemon** *(Penstemon davidsonii)* and the bright red blooms of **scarlet gilia** *(Ipomopsis aggregata)*.

As you climb higher up the ridge, the whitebark pine and subalpine fir assume a low, stunted, nearly flat form, sheared by the wind in this exposed site. Scattered among the trees are **spreading phlox** *(Phlox diffusa)*, which have whitish flowers growing low to the ground to take advantage of warmer temperatures out of the wind. Mat-forming plants, such as **phlox**, are common at timberline.

Just before the top of Cooper Spur you'll see some **pussy-toes** *(Antennaria alpina)*, **small-flowered penstemon** *(Penstemon procerus)*, and large clumps of **Davidson's penstemon**. The patches of color among the otherwise gray rock brighten this austere alpine environment.

At this point, you can enjoy unparalleled views of Eliot Glacier. As you can see, the glacier has shrunk, leaving moraines along the sides.

DAVIDSON'S PENSTEMON
Penstemon davidsonii

Davidson's penstemon, a low shrub, grows in dense mats on rocky or gravelly sites. Its purple-pink flowers are usually large compared to its rather small, evergreen leaves. The plant is named for Dr. George Davidson, who first collected it in California. The mat-like growth and evergreen leaves are both adaptations to the often-droughty sites where it flourishes: The low, sprawling growth helps the plant conserve moisture by reducing exposure to drying winds, and the evergreen leaves reduce water loss.

Elk Meadows

*Douglas' aster
cover a meadow
below Mount
Hood along Elk
Meadows Trail.*

This hike offers incredible views of Mount Hood, up close and personal. Since nearly the entire hike is through trees, with no hint of what is coming, it's a nice surprise to reach the meadows and bask in the unforgettable view. If you're interested in an overnight hike, there is a shelter at the north end of the meadow with a jaw-dropping view of the mountain. Plus, numerous trail intersections offer many opportunities for loop hikes and exploration of the region. Starting at the trailhead marker for Trail 645, you have 0.6 mile to go to reach the wilderness boundary.

The trail begins amid a western hemlock and silver fir forest. Right at the trailhead you see tons of **black huckleberry** *(Vaccinium membranaceum),*

Nearest Town	Hood River
Highlights	A spectacular meadow with terrific views of Mount Hood
Trail Rating	moderate
Trail Length	6.8 miles round-trip
Location	Mount Hood Wilderness
Elevation	4,470–5,250 feet
Contact	Mount Hood National Forest, 503-666-0700
Bloom Season	June to August
Peak Bloom	July
Directions	From Portland, take US 26 east past Government Camp to OR 35. Drive nearly 8.0 miles toward Hood River to the turn for Mount Hood Meadows Ski Area and turn left (west). Drive up this road about 0.5 mile to the trailhead and parking area, near a small campground in the trees with a few fire pits (but no water).

which ripen in August. **Beargrass** *(Xerophyllum tenax)* is also abundant, with its showy, large white blooms lighting up the forest in July.

Less than 100 yards into the forest, you reach a cut-line, about 25–30 feet wide, where the trees have been removed. Plenty of **broadleaf lupine** *(Lupinus latifolius)* and **beargrass** grow here. Shortly, the trail crosses a second cut-line, where you see western white pine scattered here and there. White pine blister rust, a disease that eventually kills trees, threatens the area and has already killed many of the larger pines here.

Where the trail crosses a fourth cut-line strip and intersects with a cross-country ski trail, turn right. **Parrot beak** *(Pedicularis racemosa)*, **grouseberry** *(Vaccinium scoparium)*, **beargrass, huckleberry,** and **lupine** grow along the trail at this junction.

When you pass Trail #667 to Umbrella Falls, keep going straight ahead for Elk Meadows. **Wild strawberry** *(Fragaria vesca)* grow abundantly on the forest floor here. Very quickly you reach Clark Creek and several more trail junctions. If you go right, the trail takes you 1.0 mile to Highway 35. Go straight ahead, across the bridge over Clark Creek, to enter the Mount Hood Wilderness. Engelmann spruce, a common species in the Rockies but relatively uncommon in the Cascades, grow along Clark Creek.

Along the level path under the trees are **trillium** *(Trillium ovatum)*, **parrot beak**, **vanillaleaf** *(Achlys triphylla)*, **arnica** *(Arnica latifolia)*, **senecio** *(Senecio triangularis)*, and **star-flowered false Solomon's seal** *(Smilacina stellata)*.

Just after crossing two small creeks, look for **black twin-berry** *(Lonicera involucrata)*, a shrub elsewhere known as **honeysuckle**, with yellow flowers and, later, dark berries. You also see **bracted lousewort** *(Pedicularis bracteosa)* and plenty of **huckleberry** and **lupine** throughout this section of trail. Cross a third small creek, and pass more **huckleberry**, **lupine**, and **trillium**. You soon reach the Newton Creek Trail, providing an alternate route to Elk Meadows and a nice loop hike.

At this trail junction, note the **beargrass**, **lupine**, and **huckleberry**, but also the **false hellebore** *(Veratrum viride)* and **queen's cup lily** *(Clintonia uniflora)*.

Logs span the glacier-fed, roaring waters of Newton Creek, so you can cross it. Beware—the creek typically rises in the afternoon because of glacial melt, which can sometimes make the crossing hazardous. Look up Newton Creek to see Mount Hood and look along the creek for small patches of **yellow monkey-flower** *(Mimulus guttatus)* and **pink monkey-flower** *(Mimulus lewisii)*, whose Latin name refers to Meriwether Lewis of the Lewis and Clark Expedition.

Once across Newton Creek, the trail winds up a slope toward Gnarl Ridge. Along the trail here you'll find **red Indian-paintbrush** *(Castilleja miniata)*, **tall bluebell** *(Mertensia paniculata)*, **Sitka valerian** *(Valeriana sitchensis)*, red **western columbine** *(Aquilegia formosa)*, more **black twin-berry**, and the evergreen shrub **mountain boxwood** *(Pachistima myrsinites)*. The trail crosses a small stream that tumbles down the steep slope. Lush **thimbleberry** *(Rubus parviflorus)* and **cow-parsnip** *(Heracleum lanatum)*, with its

ELEPHANT'S HEAD
Pedicularis groenlandica

The long, curling trunks and large ears of this flower's pink blooms give rise to its common name, **elephant's head**. Its leaves are fernlike and finely dissected. The Latin name refers to Greenland, but the plant is widely distributed in northern regions from Alaska to the southern Rockies. **Elephant's head** thrive in boggy, wet meadows— the kind of places where mosquitoes are common.

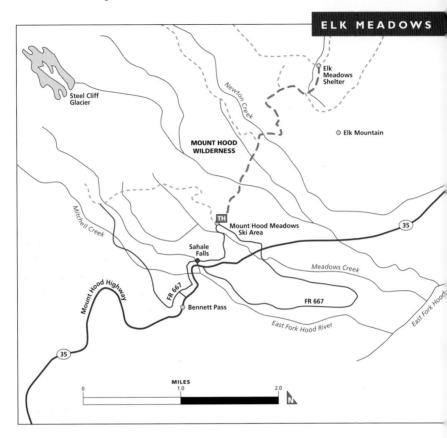

broad tropical-looking leaves, chokes the trail. You also encounter a very large Douglas fir here.

At the first switchback grow **thimbleberry**, plus **vanillaleaf, queen's cup lily, baneberry** *(Actaea rubra)*, **three-leaved anemone** *(Anemone deltoidea)*, **meadowrue** *(Thalictrum occidentale)*, and **Douglas' maple** *(Acer douglasii)*.

You cross a small, 6-foot bridge over a tiny creek along which **arnica, waterleaf** *(Hydrophyllum fendleri)*, **white bog-orchid** *(Habenaria dilatata)*, and **pink wintergreen** *(Pyrola asarifolia)* grow. Just beyond this spring creek you can find more **boxwood.**

At the second switchback, you can look through the trees and see Mount Hood. You see more **whiteveined wintergreen** *(Pyrola picta)*, also known as **pyrola, star-flowered false Solomon's seal,** and **vanillaleaf** here.

At the third switchback, plenty of **one-sided wintergreen** *(Orthilia secunda)* grow. You hike several more switchbacks, then at the sixth switchback find lots of **bracken fern** *(Pteridium aquilinum)*, plus **dwarf dogwood** *(Cornus canadensis)* and **tall bluebell**. As you pass the seventh switchback, note the beautiful white blooms of **beargrass**.

After one more switchback, the trail reaches the top of a ridge and comes to a major trail junction with the Blue Grass Ridge Trail that leads to Elk Mountain and Gnarl Ridge. Just beyond the trail junction, as the path begins to descend toward Elk Meadow, you encounter **grouseberry, lupine, huckleberry,** and **beargrass**.

A trail sign indicates a side trail to Polallie campground; the main trail that takes you around the edge of Elk Meadow is to the left. The meadow is edged by **false hellebore** *(Veratrum viride)* and **elephant's head** *(Pedicularis groenlandica)*. **Elephant's head** is a common species in wet, boggy places — places strongly associated with mosquitoes.

When the route reaches a trail junction by a creek, go left to the meadow and the open-fronted shelter that offers an outstanding view of Mount Hood. The path to the shelter is lined with **subalpine spirea** *(Spiraea densiflora),* **lupine,** and **arnica. Douglas' aster** *(Aster subspicatus)* cover the meadows, and **white bog-orchid** spot the meadow here and there.

Wildflower Hike 12

Lookout Mountain

Penstemon form the foreground of the view of Mount Hood from the top of Lookout Mountain.

Nearest Town	Hood River
Highlights	Hike through a series of meadows to a rocky, mountaintop vista
Trail Rating	moderate
Trail Length	2.5 miles round-trip
Location	Badger Creek Wilderness
Elevation	5,900–6,500 feet
Contact	Mount Hood National Forest, 503-666-0700
Bloom Season	June to August
Peak Bloom	July
Directions	From Hood River, take OR 35 south about 27 miles and turn left onto Dufur Mill Road (FR 44); from Government Camp, take US 26 and OR 35 east and north to Robinhood campground. The Dufur Mill Road (FR 44) is another 2.5 miles on the right. Take paved FR 44 for 3.8 miles to a sign for High Prairie and gravel FR 4410. Take FR 4410 about 5.0 miles to an intersection and turn left onto FR 4420, 200 yards to the trailhead and parking.

The view from Lookout Mountain is one of the most spectacular in Oregon. Immediately west lies the hulking bulk of Mount Hood, and visible to the north and south are the high, glaciated Cascade volcanoes of Mount Adams, Mount Rainier, Mount St. Helens, Mount Jefferson, the Three Sisters, and others. The good news is that getting to this rocky lookout site takes you through a series of subalpine meadows that are thick with wildflowers.

Most of the trail to the top of the mountain follows an old road, which is now a trail in the Badger Creek Wilderness. The trail grade is relatively gentle, and a sign at the trailhead even proclaims the start to be wheelchair accessible.

Right at the trailhead you enter a meadow that was covered with a pink sea of **tall mountain shooting star** *(Dodecatheon jeffreyi)* in late June. The yellow-flowered **fan-leaved cinquefoil** *(Potentilla flabellifolia)* and **Alaska saxifrage** *(Saxifraga ferruginea)* grow among the mix. In addition, poking up through the other flowers are the taller leaves of **false hellebore** *(Veratrum viride)*. In a few wet seep areas, you can also find **white marshmarigold** *(Caltha leptosepala)*.

Tree islands (groups of trees) are scattered about the meadows. Species present include lodgepole pine, whitebark pine, Engelmann spruce, Pacific silver fir, and subalpine fir.

After crossing the first meadow, you enter open forest with an understory of **Brewer's mitrewort** *(Mitella breweri)*, **Sitka valerian** *(Valeriana sitchensis)*, and **Jacob's-ladder** *(Polemonium pulcherrimum)*. **Jacob's-ladder** have blue flowers and pinnate leaves that resemble a ladder.

After passing through the forest for a short stretch, the trail turns to the left (east) and passes another meadow. Look for the brown soil castings, made by pocket gophers, that snake across the ground. Tunneling beneath the snow, the gophers pile up dirt, which remains after the snow melts.

As you enter the forest again, **grouseberry** *(Vaccinium scoparium)* cover the ground. This small blueberry has thin, green branches and tiny berries. The berries are edible, but you would likely starve before you could gather enough to make a meal. One of the trees you see here is western hemlock, identified by its drooping crown.

As you continue through another large meadow cut by a drainage ditch, you'll hear varied thrush in the surrounding forest. The meadow is full of **false hellebore, shooting star, marshmarigold,** and **fan-leaved cinquefoil**. When I visited in late June, this meadow was nearly solid pink with **shooting star**. After passing through the meadow, you enter the forest again. The ground is covered with more **Jacob's-ladder, valerian,** and **grouseberry**.

The trail curves to the right (southwest) and reaches a large, flat opening where the old road cuts back to the southeast. If you continue to follow this old road, it eventually takes you to the summit of the mountain. However, there is another trail that veers off to the right, cutting along the side of the

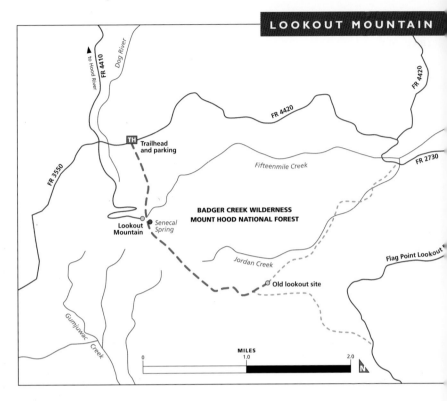

LOOKOUT MOUNTAIN

to Hood River

FR 4110

Dog River

FR 4420

FR 4420

FR 4420

FR 3550

TH Trailhead and parking

Fifteenmile Creek

FR 2730

Lookout Mountain

Senecal Spring

**BADGER CREEK WILDERNESS
MOUNT HOOD NATIONAL FOREST**

Jordan Creek

Flag Point Lookout

Old lookout site

Gumjuwac Creek

MILES
0   1.0   2.0

N

mountain. This trail affords outstanding views of Mount Hood and traverses several different flower habitats.

If you take the alternate trail, almost immediately you come to an opening that offers terrific views of Mount Hood. The hillside is gravelly and dry, with scattered whitebark pine and subalpine fir. Here you can find the blue, pealike **lupine** *(Lupinus sp.)* as well as several flowers adapted to dry, well-drained sites, including **sulfur buckwheat** *(Eriogonum umbellatum)* and **silverleaf phacelia** *(Phacelia hastata).* Both have clustered, basal leaves.

As you continue along this side hill, you can spot other drought-tolerant plants, including the small, evergreen shrub **mountain boxwood** *(Pachistima myrsinites),* and the sprawling, red-stemmed evergreen **pinemat manzanita** *(Arctostaphylos nevadensis).* Both shrubs adapt to water stress by maintaining a compact, sprawling shape that reduces the overall surface area to evaporation. Leathery, small leaves help reduce water loss as well.

Eventually the trail curves to the east and provides wonderful views to the south across Badger Creek. Badger Lake is visible to the southwest, with Mount Jefferson and the Three Sisters beyond. You encounter the Divide Trail, which continues east to Flag Point Lookout Road. The Lookout Mountain trail that you're on switchbacks northwest up to the summit ridge. As you reach the ridge, look for more **manzanita,** plus **Newberry's knotweed** *(Polygonum newberryi),* **Indian paintbrush** *(Castilleja hispida),* **Davidson's penstemon** *(Penstemon davidsonii),* and **cat's-ear lily** *(Calochortus subalpinus).* I spotted only one beautiful **scarlet gilia** *(Ipomopsis aggregata)* growing from the rocky soil, but undoubtedly others can be found here. **Scarlet gilia** is a favorite flower of hummingbirds.

The trail passes a large, flat area where there is an obvious campsite. With no water available, this is only useable early in the season when snow can be melted. The trail continues upwards at a gentle grade winding in and out among scattered whitebark pine, subalpine fir and mountain hemlock. **Grouseberry** and yellow **heart-leaf arnica** *(Arnica cordifolia)* are common beneath the trees. Views both north and south from this ridge are exceptional.

Spreading phlox *(Phlox diffusa)* grow in small mats here and there among the rocks, along with **Davidson's penstemon, sulfur buckwheat, small-flowered penstemon** *(Penstemon procerus),* **pussy-toes** *(Antennaria alpina),* and **lupine.** Here the trail intersects the old road and the two continue up to the summit area, where an old lookout once stood. Some cement foundations are the only remains, but the views are still exceptional. Soak in the scenery for a while before retracing your steps back to the trailhead.

On the way down, be careful not to miss the trail junction that leads back to the road. After descending the side hill with views of Mount Hood, you pass a huge boulder that frames the mountain. Just after the boulder, watch closely for an unmarked trail that leads a short distance to the old road.

Wildlife in the area include deer and elk; I found elk tracks in the mud during my hike.

FAN-LEAVED CINQUEFOIL
Potentilla flabellifolia

Yellow-flowered **fan-leaved cinquefoil** grow from a branched, creeping base, and the flowers grow in groups with several to a terminal stem. The leaves are compound in groups of three, and somewhat fan-shaped, as the Latin name *flabellifolia* indicates. The flower is common in moist meadows.

Wildflower Hike 13 Trillium Lake Loop

A breathtaking reflection of Mount Hood from across Trillium Lake.

Trillium Lake offers a classic vista of Mount Hood. The mountain rises dramatically above the lake, providing a fine backdrop for a hike that encircles the lake. The dominant lakeshore species include mountain hemlock, western red cedar, silver fir, and western white pine.

The hike described here starts at campsite 37. As ground cover here, you can spot **queen's cup lily** *(Clintonia uniflora)*, **dwarf dogwood** *(Cornus canadensis)*, **beargrass** *(Xerophyllum tenax)*, and **Pacific rhododendron** *(Rhododendron macrophyllum)*.

From the trailhead, turn right (north) and walk along the shore of the lake. Note the **oval-leaf huckleberry** *(Vaccinium ovalifolium)*, **foamflower**

Nearest Town	Portland
Highlights	A quiet stroll around the lake with great views of Mount Hood
Trail Rating	easy
Trail Length	2.0-mile loop
Location	Trillium Lake campground
Elevation	5,000 feet
Contact	Mount Hood National Forest, 503-666-0700
Bloom Season	June to August
Peak Bloom	July
Directions	From Portland, take US 26 toward Government Camp. Just a few miles beyond Government Camp, turn right onto FR 2656 and follow it to Trillium Lake campground and the trailhead.

(Tiarella trifoliata), **twinflower** *(Linnaea borealis),* **trail-plant** *(Adenocaulon bicolor),* **trillium** *(Trillium ovatum),* **prince's-pine** *(Chimaphila umbellata),* and **parrot beak** *(Pedicularis racemosa).*

The trail passes an open beach on the left, where you find plenty of **beargrass.** As the route passes the amphitheater, look for **mountain-ash** *(Sorbus sitchensis)* with pinnate leaves and clusters of white flowers. The flowers turn in the autumn into bright orange-red berries that are a favorite of birds. **Sitka alder** *(Alnus sinuata),* a shrubby plant common in wetlands and along streams, grow along this portion of the lakeshore.

As the trail continues along the lakeshore, it becomes a boardwalk. Along this route you will occasionally see **fireweed** *(Epilobium angustifolium),* which gets its name for its habit of invading burned forests. **Fireweed** can, however, grow anyplace where there is some disturbed soil and plenty of light. You'll also encounter the beautiful pink **subalpine spirea** *(Spiraea densiflora).* Western red cedar and hemlock plus some lodgepole pine dominate the forest here. Lodgepole pine is common east of the Cascades but is not often found on the western slope.

You pass a cove with many **pond lily** *(Nuphar lutea),* and **mountain-ash** are common on the shore. You can find **serviceberry** *(Amelanchier alnifolia),* which have white flowers in the spring, followed by dark blue berries in late summer. The berries are a favorite of wildlife, and deer and elk browse the twigs.

The trail passes through an area punctuated with old tree stumps that signal past logging. The forest here is dense second-growth timber; little light reaches the forest floor. A bridge crosses a wet, swampy area. **Skunk cabbage** *(Lysichitum americanum)* is abundant in the wetter locations; **dwarf dogwood** and pink **spirea** mark the trail borders. You see also a few **salmonberry** *(Rubus spectabilis)*, **red-osier dogwood** *(Cornus stolonifera)*, and **high-bush cranberry** *(Viburnum edule)*. **High-bush cranberry** are common in Alaska but not seen as often in Oregon. In fact, this part of Trillium's lakeshore reminds me much of Alaska.

You encounter another boardwalk surrounded by more **skunk cabbage** and some **Pacific waterleaf** *(Hydrophyllum tenuipes)*, which have large leaves that are pinnately compound with 7–13 irregular teeth. You traverse yet another boardwalk past young cedar trees mixed in with some young white pine. You also see Engelmann spruce—most frequently associated with wet basins in the Rockies and rather infrequently found in the Cascades. A side boardwalk branches from the main trail, allowing you to walk out into the marsh where **white bog-orchid** *(Habenaria dilatata)* are common.

If you continue on the main trail, you'll pass more **trillium, foamflower,** and **dwarf dogwood**. The path leads to yet another boardwalk that passes through sedges. After leaving the marsh, the trail enters a dry lodgepole pine forest with **beargrass, twinflower,** and a few **rhododendron. Cow-parsnip** *(Heracleum lanatum)*, a plant with large palmate leaves and white umbel flower clusters, live here as well.

You cross another section of marsh on another board-walk. Note the **Queen Anne's lace** *(Daucus carota)*, sometimes called **wild carrot. Queen**

DWARF DOGWOOD
Cornus canadensis

Dwarf dogwood features one white flower that is approximately an inch across. The white "petals," technically, are bracts that surround tiny purple-white flowers on this plant, which rises typically 4–8 inches tall. The plant produces red berries in the fall, hence its alternate name, **bunchberry**. *Canadensis* refers to Canada, where this flower is very common in the boreal forest. In fact, you can find **dwarf dogwood** from the East Coast across Canada to Alaska and south into the Cascades and Rockies.

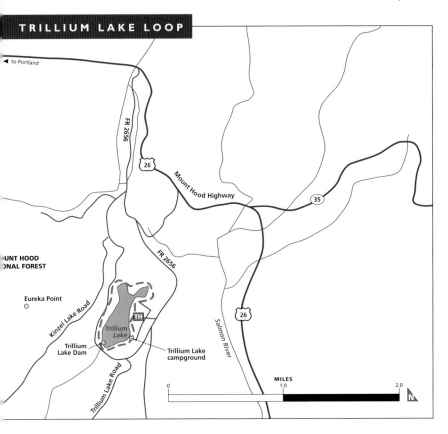

TRILLIUM LAKE LOOP

Anne's lace is indeed the wild ancestor of the domesticated garden carrot. An exotic brought in from Europe, **Queen Anne's lace** is now quite widespread in the Pacific Northwest. Another plant in this marsh area is **Cooley's mint** *(Stachys cooleyae)*, which you can easily recognize by its four-sided stems.

Just beyond the boardwalk grow **black twin-berry** *(Lonicera involucrata)* and **tall larkspur** *(Delphinium glaucum)*. Some **larkspur** are poisonous to both cattle and humans.

At this point, the trail begins to head south along the western shore of the lake. It climbs up slightly away from the lake and passes through more Engelmann spruce. **Inside-out flower** *(Vancouveria hexandra),* named for George Vancouver, a British sea captain who explored the Pacific Northwest Coast in the late eighteenth century, grow here. You can find **thimbleberry** *(Rubus parviflorus)* and **fireweed** growing thickly along this section of shore. Just beyond the very large single spruce on your left, you can enjoy a nice view of the lake.

Climb on another boardwalk that passes lots of **spirea, tall bluebell** *(Mertensia paniculata),* and **parrot beak.** The route loops in and out of some small meadows, then back into the forest with more **false hellebore** *(Veratrum viride),* **meadowrue,** and **baneberry** *(Actaea rubra).* You pass a spring seep that harbors more **white bog-orchid.** The trail eventually reaches a road that passes the dam on the lake's outlet. Walk around through the picnic area, where you can take in great views of Mount Hood. Lots of **spirea** and **thimbleberry** grow in the picnic area.

The trail picks up again at the boat launch, where you pass **huckleberry, rhododendron, dwarf dogwood, mountain-ash, salmonberry,** and other plants you encountered earlier in the hike. Continue on this path to enter the campground. **Lupine** are abundant here, and **beargrass, huckleberry,** and **alder** crowd the lake as you work back to the trail's beginning.

The lush leaves of false hellebore, or corn lily, a highly poisonous plant abundant in subalpine basins.

Timberline Trail

Wildflower Hike 14

Hikers hug the slopes of Zigzag Canyon in the Mount Hood Wilderness.

At 11,237 feet, Mount Hood dominates both its namesake wilderness and the Cascades in Oregon. The volcano, Oregon's highest peak, is draped with 11 glaciers. While exploring the Oregon coast with Captain Vancouver in 1792, Lieutenant Broughton named the mountain for British Admiral Lord Hood.

This hike follows a portion of the 38.0-mile-long Timberline Trail that circles Mount Hood and passes through numerous flowery meadows. The hike starts at Timberline Lodge ski area, where there is a huge parking lot and a confusing mix of trails that all begin at the lodge area. Fortunately, no matter which trail you choose, you will have unending views of Mount Hood and of the Cascades to the south of the mountain, including the Three Sisters and Mount Jefferson.

Nearest Town	Zigzag
Highlights	Subalpine meadows below glacier-clad Mount Hood
Trail Rating	moderate
Trail Length	6.0 miles round-trip
Location	Mount Hood Wilderness
Elevation	4,500–6,000 feet
Contact	Mount Hood National Forest, 503-666-0700
Bloom Season	July to September
Peak Bloom	August
Directions	From Portland, take US 26 east to Government Camp, then turn left onto Timberline Highway and drive 6.0 miles to the trailhead and parking at Timberline Lodge on Mount Hood's south slope.

Timberline Lodge was built in the 1930s as a Civilian Conservation Corps make-work project and is now on the National Register of Historic Places. Inside the lodge, and worth a visit before setting out, is a museum where you can learn some early history of the area and ski resort. After visiting the museum, exit the lodge and head west on a signed, paved trail that leads to the Pacific Crest Trail. If you're hiking this trail in late July or August, you are likely to see **avalanche lily** *(Erythronium montanum)*, **spreading phlox** *(Phlox diffusa)*, **alpine buckwheat** *(Eriogonum pyrolifolium)*, **alpine lupine** *(Lupinus arcticus)*, and **broadleaf lupine** *(Lupinus latifolius)* just beyond the lodge.

The trail passes a tree island where more **broadleaf lupine** grow, then comes to a sign for Timberline Lodge and PCT 2000. If you reach this sign, you're on the trail described

SITKA VALERIAN
Valeriana sitchensis

The white flowers of **Sitka valerian** are grouped in a tight white terminal cluster and the leaves are coarsely toothed. The plant has a strong odor and is common in subalpine meadows.

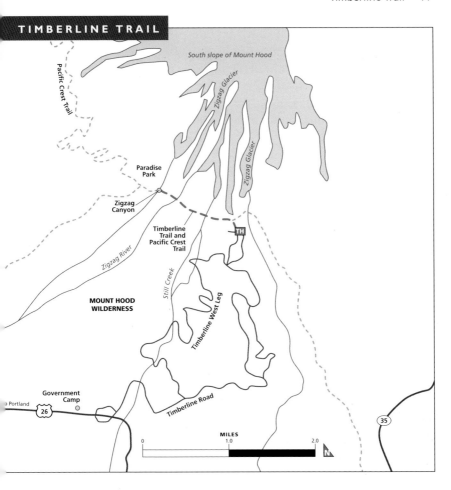

here. **Red Indian-paintbrush** *(Castilleja miniata)* and lots of **lupine** and **Cascade aster** *(Aster ledophyllus)* surround the sign. On the dry, ashy slopes, you see **partridgefoot** *(Luetkea pectinata)* and **Newberry's knotweed** *(Polygonum newberryi)*.

Just after crossing under old ski lifts, note **mountain-ash** *(Sorbus sitchensis)* on the left near some mountain hemlock. **Mountain-ash** are easy to recognize with their pinnate leaves and white flowers forming a round, top terminal cluster. The orange-red berries are a favorite of wildlife.

After a short walk, another tree island sports a riot of color with more **lupine, senecio** *(Senecio triangularis),* **heart-leaf arnica** *(Arnica cordifolia),* **parrot beak** *(Pedicularis racemosa),* **Sitka valerian** *(Valeriana sitchensis),* **slender hawkweed** *(Hieracium gracile),* and **red Indian-paintbrush.**

The route soon comes to the trail junction for Silcox Hut #798 and another sign marking the way along the PCT toward Paradise Park. The Silcox

Hut, once the upper terminal for Mount Hood's first ski lift built in 1939, is now a chalet with bunks and a café for overnight guests.

At 1.0 mile, the trail switchbacks into the spectacular and rugged Little Zigzag Canyon. The boundary for the Mount Hood Wilderness lies on the western side of the canyon. Growing here you can find plenty of **aster, lupine**, mountain hemlock, and, immediately beyond the sign, **cat's-ear lily** *(Calochortus subalpinus)*.

The trail heads down into forest with **round-leaved violet** *(Viola orbiculata)*, **dwarf bramble** *(Rubus lasiococcus)*, **heart-leaf arnica**, and a noble fir forest mixed with mountain hemlock. In the forest, you encounter **black huckleberry** *(Vaccinium membranaceum)*, **foamflower** *(Tiarella trifoliata)*, and **Oregon fawn-lily** *(Erythronium oregonum)*. A short way into the forest, you come to an open meadow slope with **lupine, false hellebore** *(Veratrum viride)*, **Sitka valerian** *(Valeriana sitchensis)*, and **mountain-ash**. A tiny stream provides a habitat for the lovely **pink monkey-flower** *(Mimulus lewisii)*, the Latin name honoring Meriwether Lewis of the Lewis and Clark Expedition.

The trail descends to an open slope with views of Mount Hood and proceeds through several patches of mountain ash. Some 1.2 miles beyond Little Zigzag Canyon, the trail circles around to a ridge above dramatic Zigzag Canyon. **Beargrass** *(Xerophyllum tenax)* grows on the ridge overlooking the canyon, plus **lupine, pearly-everlasting** *(Anaphalis margaritacea)*, and **Jacob's-ladder** *(Polemonium pulcherrimum)*.

This is the perfect spot to eat lunch, take a rest, admire the fabulous scenery, then turn around. If you are really motivated, you can continue another 1.5 miles on to Paradise Meadows—one of the most stunning flower gardens on the slopes of Mount Hood. Reaching Paradise Meadows requires a rugged climb down, then up and out of Zigzag Canyon, so it's not something to do on a lark.

Table Rock

Rhododendron blooms brighten the forest understory in the Table Rock Wilderness.

This hike into Table Rock Wilderness offers first-rate **Pacific rhododendron** *(Rhododendron macrophyllum)* blooms, plus spectacular vistas of Mount Jefferson and Mount Hood. A basalt outcrop, including the 4,881-foot Table Rock, provides commanding viewpoints. Although the hike is long and almost continuously uphill, the trail has an easy grade and makes for a very pleasant walk through a forested ecosystem.

Table Rock Wilderness is one of the few wilderness areas in the lower-elevation areas of the Cascades. Most of the Molalla drainage has succumbed to industrial forestry—it is astounding that the butchery of an entire river valley was permitted, much less legal. Yet, looking out over the steep slopes sheared of trees, you can still admire the hard work and difficult conditions

Nearest Town	Molalla
Highlights	Exceptional rhododendron blooms
Trail Rating	moderate
Trail Length	7.0 miles round-trip
Location	Table Rock Wilderness
Elevation	3,600–4,881 feet
Contact	BLM, Salmon District, 503-375-5646
Bloom Season	May to August
Peak Bloom	June
Directions	From I-5, take the Woodburn Exit 271 east onto OR 214 to OR 211 and continue east to Molalla. Turn right onto Mathias, then left onto Feyrer Park Road, then right again onto Dickey Prairie Road along the Molalla River to Upper Molalla Road. Drive 12.0 miles on this road, following signs at all major road junctions to gravel Table Rock Road and another 4.0 miles or so to the trailhead. This last stretch takes longer than you might expect—allow plenty of time to make the drive from I-5. The logging road that formerly provided trailhead access recently fell away in a landslide. The new trailhead adds a mile or so to the hike.

faced by loggers who risked life and limb to get the cut out. Unfortunately, they were all too successful, and Table Rock remains an island of forested habitat in the midst of regrowing clear-cuts. Forests of Douglas fir and western hemlock cloak the wilderness area's lower slopes, while Alaskan cedar and noble fir grow at higher elevations.

Despite the fact that it's only 40 air miles from Portland—many more by road—the area receives few visitors. This 5,750-acre wilderness, designated in 1984, is managed by the BLM.

From the trailhead, you walk a mile or more on the old roadbed. The road is lined with **alder** *(Alnus crispa)*, a shrub, and the occasional tree. **Alder**, a nitrogen-fixing species, enriches the soil. You can also see the white blooms of **oxeye daisy** *(Leucanthemum vulgare)*, an exotic that colonizes disturbed habitat. **Woodland penstemon** *(Nothochelone nemorosa)*, **Oregon sunshine** *(Eriophyllum lanatum)*, and **rhododendron** grow on roadside slopes. The large, leathery, evergreen leaves of **rhododendron** are an adaptation to drought. Despite heavy rains in winter, Oregon summers are typically rainless. With leaves that resist water loss, **rhododendron** can better survive the dry summers.

About 0.25 mile up from the new trailhead, you pass a small stream on the right. Here you see **yellow monkey-flower** *(Mimulus guttatus)*, a species common along seeps and waterways.

A 1996 landslide wiped out most of the roadway just as it reaches the corner of the slope. A new trail now goes up into a western hemlock forest and rejoins the road beyond the slide. A few **huckleberry** *(Vaccinium sp.)*, deciduous shrubs with delicious fruit that ripens in August, are here. Look for **prince's-pine** *(Chimaphila umbellata)*, another species with evergreen leaves adapted to drought. **Oregon grape** *(Mahonia nervosa)*, which grow on the forest floor, have hollylike evergreen leaves that are drought-tolerant as well. The common understory shrub-tree **vine maple** *(Acer circinatum)* also live here.

The trail reaches the old road that now heads eastward. More **alder** mark the roadside, and **paintbrush** *(Castilleja sp.)* are also common in this section. Because there are many different *Castilleja* in Oregon, keying out the various **paintbrush** species is not always easy. **Paintbrush** "flowers" are actually the leafy bracts surrounding the flowers. Most species are partly parasitic and live on the roots of other plants.

As you follow the old road eastward, you pass an area where the roadcut exposes an ash flow covered by a lava flow. All of Table Mountain is part of the western Cascades volcanic region, so evidence of past eruptions and lava flows is abundant.

The roadcut provides habitat for multiple species that are abundant on disturbed sites. For example, **fireweed** *(Epilobium angustifolium)* grow here—and when they're flowering the bright pink blossoms are quite striking.

On the uphill slope of the road, you will pass an old clear-cut. Among the small trees are **beargrass** *(Xerophyllum tenax)* and **goatsbeard** *(Aruncus dioicus)*. The showy **beargrass** is a member of the lily family and has thin, grasslike leaves. All along the edge of the forest in this section you can see **rhododendron** in bloom.

About 1.0 mile from the parking area, you reach the old trailhead. The road continues eastward to other clear-cuts, but the signed trail is on the right.

As you enter a lovely forest dominated by Douglas fir and Pacific silver fir, the change in vegetation from the disturbed habitat along the road is evident. You will find typical interior forest species such as **dwarf dogwood** *(Cornus canadensis)*, **vanillaleaf** *(Achlys triphylla)*, **queen's cup lily** *(Clintonia uniflora)*, **twinflower** *(Linnaea borealis)*, and **foamflower** *(Tiarella trifoliata)*. **Twinflower's** Latin name *Linnaea* honors Swedish scientist Linnaeus, who developed the binomial nomenclature system of genus and species name that we use today.

Several larger flowers and shrubs, including **gooseberry**, also known as **currant** *(Ribes lobbii)*, **thimbleberry** *(Rubus parviflorus)*, more **huckleberry**, **false hellebore** *(Veratrum viride)*, and **devil's club** *(Oplopanax horridum)*, thrive

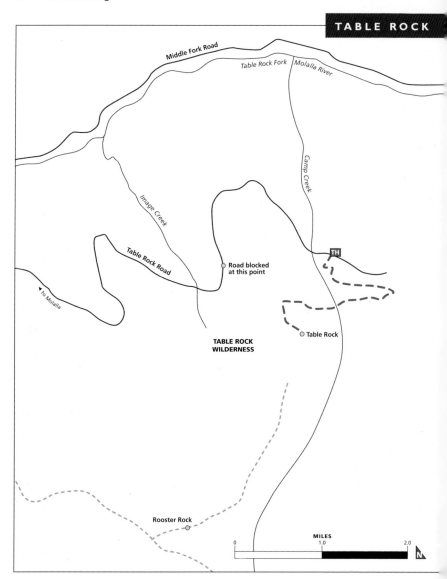

TABLE ROCK

Middle Fork Road

Table Rock Fork | Molalla River

Camp Creek

Image Creek

Table Rock Road

to Molalla

TH

Road blocked
at this point

○ Table Rock

**TABLE ROCK
WILDERNESS**

Rooster Rock
○

MILES
0   1.0   2.0

N

in the understory. The appropriately named **devil's club** has large thorns on its leaves and stems that contain a toxin, which causes swelling and pain upon contact. The large evergreen **sword-fern** *(Polystichum munitum)* is common here and there on the forest floor as well.

After a very short walk, you encounter a sign explaining a few things about the wilderness area. Note the uneven topography of the forest floor in this area. As trees fall, they pull up a mass of soil with the root wad, creating a lumpy forest floor.

As you proceed up the trail, some sections have almost no understory growth because of the intense shade under the forest canopy. Most of the forest in this area is relatively young and has a very closed canopy, allowing little light penetration.

Off to the left, you'll pass a big patch of **devil's club**. A few new interior forest plants grow in this section of trail, including the white-flowered **three-leaved anemone** *(Anemone deltoidea)*, **trillium** *(Trillium ovatum)*—very showy in early spring—and **star-flowered false Solomon's seal** *(Smilacina stellata)*.

The trail curves up to a viewpoint featuring an expansive look at the clear-cuts stretching up the Molalla drainage. **Rhododendron** and **beargrass** are very common along this section of trail—and quite beautiful when all the blossoms are in bloom.

As the trail curves back into the mountain, you again encounter more **dwarf dogwood, queen's cup lily**, and **Oregon grape** along the path. You'll hear varied thrush calling in the distance.

The trail cuts around to the west again. Here you'll find **sorrel** *(Oxalis oregana)* and **round-leaved violet** *(Viola orbiculata)*. **Sorrel**, easy to identify by their cloverlike leaves, often forms almost continuous cover on the forest floor in favorable locations.

The trail continues west, gently rising along a bench where there is little growing on the forest floor. As the trail curves into a valley with a small stream, there are more **rhododendron**. Right along the trail sits an Alaskan cedar tree with a yellow arrow painted on it. Although Alaskan cedar are relatively rare in the Cascades, they are common along the Table Rock trail.

The streamside area is relatively lush, and you can spot more **vanillaleaf, huckleberry, devil's club, queen's cup lily**, and **false hellebore**. Salmonberry *(Rubus spectabilis)*, shrubs that sport bold pink blooms early in the spring, also grow here along with **Sitka valerian** *(Valeriana sitchensis)*, which sport terminal clusters of small, white flowers.

Off to the right through the trees you can see a talus slope and cliff—and if you're lucky you may hear pikas cry

OREGON SUNSHINE
Eriophyllum lanatum

Oregon sunshine, a member of the sunflower family, certainly resembles a sunflower with its bright yellow blossoms that grow on the end of long stalks. The leaves are narrowly lobed, and the plant thrives in dry, open habitats.

from the rocks. Pikas, which look like tiny rabbits, emit a loud "eek" when alarmed.

The path climbs southeast, passing more **sorrel, dwarf dogwood, round-leaved violet, foamflower,** and **vanillaleaf.** You pass another talus slope, strewn with **vine maple,** that lies directly below another rocky cliff.

The trail curves around the eastern shoulder of the ridge, passing through more **beargrass** and lots of **rhododendron** in bloom. You pass below some cliffs and encounter more **Oregon grape, false Solomon's seal** *(Smilacina racemosa),* and **alumroot** *(Heuchera micrantha).* **Thimbleberry** is very thick along the path and nearly encloses the trail within a wall of green.

As the trail passes the rocky area, you find a lot more **rhododendron,** plus **mountain boxwood** *(Pachistima myrsinites),* a small evergreen shrub. **Wild rose** *(Rosa gymnocarpa)* and **parrot beak** *(Pedicularis racemosa)* also grow here.

A side trail breaks off to the right and climbs up a rocky ridge that offers superb views of Mount Hood and Mount Jefferson. On those dry, rocky slopes grow **kinnikinnick** *(Arctostaphylos uva-ursi).* With their evergreen leaves and sprawling habit, the plants look like tiny **manzanitas.** Also growing among the dry slopes are **cat's-ear lily** *(Calochortus subalpinus),* **spreading phlox** *(Phlox diffusa),* and **rock penstemon** *(Penstemon rupicola).*

The main trail continues upward through more **rhododendron, beargrass,** and Alaskan cedar. After taking you more than 1.5 miles from the trailhead, the trail eventually winds up to the base of Table Rock, a massive, 500-foot cliff of basalt, the relic of an ancient volcano plug. Among the talus boulders are **Pacific bleedingheart** *(Dicentra formosa),* red **western columbine** *(Aquilegia formosa),* **valerian, huckleberry,** and **red elderberry** *(Sambucus racemosa).* Savor the great views from this point.

The trail traverses the face of the cliff, then winds up a ridge to where the path to the summit of Table Rock leaves the trail to Rooster Rock. The last 0.5 mile zigzags up to the summit and affords superb views on clear days.

Trail of Ten Falls Loop

South Falls, a main attraction on the
Trail of Ten Falls, Silver Falls State Park.

Salem	***Nearest Town***
Lovely forest hike past spectacular waterfalls	***Highlights***
moderate	***Trail Rating***
Entire trail is a 2.5-mile loop	***Trail Length***
Silver Falls State Park	***Location***
1,080–1,330 feet	***Elevation***
Silver Falls State Park, 503-873-3495	***Contact***
April to July	***Bloom Season***
May to June	***Peak Bloom***
From I-5 in Salem, take OR 22 east about 8 miles to OR 214, turn left and continue east to Silver Falls State Park. Park by the Nature Center.	***Directions***

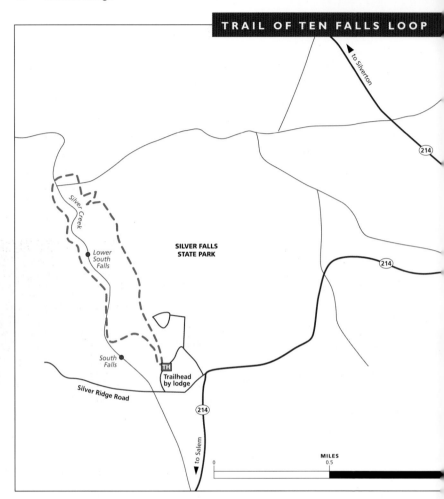

The canyons at Silver Falls State Park boast 10 major waterfalls, with five higher than 100 feet. A resistance layer of lava created the falls. The forested canyon of second-growth forest includes many flowers and shrubs common in the Cascade foothills. Open year-round, the park provides wonderful hiking options throughout the year. Spring, however, with its numerous blooming shrubs and ground cover, is absolutely enchanting.

The 8,706-acre Silver Falls State Park is Oregon's largest state park and is set in the foothills of the Cascades. Its scenic splendor continues to attract a national following, and it was once considered a candidate for national park status. The major scenic features of the park include the waterfall-riddled canyons of the North Fork and South Fork of Silver Creek. The park was the site of Silver Falls City, but the surrounding forests were logged, and in time the town disappeared. The federal government acquired the land during the 1930s and created a recreation demonstration site, constructing a lodge, camp facilities, and trails. In the 1940s, this site was finally ceded to Oregon to be maintained as a state park.

The trailhead is to the east of the nature center—away from the parking area and restrooms. The trail is paved as it descends toward the 177-foot South Falls. As you descend into the canyon of the North Fork of Silver Creek, you encounter the delicate, branching **vine maple** *(Acer circinatum),* a common understory species in the region's Douglas fir forests. Below the **vine maple**, a number of common shrubs grow, including the hollylike evergreen leaves of **Oregon grape** *(Mahonia nervosa),* **red huckleberry** *(Vaccinium parvifolium),* and the tough, leathery-leaved **salal** *(Gaultheria shallon).* The lovely, pink-flowered **salmonberry** *(Rubus spectabilis)* is common as well. Ground cover consists of the evergreen **sword-fern** *(Polystichum munitum)* along with flowers such as **false lily-of-the-valley** *(Maianthemum dilatatum),* **Pacific bleedingheart** *(Dicentra formosa),* and **yellow violet** *(Viola glabella).*

As you descend into the canyon, you'll enjoy some great views of South Falls. You also encounter more **sword-fern** and **vine maple**, plus **candyflower** *(Claytonia sibirica)* with its distinctive egg-shaped paired leaves.

At the first switchback is a sign for Frenchie Falls. Some good examples of lacy **maidenhair fern** *(Adiantum pedatum)* and **Brewer's mitrewort** *(Mitella breweri)* edge a wet bank above the trail.

After making the turn, you encounter **wild rose** *(Rosa sp.)* on the right downslope side of the trail just before you reach a fence. On the left, you can see more **maidenhair fern**. Showy, white cluster blooms of **false Solomon's seal** *(Smilacina racemosa)* are also abundant here.

You soon reach a trail junction. To the left, the trail winds around behind South Falls. If you've never done this hike before, it's worth taking a diversion to walk behind the falls and experience the amazing rush of water pouring past you just a few feet away. If you don't take the left fork, spend a moment admiring the falls, then take the right fork.

At the switchback, **Oregon saxifrage** *(Saxifraga oregana)* thrive in a wet seep. Along

WESTERN CORYDALIS
Corydalis scouleri

Western corydalis often form dense patches of pinkish-white blooms in moist forests. The flowers have long spurs and grow in long, spikelike racemes with 10–35 flowers. The leaves are much divided. The plant is named for Dr. John Scouler, an early Pacific Northwest botanist.

the trail you can also find the white-flowered **sorrel** *(Oxalis oregana)* with their cloverlike, heart-shaped leaves. Lots of **salmonberry, sword-fern,** and **vine maple** also border the trail. **Indian plum** *(Osmaronia cerasiformis),* one of the earliest-flowering shrubs in the region, is also found here.

When you reach the creek and a bench, you will find **Pacific waterleaf** *(Hydrophyllum tenuipes).* Clusters of **yellow violet, bleedingheart,** and **sorrel** surround the bench, and this spot offers wonderful views of the falls.

The trail crosses a bridge over the North Fork of Silver Creek. On the other side, the main trail heads right down the canyon, following closely along the creek. About 30 feet down the trail, you'll see some **thimbleberry** *(Rubus parviflorus),* which feature lovely white blossoms and large, tropical-looking leaves. The berries, which ripen in July and August, are edible and sweet.

You continue to encounter **false lily-of-the-valley, yellow violet, sorrel, bleedingheart,** and **salmonberry** along the trail. In addition, you'll see tall shrubs of **red elderberry** *(Sambucus racemosa),* which sport clusters of creamy-white blossoms. You can identify **Hooker fairy-bell** *(Disporum hookeri)* here by their two or three bell-shaped white blossoms and lance-shaped leaves. You pass another bench that is surrounded by **salmonberry** and lots of **candyflower.**

In patches along the way, you find abundant clumps of **western corydalis** *(Corydalis scouleri)* with their terminal clusters of pinkish flowers. At another bench by a large stump, **corydalis** are practically the only ground cover you will find. Eventually, the trail takes you down a switchback and under the Lower South Falls, which are only 93 feet high but broader than South Falls.

The trail takes you back down along the creek, passing through forests of bigleaf maple, along with some western red cedar and Douglas fir. You will pass more **false lily-of-the-valley, bleedingheart, yellow violet,** and **salmonberry.** Finally the trail climbs out of the canyon to join the ridge trail. Here the forest becomes somewhat drier and you see more **salal** along with **red huckleberry.**

When you reach a sign that says the trailhead for Ridge Trail is 1.2 miles, there is a bench surrounded by old-growth Douglas fir and **huckleberry.** The trail leads up to a switchback with another bench. Along the way you pass more **salmonberry, waterleaf, sorrel,** and lots of **vine maple.**

Once you reach the ridge, you see more Douglas fir along with **Oregon fawn-lily** *(Erythronium oregonum)* and **striped coral-root orchid** *(Corallorhiza striata).* The **vine maple's** stunning, lime-green foliage—with light filtering through it—creates an arch across the trail and is particularly beautiful in the spring. The ridge trail takes you back to the main trailhead by the lodge. You pass a "No Dogs Allowed" sign, near which grows **skunk cabbage** *(Lysichitum americanum),* with large leaves lending them a tropical look.

As you approach the picnic area and the original trailhead by the lodge, the vegetation along the trail doesn't differ much. You encounter a few western hemlock along with western red cedar.

Elk Lake Creek

Wildflower
Hike 17

Serene Elk Lake in the Bull of the Woods Wilderness.

Salem	***Nearest Town***
Open old-growth forest	***Highlights***
moderate	***Trail Rating***
1.0 mile each way	***Trail Length***
Bull of the Woods Wilderness	***Location***
3,900–3,500 feet (descent)	***Elevation***
Willamette National Forest, 541-465-6521	***Contact***
June to August	***Bloom Season***
July	***Peak Bloom***

Directions

From Salem, take OR 22 (North Santiam Highway) east to Detroit and follow signs for FR 46 (Breitenbush Road) and the Breitenbush River. After 4.4 miles, turn left for Elk Lake on FR 4696. The road is steep and very rough, but passable in two-wheel-drive vehicles. Follow this road less than 0.5 mile, and then turn left on FR 4697. After 4.7 miles, turn left at the sign for Elk Lake. Here the road narrows and is again rough; go slowly. After about 1.0 miles of crawling along this road, you reach parking by the lake and its outlet. The trailhead is 100 feet or so beyond the creek.

Elk Lake, a beautiful, glacially-carved lake, rests below Battle Ax Mountain (the highest peak in the Bull of the Woods Wilderness). An absolutely terrible road leads to a campground at the west end of the lake, 1.0 mile beyond the trailhead. Flowery meadows decorate the far end of the lake.

The hike down Elk Lake Creek passes through the Bull of the Woods Wilderness. Established in 1984, the 34,900-acre wilderness preserve, 40 miles east of Salem, protects a relict of the old Cascades forests, including huge, old specimens of Douglas fir, silver fir, and western hemlock.

SKUNK CABBAGE
Lysichitum americanum

With their giant, tropical-looking leaves, **skunk cabbage** seem out of place in the Pacific Northwest. The leaves may extend up to 6 feet long in very large specimens. The greenish-yellow flower on a spike is surrounded on three sides by a large yellow hood. **Skunk cabbage** is found in swamps and seeps as far north as southeast Alaska.

The entire Elk Lake Creek Trail (#559) gradually descends 8.9 miles to a lower trailhead on the eastern side of the wilderness. You could easily spend a weekend backpacking this trail, but I defined only the first mile or so for this wildflower hike.

An abundance of Alaskan cedar sits right at the trailhead. Alaskan cedar are not very common in the Cascades, reaching their southern limits in northern California. Other trees common in this forest include silver fir, Douglas fir, and western hemlock. **Red huckleberry** *(Vaccinium parvifolium)* are common an understory plants. You also can see **twinflower** *(Linnaea borealis),* **dwarf dogwood** *(Cornus canadensis),* and **parrot beak** *(Pedicularis racemosa).*

Very shortly, you will pass a sign that announces the border of the Bull of the Woods Wilderness. Just beyond the sign grow **queen's cup lily** *(Clintonia uniflora)* and **vanillaleaf** *(Achlys triphylla).* **Vanillaleaf**, a common species on the floor of shady forests, has three-part leaves that resemble large maple leaves.

You reach a small, wet, muddy area where **vine maple** *(Acer circinatum)* can grow. **Vine maple**, one of the most beautiful and common understory shrub-trees, add a splash of color to the otherwise somber, conifer-dominated forests. Their lime-green leaves glow in the summer forest and turn bright crimson in fall.

Here you also see **foamflower** *(Tiarella trifoliata),* featuring small, very delicate white

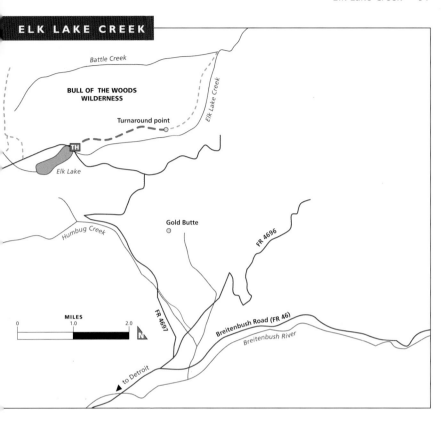

flowers and three-lobed leaves. When dense, the flowers look like foam on the forest floor, hence the name.

In another 100 yards you reach a second wet area. **Alder** *(Alnus crispa)*, **huckleberry,** and **skunk cabbage** *(Lysichitum americanum)* are all conspicuous here. You'll also see **false hellebore** *(Veratrum viride),* a robust plant that grows up to 6 feet tall and has ovate, strongly veined, cabbagelike leaves. The plant grows in meadows and wet areas throughout the West.

The trail curves along the slope to the northeast through amazing large trees. You also encounter **inside-out flower** *(Vancouveria hexandra),* named for Captain George Vancouver, who explored the coast of the Pacific Northwest in the 1790s. A few **Pacific rhododendron** *(Rhododendron macrophyllum)* and **beargrass** *(Xerophyllum tenax)* grow in the forest among scattered and very ancient Douglas fir. Other plants you see include more **vanillaleaf, trail-plant** *(Adenocaulon bicolor)*, and **whiteveined wintergreen** *(Pyrola picta).*

You come to a bridge that passes over a wet seep. The beautiful white flowers of **three-leaved anemone** *(Anemone deltoidea)* are scattered about the ground. You also see **salmonberry** *(Rubus spectabilis),* **red huckleberry, senecio**

(Senecio triangularis), and **false bugbane** *(Trautvetteria caroliniensis).* **False bugbane**, a member of the buttercup family, has a chemical compound that causes skin irritation upon contact. Other plants by the seep include **deer-fern** *(Blechnum spicant),* **false hellebore, thimbleberry** *(Rubus parviflorus),* and **false Solomon's seal** *(Smilacina racemosa).*

Slightly farther down the trail is another seep. Here, you can spot more **skunk cabbage, trillium** *(Trillium ovatum),* **foamflower, thimbleberry, vanilla-leaf,** and green **slender bog orchid** *(Habenaria stricta).* **Huckleberry** are thick, and there are more Alaskan cedar.

Yet another seep is passed with more **trillium, false bugbane, dwarf dogwood,** and **prince's-pine** *(Chimaphila umbellata).* The trail crosses a spring with a larger wet area that is dense with **skunk cabbage, false hellebore,** and **thimbleberry.** You also pass a dense stand of **rhododendron.**

This spot makes a good turnaround point as the trail begins to sidehill above the creek slightly ahead.

Hikers enjoy the coniferous forests along the Elk Lake Creek Trail.

Middle Santiam

Old-growth groves still stand in the Middle Santiam Wilderness.

Sweet Home	*Nearest Town*
Some of the most extensive old-growth forest remaining in the Cascades	*Highlights*
moderate	*Trail Rating*
5.0 miles round-trip	*Trail Length*
Middle Santiam Wilderness	*Location*
1,900–2,400 feet	*Elevation*
Willamette National Forest, 541-465-6521	*Contact*
May to August	*Bloom Season*
June	*Peak Bloom*
From Sweet Home, take US 20 (Santiam Highway) east for 25.0 miles to tiny Upper Soda, and turn left (north) on FR 2041 (Soda Fork Road) just before Mountain House Restaurant. Take FR 2041 for 16.0 miles past many confusing road crossings in a maze of clear-cuts and logging roads. If you top over a ridge and begin to descend into the Middle Santiam drainage, you have successfully negotiated the road network. At a big bend on FR 2041, turn right onto FR 646, then bear left onto FR 647 to at its end at the Chimney Peak Trailhead.	*Directions*

This is a quiet hike through old-growth forest on the eastern border of the Middle Santiam Wilderness, about 36 miles east of Sweet Home. Here are some of the best examples of old-growth forest remaining on the western slope of the Cascades. According to some, this wilderness contains the largest continuous concentration of large trees left in the state. A special botanical feature of this region is sugar pine, which sports 12-inch-long cones. Sugar pine reaches its northern limits here.

Although the 1984 Oregon Forest Wilderness Act designated the 8,553-acre Middle Santiam Wilderness, more than 16,000 roadless acres adjacent to the new wilderness were left out of protection. The elevation in the wilderness varies from 1,500 to 4,965 feet at the top of Chimney Peak.

This hike takes you into the Pyramid Peak roadless area (immediately east of the designated wilderness) via the Chimney Peak Trail. Although the area is not particularly high in elevation, it's typically impossible to get to the trailhead much before the end of May due to lingering snowdrifts blocking the access roads.

From the Chimney Peak Trailhead (Trail #3382), the path descends to the Shedd Camp Shelter, crosses the Middle Santiam River on a logjam, and then continues uphill and around a shoulder of a mountain before descending into Pyramid Creek Valley. Pyramid Creek requires wading as it has no bridge. If you continue on this trail, you will eventually enter the Middle Santiam Wilderness and reach Donaca Lake, the only water body in the wilderness.

The forest immediately surrounding the trailhead consists of Douglas fir and western hemlock with an understory of **bracken fern** *(Pteridium aquilinum)*, **Oregon grape** *(Mahonia nervosa)*, **salal** *(Gaultheria shallon)*, **red huckleberry** *(Vaccinium parvifolium)*, **dwarf dogwood** *(Cornus canadensis)*, and **twinflower** *(Linnaea borealis)*.

The trail heads downhill and quickly crosses a small creek featuring the tropical-looking **skunk cabbage** *(Lysichitum americanum)*. **Sword-fern** *(Polystichum munitum)*, **thimbleberry** *(Rubus parviflorus)*, and **foamflower** *(Tiarella trifoliata)* also grow here. While **bracken fern** is deciduous, dying back each winter, the leathery evergreen fronds of **sword-fern** remain all winter.

The trail goes through an old clear-cut that consists mostly of the regrowth of small trees. The trail follows a small creek through a forest of **red alder** *(Alnus rubra)*, a colonizing species that often comes in after a fire or logging. Immediately next to the stream grows **coast boykinia** *(Boykinia elata)*, which have thin, wispy stems with small, delicate white flowers. Growing beneath the **alder** are **candyflower** *(Claytonia sibirica)* and **trillium** *(Trillium ovatum)*, both early spring bloomers. **Trillium** is sometimes known as **wake robin**. **Oregon grape** and **salal** continue to be common.

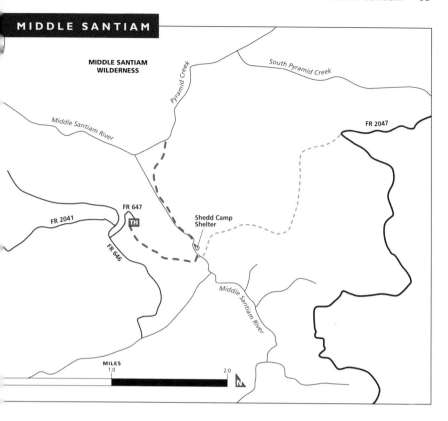

MIDDLE SANTIAM

MIDDLE SANTIAM
WILDERNESS

Pyramid Creek

South Pyramid Creek

Middle Santiam River

FR 2047

FR 647

FR 2041

TH

Shedd Camp
Shelter

FR 646

Middle Santiam River

MILES
1.0   2.0

You pass a few **Pacific rhododendron** *(Rhododendron macrophyllum)*, the beautiful, large pink blooms lighting up the forest. In a few places, **dwarf dogwood** create an almost continuous carpet on the forest floor. Where you don't find dogwood, **vanillaleaf** *(Achlys triphylla)* seem to take their place.

The trail passes into a more mature, uncut forest and starts to descend by switchbacks toward the Middle Santiam River. The forest is dominated by older Douglas fir with a nice understory of **rhododendron**. A few western red cedar and western hemlock are mixed in with the Douglas fir. **Red huckleberry**, with pale-green oval leaves, grow in abundance along this section of trail.

After the second switchback, you can spot the lacy fronds of **maidenhair fern** *(Adiantum pedatum)* growing along the trail. **Trail-plant** *(Adenocaulon bicolor)*, which also grows here, is named for its ability to mark the trail. The bottom part of the leaf is lighter than the surface, so when something disturbs it, the lighter parts remain upright, marking the "trail."

You come to a point where a major elk trail intersects the trail, and just beyond you see a western yew, also known as Pacific yew. Once considered only a "trash" tree by loggers, yew is now used to treat cancer.

The trail levels off in a valley. You pass a thick cluster of **thimbleberry** and more yew trees, then cross another small creek with lots of **maidenhair fern** and **sorrel** *(Oxalis oregana)*. You can discover **Star-flowered false Solomon's seal** *(Smilacina stellata)* and **broad-leaved starflower** *(Trientalis latifolia)* both flourishing beside the stream, just beyond which lies a seep in which **devil's club** *(Oplopanax horridum)* grow.

The trail finally reaches the Middle Santiam River and the Shedd Camp Shelter. The wooden lean-to shelter sits on a high bank above the river by a deep swimming hole. The trail heads right to a ford across the river, where giant logs are stacked to provide a crossing place.

After you cross the Middle Santiam River, the trail takes you up into the forest on a rocky ridge. As you enter the forest, look for the **serviceberry** shrub *(Amelanchier alnifolia)*. **Serviceberry** has white blossoms in the spring and dark purple-black berries in the fall. On this same rocky site grow **Douglas' maple** *(Acer douglasii)*, which is related to Rocky Mountain maple and similar to the more common **vine maple** *(Acer circinatum)*. **Broadleaf lupine** *(Lupinus latifolius)* also grow here, along with more **Oregon grape** and **salal**.

The trail now heads northwest above the river, gradually pulling away from the stream. You pass through very large Douglas fir with a **rhododendron** understory. Here you also see **dwarf dogwood, foamflower, vanillaleaf,** and **red huckleberry**.

As you walk the trail in this area, note the large trees, plus the abundance of downed woody material, fallen logs, and snags. These are all classic characteristics of old-growth forest. Logged forests lack fallen logs and woody debris, and given the short rotations in commercially managed forests, are unlikely to ever have them again.

You come to a trail junction. The right fork is the South Pyramid Creek Trail; take the left fork that goes on to Chimney Peak. The trail

SORREL
Oxalis oregana

Sorrel feature white to pale pink flowers that are often closed. Delicate, cloverlike leaves make them easy to recognize. Known sometimes as **redwood sorrel**, the plant is a common ground cover in shady old-growth forests and sometimes forms continuous patches of emerald green.

crosses a small drainage that features good examples of nurse logs—fallen, old, partially-rotted tree trunks that provide seed beds and nutrients for new trees.

After crossing the creek, the trail heads southwest, passing lots of **red huckleberry** and a few **Pacific dogwood** *(Cornus nuttallii)*. The trail climbs into a small tributary creek valley and crosses a small bridge over a seep with lots of **maidenhair fern**. You cross another small creek that sports **skunk cabbage** and **salmonberry** *(Rubus spectabilis)*. **Palmate coltsfoot** *(Petasites palmatus)* also grow near the stream.

As the trail winds up and away from the creek, you cross a level bench with very large old trees. **Salal, rhododendron, Oregon grape**, and western yew dominate the understory here.

As you continue, the trail crosses a sidehill above Pyramid Creek with occasional views of Chimney Peak and the unlogged slopes of the Middle Santiam Wilderness. Along the trail you'll see a few Incense cedar—a tree more typical of the Sierra Nevadas and areas in southern Oregon's Cascades. The trail passes a rock ledge bearing seeps festooned with **maidenhair fern**. A bit of **beargrass** *(Xerophyllum tenax)* lives on the open slope just before you reach a flat by Pyramid Creek.

Finally, the trail descends to Pyramid Creek, where a beautiful, flat campsite lies beside the stream. The stream makes a good place to turn around and retrace your steps to the trailhead.

Wildflower Hike 19

House Rock Loop

The South Santiam River, Willamette National Forest.

Nearest Town	Sweet Home
Highlights	A loop through old-growth forest with a waterfall
Trail Rating	easy
Trail Length	0.8-mile loop
Location	House Rock campground
Elevation	1,680–2,000 feet
Contact	Willamette National Forest, 541-465-6521
Bloom Season	April to July
Peak Bloom	May to June
Directions	From Sweet Home, take US 20 (Santiam Highway) east 25.3 miles, and take a right at the turnoff for House Rock campground (FR 2044). Drive 0.5 mile, crossing the South Santiam River. The trailhead and parking are in the picnic/hiker area just before Sheep Creek and the campground.

House Rock is a large, overhanging boulder that lies just across a footbridge over the South Fork of the Santiam River. The trail wanders through an old-growth forest and takes you over a portion of the old Santiam Wagon Road.

From the parking lot, head west along Sheep Creek through the picnic grounds. As soon as you begin walking toward the bridge over the South Fork of the Santiam River, you encounter bigleaf maple, **red alder** *(Alnus rubra)*, and **vine maple** *(Acer circinatum)* mixed with Douglas fir, western red cedar, and western hemlock. As you approach the bridge, you find the cloverlike **sorrel** *(Oxalis oregana)*, **candyflower** *(Claytonia sibirica)*, **snowberry** *(Symphoricarpos albus)*, and **meadowrue** *(Thalictrum occidentale)* in the understory. **Sword-fern** *(Polystichum munitum)* and the leathery-leaved **salal** *(Gaultheria shallon)* also grow under the forest. Just before you reach the bridge, you can find the oval leaves of **false lily-of-the-valley** *(Maianthemum dilatatum)*.

You cross the South Fork of the Santiam River on a wooden bridge. On the opposite side, note **red huckleberry** *(Vaccinium parvifolium)* and **Oregon grape** *(Mahonia nervosa)*. You can also spot **star-flowered false Solomon's seal** *(Smilacina stellata)*, recognizable by their large clusters of small, white blossoms.

Just after you cross the bridge is a sign for the loop. Go left. As you climb the trail up the hill, you see Pacific yew, which has gained fame as a potential cure for ovarian cancer. You soon reach House Rock; **western saxifrage** *(Saxifraga occidentalis)* and **maidenhair fern** *(Adiantum pedatum)* grow on its face. Here also are **red elderberry** *(Sambucus racemosa)*, whose berries are enjoyed by bears and humans, who make wine and jelly from them.

The trail proceeds past House Rock up the South Fork of the Santiam River. Here you find **vanillaleaf** *(Achlys triphylla)* and **queen's cup lily** *(Clintonia uniflora)* growing along with **Brewer's mitrewort** *(Mitella breweri)*. The beautiful pink flowers of **salmonberry** *(Rubus spectabilis)* overhang the trail.

You soon pass a giant cut log, and across the creek you can see the campground. **Yellow violet** *(Viola glabella)* and **sweet coltsfoot** *(Petasites frigidus)* thrive among the **salal, vine maple,** and **sword-fern.** In a wet seep, you see

FALSE LILY-OF-THE-VALLEY
Maianthemum dilatatum

False lily-of-the-valley sport small white flowers in a terminal cluster and have a perfumed scent. The somewhat heart-shaped leaves have long stalks and parallel veins. *Maianthemum* refers to May, the month in which these plants reach their height of bloom. **False lily-of-the-valley** are common in moist, shady woods.

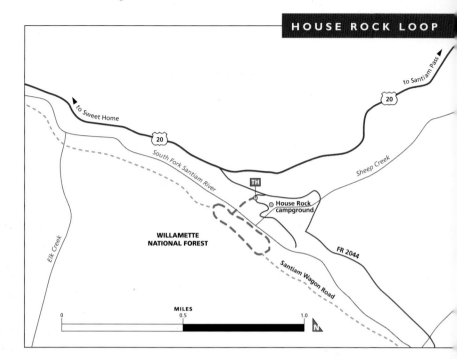

HOUSE ROCK LOOP

to Santiam Pass

to Sweet Home

South Fork Santiam River

Sheep Creek

TH

House Rock
campground

Elk Creek

WILLAMETTE
NATIONAL FOREST

FR 2044

Santiam Wagon Road

MILES
0   0.5   1.0

the large, tropical-looking leaves that distinguish **skunk cabbage** *(Lysichitum americanum).* Upslope you can find some very large Douglas fir.

When you get to the trail junction, turn left for a fine view of a waterfall. Right by the fence you see Pacific yew. **Lady-fern** *(Athyrium filix-femina),* **maidenhair fern,** and **sword-fern** are common along this short trail to the waterfall viewpoint. After viewing the falls, backtrack to the trail junction and continue up the slope to the Santiam Wagon Road. Tall **red alder** create a sense of openness and light, and **sorrel** covers the ground here. Once on the road, head right, passing some large old growth on the left and several small creeks. You'll come to a sign about the Santiam Wagon Road, which used to link the Willamette Valley with Sisters. To finance the road, the government granted the road builders 800,000 acres of public land—an astoundingly good deal for the road builders but not such a good deal for the public. A toll road operated from 1867 to 1915, and the state took possession in 1925.

At the sign is a trail junction looping back to the river. You'll wander through **salal, sword-fern, sorrel,** and **trillium** *(Trillium ovatum).* About 50 feet down the trail, look right to see notches cut into a stump. In the days before chainsaws, loggers cut notches into the very broad lower trunks of trees (the swollen bole) at about 8–10 feet off the ground. They placed long boards, called springboards, into the notches and used them as platforms, cutting the trees above the swollen bole. Continue following the trail back to the bridge over the South Fork of the Santiam River.

Iron Mountain/Cone Peak

*Wildflower
Hike 20*

*Cat's-ear lily and paintbrush dot a
meadow along the Cone Peak Trail.*

Sweet Home	***Nearest Town***
One of the most spectacular wildflower displays in Oregon	***Highlights***
difficult	***Trail Rating***
5.0 miles round-trip	***Trail Length***
Tombstone Pass	***Location***
4,100–5,646 feet	***Elevation***
Willamette National Forest, 541-465-6521	***Contact***
June to August	***Bloom Season***
July	***Peak Bloom***
From Sweet Home, drive east on US 20 (Santiam Highway) to Tombstone Pass. Park just beyond the pass at the Sno-Park. To reach the Cone Peak trailhead, walk east along the shoulder of US 20 downhill from the pass for 0.33 mile, watching for the trail heading off into the trees on the left (north).	***Directions***

The Iron Mountain/Cone Peak area is known as Oregon's most accessible and spectacular wildflower haven. From late June through August, an amazing diversity of flowers blooms within the old-growth forests, meadows, and rocky ridges of the area. At least 300 species of flowering plants have been documented here. In addition, the Iron Mountain/Cone Peak basin supports 17 types of trees—more than any other similar-size area in Oregon. The basin is so well-known among plant lovers that it has its own plant guide, *Wildflowers of the Western Cascades* by Robert A. Ross and Henrietta L. Chambers, with illustrator Shirley A. Stevenson.

You can take a popular 6.4-mile loop hike up Iron Mountain, the site of a former lookout, then over to a ridge on Cone Peak and back to the highway. It would be difficult, however, to have time to identify any plants on the loop hike, so I recommend the 5.0-mile round-trip hike up Cone Peak detailed here.

Iron Mountain/Cone Peak forms a part of the proposed Old Cascades Wilderness, a series of small roadless areas that includes the nearby Three Pyramids, Crescent Mountain, and Browder Ridge.

Immediately after stepping off the highway onto the trail, you enter a forest of silver fir and western hemlock. Right beyond the trailhead sign you find a tremendous diversity of species. You'll see **star-flowered false Solomon's seal** *(Smilacina stellata),* **vanillaleaf** *(Achlys triphylla),* **thimbleberry** *(Rubus parviflorus),* **false Solomon's seal** *(Smilacina racemosa),* **ocean-spray** *(Holodiscus discolor),* **foamflower** *(Tiarella trifoliata),* **queen's cup lily** *(Clintonia uniflora),* **dwarf dogwood** *(Cornus canadensis),* **Pacific bleedingheart** *(Dicentra formosa),* **trillium** *(Trillium ovatum),* **waterleaf** *(Hydrophyllum fendleri),* **inside-out flower** *(Vancouveria hexandra),* **three-leaved anemone** *(Anemone deltoidea),* and **round-leaved violet** *(Viola orbiculata).* A common understory shrub-tree throughout this area is **vine maple** *(Acer circinatum).*

At first, the trail passes near a small creek that flows off to the left, then it switchbacks up a small meadow. **Western columbine** *(Aquilegia formosa),* **tall bluebell** *(Mertensia paniculata),* **Sitka valerian** *(Valeriana sitchensis),* **cow-parsnip** *(Heracleum lanatum),* and **bracken fern** *(Pteridium aquilinum)* bloom in the meadow. **Alpine knotweed** *(Polygonum phytolaccaefolium)* are abundant in the meadow, and some **red elderberry** *(Sambucus racemosa),* a flowering shrub, grow along the edge.

The trail enters the forest again. Here you see **wild strawberry** *(Fragaria vesca),* **candyflower** *(Claytonia sibirica),* **star-flowered Solomon's seal, thimbleberry, round-leaved violet,** and **trail-plant** *(Adenocaulon bicolor).* The delicate fronds of **oak-fern** *(Gymnocarpium dryopteris)* grow in the shady forest. You also see **great polemonium** *(Polemonium carneum),* showy plants that edge forest borders and meadows. The flowers occur in a wide variety of colors including orange-yellow, yellow, and lavender-yellow. **Salmonberry**

(Rubus spectabilis), **candyflower**, and **western columbine** thrive along this section of trail as well.

The path crosses a second small meadow with more **knotweed, bluebell, western columbine, bracken fern, cow-parsnip**, and **thimbleberry**.

After crossing the meadow, the path heads back into a forest with some very large trees. Again you encounter forest-loving species such as **foamflower, trillium, vanillaleaf, anemone, Oregon grape** *(Mahonia nervosa)*, and **broad-leaved starflower** *(Trientalis latifolia)*. You'll also see the occasional **wild rose** *(Rosa gymnocarpa)*.

The trail passes a rocky outcrop full of **cliff larkspur** *(Delphinium menziesii)* on the left. A western yew tree sits just beyond the rock ledge, and **Cascade penstemon** *(Penstemon serrulatus)*, **mountain boxwood** *(Pachistima myrsinites)*, and lots of **dwarf dogwood** *(Cornus canadensis)* also grow here.

Beargrass *(Xerophyllum tenax)*, a showy member of the lily family, lives on the left upslope just before a switchback. The spectacular white blossoms grow from a tussock mount of narrow, tough leaves.

Just as you reach the switchback, look for Alaskan cedar. As its name implies, the Alaskan cedar is more common in Alaska, but it is scattered here and there down the spine of the Cascades. The tree is exceedingly long-lived, with some specimens of 1,000 years or more recorded.

Prince's-pine *(Chimaphila umbellata)*, an evergreen member of the heath family, sits by a large Douglas fir immediately after the switchback. You can also spy **black huckleberry** *(Vaccinium membranaceum)* all along the trail. It is the most common **huckleberry** of the three species on the mountain.

Cardwell's penstemon *(Penstemon cardwellii)*, one of several **penstemon** found along the trail, grows on rocky outcrops and forest edges. It has opposite leaves and large, purple blue flowers. Since nearly 50 **penstemon** species grow in Oregon, keying them all out is difficult.

ROCK PENSTEMON
Penstemon rupicola

Rock penstemon grow on rocky outcrops in the Western Cascades. This species of **penstemon** has deep pink flowers, thick woody branches, and opposite, often hairy, ovate-shaped leaves.

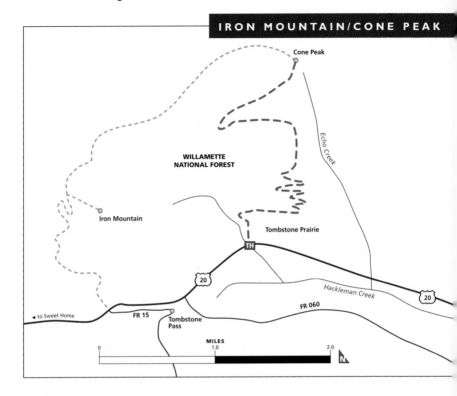

IRON MOUNTAIN/CONE PEAK

Cone Peak

Echo Creek

WILLAMETTE
NATIONAL FOREST

Iron Mountain

Tombstone Prairie

TH

20

Hackleman Creek

FR 060

20

to Sweet Home

FR 15

Tombstone
Pass

MILES
1.0   2.0
0

The trail passes through an opening, where you see lots of **thimbleberry**, **beargrass**, and **goatsbeard** *(Aruncus dioicus)*. Just before the third switchback, watch for **spotted coral-root orchid** *(Corallorhiza maculata)*, one of the most common **coral-root orchids** found in the western Cascades. **Coral-root orchids** lack green leaves—rather, they depend on nutrients derived from other plants.

The fourth switchback is very short. You see more **coral-root orchid**, plus a lot of **queen's cup lily, dwarf dogwood, vanillaleaf,** and **star-flowered false Solomon's seal** at this point in the trail.

Just beyond the fifth switchback, find more **beargrass, thimbleberry, black huckleberry,** and scattered **dwarf dogwood** and **anemone.**

After turning on the sixth switchback, watch for **valerian, false Solomon's seal** *(Smilacina racemosa)*, and **Pacific waterleaf** *(Hydrophyllum tenuipes)*.

The seventh switchback takes you through more **huckleberry** as the forest canopy begins to open up. During sunny times, you find **Oregon sunshine** *(Eriophyllum lanatum)*, a yellow member of the sunflower family. Other sun-loving plants such as **cat's-ear lily** *(Calochortus subalpinus)*, **small-flowered penstemon** *(Penstemon procerus)*, **pinemat manzanita** *(Arctostaphylos nevadensis)*, **cliff larkspur, ocean-spray** *(Holodiscus discolor)*, and **virgate phacelia** *(Phacelia* *heterophylla)* grow here. There is a particular abundance of **larkspur** and **cat's-ear lily,** and a rocky outcrop bears some **stonecrop** *(Sedum oregonense).* The rocky outcrop and opening provide the first views of Browder Ridge, Echo Peak, and the goal of this hike, Cone Peak.

When you reach the eighth switchback, note a rocky ledge with an abundance of **larkspur, cat's-ear lily, small-flowered penstemon, ocean-spray,** and **sticky cinquefoil** *(Potentilla glandulosa).* This area affords excellent views of Cone Peak.

The trail cuts back into the forest and traverses the hill to a small, rocky outcrop featuring more **stonecrop, larkspur,** and **Oregon sunshine.**

You reach the ninth, then the tenth switchback, where you find another rocky outcrop and a small meadow. **Scarlet gilia** *(Ipomopsis aggregata),* their bright red flowers loved by hummingbirds, live in the rocky meadow. Flowering **serviceberry** *(Amelanchier alnifolia)* shrubs grow along the margins of the meadow. Although **sagebrush** *(Artemisia ludoviciana)* is typically found in arid environments east of the Cascades, small **sagebrush** also can be found in droughty sites along this trail.

You soon reach the eleventh switchback, and the trail cuts up to the ridge and to another rocky outcrop with **northern buckwheat** *(Eriogonum compositum)* and **broadleaf lupine** *(Lupinus latifolius).* At the twelfth switchback, you can find **bracken fern, cat's-ear lily, Indian paintbrush** *(Castilleja hispida),* and more **sagebrush.** The trail heads up toward Cone Peak, lending great views of the entire upper basin between Cone and Echo peaks. The basin is flower-studded with a thick blanket of **red Indian-paintbrush** *(Castilleja miniata),* **cat's-ear lily, larkspur,** and **buckwheat.**

The trail heads up a ridge with Alaskan cedar. Here you can spy the lookout on Iron Mountain. The trail passes into a wet swale that houses **great polemonium, valerian, senecio** *(Senecio triangularis),* **lupine,** and **sagebrush.**

You encounter another rocky outcrop, where you can see some **meadow death-camas** *(Zigadenus venenosus)* and **spreading stonecrop** *(Sedum divergens)* among the rocks. The trail then winds around a rocky ridge; stop to enjoy the gorgeous views. You enter a forest with small, lush meadows full of **alpine knotweed, thimbleberry, western columbine, valerian, cow-parsnip,** and **lupine.** You cross several small creeks, including one with **waterleaf** and a lot of **Sitka alder** *(Alnus sinuata)* shrubs bordering the stream.

The trail then reaches a shoulder between Iron Mountain and Cone Peak. The trail to Iron Mountain is straight ahead. To head up Cone Peak, veer to the right to the top of the nearby rocky ridge. There is a terrific view to the north here with many clear-cuts visible in the near and far distance. **Pearly-everlasting** *(Anaphalis margaritacea),* **scarlet gilia, Oregon sunshine,** and **yarrow** *(Achillea millefolium)* grow along the rocky ridge.

If you want to head up Cone Peak, head into the trees and climb the steep slope to the east. After you pass through some trees, the shoulder of Cone Peak is mostly open meadows with **Oregon sunshine, sagebrush, sticky cinquefoil, northern buckwheat,** and **small-flowered penstemon.**

The summit of Cone Peak features some clumps of **rock penstemon** *(Penstemon rupicola)* and terrific views. You can see Mount Jefferson, Three Fingered Jack, Three Sisters, Mount Washington, and even Diamond Peak, far to the south.

After enjoying the views, retrace your steps back to the trailhead.

A view of neighboring Iron Mountain from the ridge of Cone Peak.

Crescent Mountain

Cascade flowers fill a meadow slope along the Crescent Mountain Trail.

Crescent Mountain is part of the Old Cascades—a lower and more eroded segment of the Cascade Mountains. Wildflowers thrive in the area's deep soils, and you can enjoy outstanding vistas of the Three Sisters and Mount Jefferson. The Crescent Mountain roadless area is one unit of the proposed Old Cascades Wilderness.

At the trailhead, a sign declares that the distance to Crescent Mountain is 4.0 miles. The first 1.5 miles of this trail, which leads to Maude Creek, is almost level. If you have limited time, the hike to the creek makes a good turnaround point, although you will end up walking through forests the entire time. If you're really ambitious (and you make arrangements for a shuttle), instead of turning around at the summit of the mountain, you can hike another 5.0 miles

Nearest Town	Sweet Home
Highlights	Lovely hike through forests up to subalpine meadows with terrific views
Trail Rating	difficult
Trail Length	8.0 miles round-trip to the summit, 6.0 miles to major subalpine meadows
Location	Willamette National Forest
Elevation	3,500–5,760 feet
Contact	Sweet Home Ranger District, Willamette NF, 541-465-6521
Bloom Season	June to August
Peak Bloom	July
Directions	From Sweet Home, drive east on US 20 (Santiam Highway) for 44.0 miles. Just before you reach the junction with OR 126, turn left (north) onto Lava Lake Road (FR 2067) and take it 1.0 mile to gravel FR 508. Drive less than a mile to the trailhead and ample parking.

to the South Pyramid Creek Trailhead. From the top of the mountain, continue north along the crest of Crescent Mountain and down the north side to the trailhead located on spur road 2067-572.

The first part of the trail is through a forest of western hemlock with an understory of **dwarf dogwood** *(Cornus canadensis),* which is sometimes called **bunchberry.** The plant's lovely white blossoms turn into bright red berries in the autumn. Other ground cover you can find here includes **prince's-pine** *(Chimaphila umbellata),* **Oregon grape** *(Mahonia nervosa),* **twinflower** *(Linnaea borealis),* and **vanillaleaf** *(Achlys triphylla).* **Oregon grape** is easily identified by its leathery hollylike leaves, while **vanillaleaf** has large, fan-shaped, blunt-toothed leaflets.

The trail descends from the trailhead, passing through a Douglas fir forest that features **trillium** *(Trillium ovatum).* An early spring bloomer, **trillium** typically goes to seed by late July. As you descend gradually toward Maude Creek, you pass patches of **Pacific rhododendron** *(Rhododendron macrophyllum)* and small patches of **beargrass** *(Xerophyllum tenax).* A member of the lily family that sports showy, white blossoms, **beargrass** isn't a grass at all. The plant is named for its tough, wiry, grasslike leaves that form large clumps on the forest floor. Among the Douglas fir you can find an occasional Pacific yew, a smallish tree with bark that is now used to treat cancer.

Continuing along the trail, you'll find more **Oregon grape**, plus **one-sided wintergreen** *(Orthilia secunda)*. The bell-shaped flowers, which range from pale green to whitish, tend to nod downward. Occasionally you see **black huckleberry** *(Vaccinium membranaceum)*, the delicate white flowers of **foamflower** *(Tiarella trifoliata)*, and the evergreen shrub **mountain boxwood** *(Pachistima myrsinites)*, which is seldom more than 2 feet tall. **Vanillaleaf** and **dwarf dogwood** are quite common in this area.

You see several **wintergreen** species in the forest, including **whiteveined wintergreen** *(Pyrola picta)*. The basal rosette leaves, reddish stem, and white flowers make this species easy to identify. **Pink wintergreen** *(Pyrola asarifolia)* are also found here and show basal leaves, but sport pinkish flowers.

The trail descends to Maude Creek and levels off. You can hear the creek to your right and catch occasional glimpses of it through the trees. The mostly younger forest of silver fir includes a few very large Douglas fir. **Bracken fern** *(Pteridium aquilinum)*, a deciduous fern, is common in patches along the trail. Here and there in the forest you'll see **queen's cup lily** *(Clintonia uniflora)* and **Merten's coral-root orchid** *(Corallorhiza mertensiana)*, sometimes known as **candystick**. In the deeper soils near the stream, you can find **star-flowered false Solomon's seal** *(Smilacina stellata)*.

You pass a huge Douglas fir on the right, and then two big Douglas fir on the left. A small meadow here blooms with **leafy aster** *(Aster foliaceus)* and **senecio** *(Senecio triangularis)*. Beyond the meadow, you find some **Sitka valerian** *(Valeriana sitchensis)*, **Oregon bedstraw** *(Galium oreganum)*, and **yellow violet** *(Viola glabella)*. As the trail pulls away from the creek, you'll see lots of **bracken fern**.

You cross a 6-foot-wide wooden bridge with lots of small openings for **cow-parsnip** *(Heracleum lanatum)* to grow. **Cow-parsnip** have large, palmate leaves and umbrellalike clusters of white flowers.

SCARLET GILIA
Ipomopsis aggregata

You can't miss the stunning red hue of **scarlet gilia,** also known as **skyrocket**. The highly dissected basal leaves, when crushed, smell something like a skunk, but the trumpet-shaped flowers, 1–2 inches long, are very attractive to hummingbirds—you can often hear them buzzing through fields of **scarlet gilia**. The plant is named for Spanish botanist Felipe Gil.

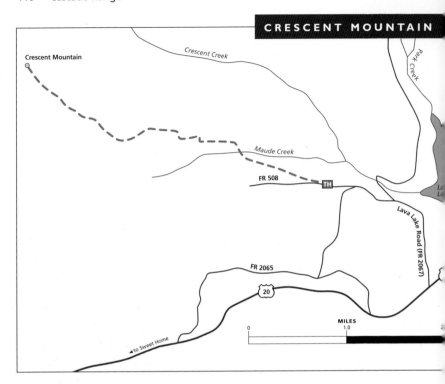

As you approach Maude Creek, note the Engelmann spruce, much more common in the Rockies but also found in cool, snowy locations in the Cascades. A bridge crosses Maude Creek. On the other side, you'll find plenty of **star-flowered false Solomon's seal. Palmate coltsfoot** *(Petasites palmatus),* with their large, pinnately divided leaves, grow near the bridge. If you don't want to climb the mountain, the bridge over Maude Creek makes a good turnaround point. From this point on, the trail climbs quite a bit.

The trail begins its ascent of Crescent Mountain via many switchbacks through a lovely fir forest. You continue to see **vanillaleaf, prince's-pine, dwarf dogwood, broad-leaved starflower** *(Trientalis latifolia),* **foamflower, Oregon grape,** and **trillium.** Each switchback features a major log construction. By the time you reach the sixth switchback, the forest starts to open up into small meadows with **bracken fern, thimbleberry** *(Rubus parviflorus),* and **western columbine** *(Aquilegia formosa).* From this point onward, you catch occasional glimpses of the Three Sisters.

You encounter new flowers in the meadows and open forest, including **wild strawberry** *(Fragaria vesca),* **cat's-ear lily** *(Calochortus subalpinus),* and a few **Pacific bleedingheart** *(Dicentra formosa).* As the path alternates between forested sections and meadow glades, the trail crosses a shrubby area of **Douglas' maple** *(Acer douglasii)* and **Sitka alder** *(Alnus sinuata)* that provides good views of the Three Sisters. Through here you can see **red elderberry** *(Sambucus racemosa)* along with **sagebrush** *(Artemisia ludoviciana)* and **broadleaf lupine** *(Lupinus latifolius).*

The trail passes a rocky outcrop. **Oregon sunshine** *(Eriophyllum lanatum),* a sunflowerlike plant, plus **cliff larkspur** *(Delphinium menziesii)* grow here. Since **larkspur** are poisonous to livestock, these beautiful plants were sometimes sprayed with herbicides on rangelands. You'll also see a **saxifrage** known as **Brewer's mitrewort** *(Mitella breweri)* and **silverleaf phacelia** *(Phacelia hastata)* growing among the rocks. **Ocean-spray** *(Holodiscus discolor),* shrubs that sport clusters of white flowers, live here as well. **Ocean-spray's** wood is extremely strong, so Pacific Northwest American Indian tribes used it for arrow shafts and digging sticks.

After passing the rocky outcrop, the trail enters another small meadow filled with more **sagebrush, lupine, bracken fern, larkspur,** and **scarlet gilia** *(Ipomopsis aggregata).* You pass through another section of trees and enter a third meadow, which offers great views of the Maude Creek drainage. Just beyond a small sign indicating the 3.0-mile mark, the trail breaks out into the open and switchbacks up the slope. At the switchback, you find **false hellebore** *(Veratrum viride),* a member of the lily family that have beautiful, large leaves but relatively unattractive flowers. The **Washington lily** *(Lilium washingtonianum)* you spot here, however, have spectacular and delightful-smelling flowers.

These meadows also house more **lupine, scarlet gilia, Oregon sunshine,** and **sagebrush**. With so many flowers, you will undoubtedly hear humming-birds patrolling the meadows in search of nectar-bearing flowers. The lovely, pink **owl-clover** *(Orthocarpus imbricatus)* are abundant.

You can spend hours exploring flowers in these large meadows and savoring the terrific views of the Three Sisters, Mount Washington, and other peaks. I turned around at this point, but in the past I've hiked to the top of the mountain. If you continue to the summit, you're treated to a horizon-to-horizon view of all the Cascades—and Mount Jefferson is strikingly close.

Wildflower
Hike 22 # Browder Ridge

The Browder Ridge Trail affords great views of some major Cascade volcanoes.

This hike features a pleasant stroll through wonderful forests with some fantastic views of Cascade volcanoes. The Gate Creek Trail (#3412) up Browder Ridge takes you into a relict roadless area in the western Cascades that has been proposed as wilderness. The trail first climbs up the slope above Gate Creek by a series of switchbacks, then enters a beautiful section of old-growth Douglas fir forest, which sports some trees with trunks more than 6 feet in diameter. The trail eventually climbs up through a series of long meadows to the top of the ridge, and then more or less follows the ridge to a junction with the Browder Ridge Trail (#3409), an alternate route into the area.

Nearest Town	Sweet Home
Highlights	Western Cascades old-growth forest with many steep ridgetop meadows
Trail Rating	moderate
Trail Length	6.0 miles round-trip
Location	Willamette National Forest
Elevation	3,650–5,300 feet
Contact	Sweet Home Ranger District, Willamette NF, 541-465-6521
Bloom Season	May to August
Peak Bloom	July
Directions	From Sweet Home, drive east on US 20 (Santiam Highway) for 38.0 miles. Just 2.0 miles before reaching the junction with OR 126, turn right (south) onto Hackleman Creek Road (FR 2672). Turn right again onto gravel FR 1598, and drive south, following signs for Gate Creek Trailhead. At a sharp 90-degree turn, the road crosses small Gate Creek; the trailhead, just beyond the creek, is easily missed.

Starting at the Gate Creek Trailhead, you enter a forest full of western hemlock with a **vine maple** *(Acer circinatum)* understory. **Foamflower** *(Tiarella trifoliata),* **dwarf dogwood** *(Cornus canadensis),* **trillium** *(Trillium ovatum),* **lady-fern** *(Athyrium filix-femina),* **oak-fern** *(Gymnocarpium dryopteris),* **black huckleberry** *(Vaccinium membranaceum),* **thimbleberry** *(Rubus parviflorus),* and **vanillaleaf** *(Achlys triphylla),* comprise most of the ground cover and shrub layer. Gate Creek is off to the right. This is the last you will see or hear of it, so if you need water, fill your canteen now.

After about 100 yards, you come to a sign indicating mileage to the Browder Ridge Trail and Lake Trail. At the sign, look for **vanillaleaf, broad-leaved starflower** *(Trientalis latifolia),* **star-flowered false Solomon's seal** *(Smilacina stellata),* and **dwarf dogwood.**

A few **Pacific rhododendron** *(Rhododendron macrophyllum)* grow along this section of trail. In the shade of the forest grow Pacific yew, a semi-shrub-tree with bark containing the chemical taxol, which is used to fight cancer.

The trail climbs directly up the slope, through **beargrass** *(Xerophyllum tenax),* **queen's cup lily** *(Clintonia uniflora),* **Oregon grape** *(Mahonia nervosa),* **twinflower** *(Linnaea borealis),* and **prince's-pine** *(Chimaphila umbellata).* Where the trail makes its first switchback, you can spot more **queen's cup lily, dwarf dogwood, vanillaleaf, twinflower,** and a few **beargrass.**

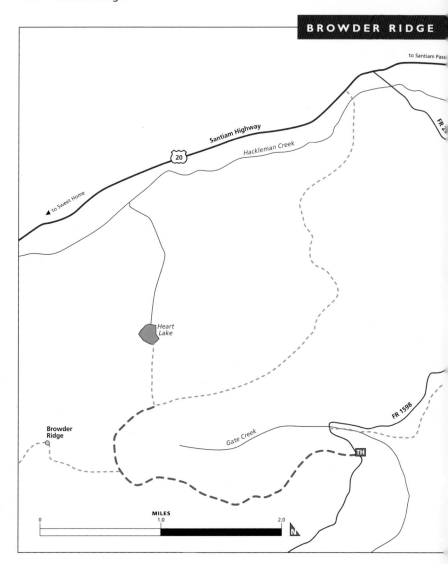

As the trail cuts back to the left, it passes through a nice stand of **Pacific rhododendron**. The trail makes a second switchback, where you can find **dwarf dogwood**, **vanillaleaf**, **prince's-pine**, **trillium**, and a few small **rhododendron.**

At the third switchback, more **rhododendron**, **beargrass**, and **Oregon grape** grow. You climb another switchback and pass through a forest with little ground cover. At the fifth switchback, the forest is very open, still with sparse ground cover. By the time you come to the sixth switchback, you're practically on the ridge, and the trail eases up a bit. Ground cover here includes **queen's cup lily**, **vanillaleaf**, **dwarf dogwood**, and **foamflower**. Finally, the trail levels on a bench, and here you encounter an abundance of Pacific yew and **huckleberry.**

Because of deeper soils, the trees here are larger and taller than anything found up to this point. The forest is peaceful, and it is a real delight to amble through these woods. The trail crosses a lush, verdant section with plenty of **bracken fern** *(Pteridium aquilinum)* and white-flowered **three-leaved anemone** *(Anemone deltoidea).* About 50 feet off the trail you'll spy a clump of **devil's club** *(Oplopanax horridum)* with their large, maplelike leaves giving the site an almost tropical look.

The trail heads upslope gently in a southwest direction, passing through a thick covering of **bracken fern** with an overstory multilayer forest above. The trail crosses a small meadow nearly covered with **bracken fern** and **false hellebore** *(Veratrum viride).* I spied one orange-flowered **tiger lily** *(Lilium columbianum)* growing among the ferns. Western white pine, a relatively uncommon tree in the Cascades, grows here and higher up on the trail. The tree has long, narrow cones and five needles to a bract.

As the trail crosses the meadow, you see **Sitka valerian** *(Valeriana sitchensis)* and **senecio** *(Senecio triangularis)* among the ferns. Once you are through the meadow, you will climb a bit. The trail turns to the southwest and through a fern-dominated meadow with some **tall bluebell** *(Mertensia paniculata)* and **cow-parsnip** *(Heracleum lanatum).* The trail continues to skirt meadows and then climbs uphill into a more open forest, providing the first good view of Three Fingered Jack.

The trail cuts across another large meadow with chest-deep **bracken fern.** You encounter **tall bluebell, false hellebore,** a few more **tiger lily, western columbine** *(Aquilegia formosa),* and **Queen Anne's lace** *(Daucus carota).*

CAT'S-EAR LILY
Calochortus subalpinus

This showy perennial grows in open forests and rocky meadows from the Cascades of southern Washington to the Three Sisters Wilderness in central Oregon. The bulbs are edible, and Indians formerly harvested and ate them. The plant's common name, **cat's-ear lily,** refers to the hairy throats of the flower. The Spanish named the flower *mariposa,* "butterfly," giving rise to an alternate common name, **subalpine mariposa lily.** *Calochortus* is Greek for "beautiful grass."

As you head up and back into the trees, lots of **violets** grow along the trail. The path passes some Alaskan cedar, common in its namesake state but rare in Oregon. At the switchback, you can see three or four Alaskan cedar.

The route turns back to the southwest, climbing up to a rocky flat before turning into the forest. The flat grants great views of Mount Jefferson, Three Sisters, and other Cascade volcanoes. Plus you find **cat's-ear lily** *(Calochortus subalpinus)*, **cliff larkspur** *(Delphinium menziesii)*, **broadleaf lupine** *(Lupinus latifolius)*, and **buckwheat** *(Eriogonum sp.)* growing in the rocky, shallow soils.

Upon re-entering the woods, you'll see more **starflower** on the forest floor along with **queen's cup lily** and some **beargrass.**

As the trail winds up the ridge, it levels off. In the few rocky places, look for creamy **stonecrop** *(Sedum oregonense)* and **small-flowered penstemon** *(Penstemon procerus)*. You'll come to a spot that offers another great view of the Three Sisters. The trail continues to climb higher, passing through more **beargrass** and **huckleberry**. Once the trail hits the ridge, you can see off into the valleys on either side. I encountered elk scat and tracks here.

After passing more forest, the route comes to a rocky opening with lots of **lupine** and **cat's-ear lily. Queen Anne's lace** is particularly abundant. You skirt a few more meadows, then pass over a rocky outcrop with **sagebrush** *(Artemisia ludoviciana)*. You trace the top of a steep open bowl and come out on a ridge with relatively flat, fern-filled meadows off to the south.

After crossing yet another meadow, you reach the trail junction with the Browder Ridge and Heart Lake trails. To continue up to Heart Lake, turn right. For the Browder Ridge trailhead, turn left. For most people, this makes a good turnaround point.

I continued up the ridge toward Heart Lake. If you take this trail, you will pass through several smaller meadows and some beautiful forests before breaking out into a large, sloping meadow directly below a rocky cliff. This meadow affords outstanding views of the Three Sisters. If you follow the trail across this slope to the ridge, you can then climb cross-country to the summit, from which you can enjoy a tremendous view. Look for **cat's-ear lily** and **spreading phlox** *(Phlox diffusa)* in this region.

Patjens Lakes Loop

Coniferous stands above one of the Patjens Lakes.

This easy hike around the Patjens Lakes is excellent for children. Although rated moderate because of its 6.0-mile length, the hike is almost level, gaining/losing only 400 feet of elevation. What the path lacks in the diversity of flowers it makes up for in the total number of flowers. Abundant **beargrass** (*Xerophyllum tenax*) blooms make this hike especially worthwhile. The trail passes through mostly open forest with few meadows. Much of the forest consists of small-diameter lodgepole pine, regrowth after a major fire.

The signed trailhead has parking for four or five vehicles. You start out hiking in a lodgepole pine forest with an understory largely of **beargrass**. **Broadleaf lupine** (*Lupinus latifolius*) and a few **yellow violet** (*Viola glabella*) are also in the mix.

Nearest Town	Santiam Junction
Highlights	Extensive beargrass accessed by a relatively easy trail
Trail Rating	moderate
Trail Length	6.0-mile loop
Location	Mount Washington Wilderness
Elevation	4,450–4,800 feet
Contact	McKenzie Ranger District, Willamette NF, 541-465-6521
Bloom Season	June to August
Peak Bloom	July
Directions	From Sweet Home, drive east on US 20 (Santiam Highway) to Santiam Pass, then turn right (south) onto FR 2690 toward Big Lake. (The road also provides access for Hoodoo Ski Area.) Follow FR 2690 for nearly 4.0 miles and around to the West Big Lake campground entrance and trailhead.

After only 0.1 mile, you reach a fork in the trail. The sign to Patjens Lakes points both ways—it's a loop, so you can go either way. To follow this hike, turn right. The trail curves west, and you can discover a few fir mixed in with the lodgepole pine. Look closely and you may spot some **prince's-pine** *(Chimaphila umbellata),* which have evergreen leaves and drooping, waxy white flowers. The dominance here of smaller lodgepole, which are all nearly the same size, tells something of its history. In all likelihood, this area burned in a forest fire some time ago. Lodgepole pine are adept at recolonizing burned areas. The heat of a fire opens the trees' cones slowly, releasing thousands of seeds on the site.

You pass a small pond with a wet meadow complex around its edge—a good place for mosquitoes. Note that more fir than pine live near the lake. In all likelihood, the wetter conditions near the lake favored the recruitment of the fir.

Grouseberry *(Vaccinium scoparium),* also known as **whortleberry** and members of the **huckleberry** family, grow under the forest. The plants have tiny, urn-shaped flowers, and you can identify them by their small, elliptical leaves. You'll also see a few **queen's cup lily** *(Clintonia uniflora)* here.

You come to a small swale, where you find **senecio** *(Senecio triangularis)* and **parrot beak** *(Pedicularis racemosa)* plus more **yellow violet** and **grouseberry.**

The trail rises and falls in roller-coaster fashion, finally heading up a hill to reach the wilderness boundary about 1.6 miles from the trailhead. The trail

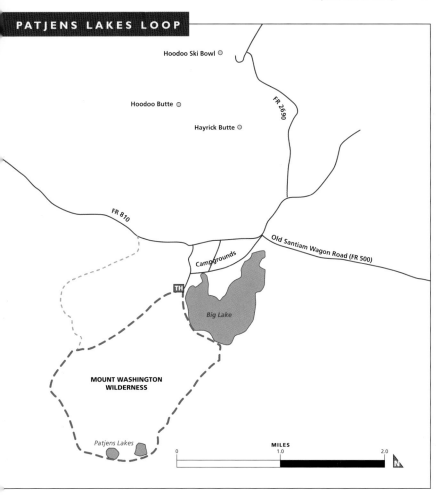

PATJENS LAKES LOOP

Hoodoo Ski Bowl

Hoodoo Butte

Hayrick Butte

FR 2690

FR 810

Old Santiam Wagon Road (FR 500)

Campgrounds

TH

Big Lake

MOUNT WASHINGTON
WILDERNESS

Patjens Lakes

MILES
0   1.0   2.0

N

reaches the top of the hill at about 4,800 feet and begins to descend. Through the open forest is a view of Three Sisters. **Bracken fern** *(Pteridium aquilinum)*, **beargrass**, and **lupine** *(Lupinus sp.)* dominate the forest floor.

On the rather dry, south-facing slope, **pinemat manzanita** *(Arctostaphylos nevadensis)* grow. The small, evergreen leaves resist water loss as an adaptation to the droughty soil conditions.

The trail enters a small meadow with great views of Mount Washington. The meadow, dominated by the white blooms of **beargrass**, almost looks like a snowbank. Other flowers you can find in the meadow include **small-flowered penstemon** *(Penstemon procerus)*, **strawberry** *(Fragaria virginiana)*, and **scarlet gilia** *(Ipomopsis aggregata)*.

The trail cuts across the lower end of the meadow, entering denser forest again. **Star-flowered false Solomon's seal** *(Smilacina stellata)* and **vanillaleaf**

(Achlys triphylla) grow along with **beargrass**. Many wind-sheared trees lie across the trail in the same east-west direction of the wind that toppled them.

As the route continues downward the trees are larger, dominated by fir and hemlock. **Three-leaved anemone** *(Anemone deltoidea)* and **broad-leaved starflower** *(Trientalis latifolia)* brighten the forest floor with white blooms.

A few western white pine appear along the trail. Previously common, the pine has suffered from the white pine blister rust disease and just about disappeared from much of the West. A fire-dependent species, white pine invades recently burned sites, so no doubt fire suppression has hurt its distribution and numbers as well.

The trail passes a small pothole pond on the right, the first of the Patjens Lakes. You pass a huge Douglas fir, which has obviously survived many fires. **Trillium** *(Trillium ovatum)*, **anemone**, and **vanillaleaf** are common near its base, but **beargrass** remains the most common species.

BEARGRASS
Xerophyllum tenax

Beargrass, a member of the lily family, features white, showy blossoms that are clustered in a dense terminal raceme. Growing from a basal tussock, the leaves are thin and grasslike, hence the common name. The flowering stalk is 2–3 feet tall. **Beargrass** do not bloom every year, so the floral displays vary in intensity from place to place. Despite the reference to bears, almost nothing eats **beargrass**, as its tough leaves are difficult to digest.

The trail climbs up a slight hill, and soon you arrive at the larger of the Patjens Lakes. **Beargrass** and trees surround the lakes. There are several confusing trails in this area, but no signs. To be sure you're on the right trail, always look for the standard FS trail blaze—a long slash with a shorter slash below it —on the trees along the trail.

After viewing the lakes, head northeast toward the shore of Big Lake. You soon pass the wilderness boundary sign. The trail reaches Big Lake at a small beach, which offers nice views of Hayrick Butte across the lake. As you continue along the trail, you come to another fork. Both trails take you back to your car— one via a trail that skirts the West Big Lake campground and one that simply leads you to the campground and parking area. The trail around the campground offers a good view of the lake and Mount Washington. **Beargrass** again dominate the path back to the trailhead.

Canyon Creek Meadows

Canyon Creek Meadows below Three Fingered Jack creates a scenic vista.

This hike leads into the Mount Jefferson Wilderness and to a meadow just below the looming Three Fingered Jack. The hike passes through mostly younger lodgepole pine forest mixed with mountain hemlock and some fir. For the most part, the trail is gentle and easy to follow. It also appears to be popular with horse riders and can be quite dusty. You can make a loop of the hike and take in Canyon Creek Falls. (The loop is actually only slightly longer than the in-and-out hike described here.)

Two trails start from the parking area at Jack Lake campground. To make sure you're on the hike to Jack Lake, follow the sign to Old Summit Trail and Canyon Creek Meadows, which heads off to the right (north) from the parking area. You will almost immediately skirt shallow Jack Lake.

Nearest Town	Sisters
Highlights	Beautiful meadow laced by streams below Three Fingered Jack
Trail Rating	moderate
Trail Length	4.0 miles round-trip
Location	Mount Jefferson Wilderness
Elevation	5,130–5,500 feet
Contact	Deschutes National Forest, 541-388-2715
Bloom Season	July to August
Peak Bloom	late July
Directions	From Sweet Home, take US 20 (Santiam Highway) 8.0 miles beyond Santiam Pass and turn left at the wilderness trailhead sign onto FR 12. Drive 3.7 miles to gravel FR 1230 and take this road 1.5 miles, then turn left on FR 1234 and drive about 5.0 miles up to the trailhead by Jack Lake campground.

The forest around the trailhead and most of the way into the meadows is dominated by lodgepole pine, plus pockets of mountain hemlock and subalpine fir. Lodgepole pine, common along the east side of the Cascades, is easily recognized by its two-paired needles and small, roundish cones. The species tends to grow on droughty or extremely acidic soils and dominates areas with cold air drainage. More than almost any other species, lodgepole pine depends on fire to perpetuate itself on a site. After a blaze, the cones open and shed thousands of seeds that grow rapidly, easily outcompeting other conifers.

Grouseberry *(Vaccinium scoparium),* a small member of the blueberry family, are a common ground cover in lodgepole pine forests. These shrubs have tiny urn-shaped flowers but are best identified by their lime-green leaves. Other plants along the shore of Jack Lake include **parrot beak** *(Pedicularis racemosa),* **arnica** *(Arnica latifolia),* **queen's cup lily** *(Clintonia uniflora),* and **Sitka valerian** *(Valeriana sitchensis).*

You reach a small wooden sign that says Canyon Creek Meadows/Wasco Lake. At the base of the sign, look for **pinemat manzanita** *(Arctostaphylos nevadensis),* a sprawling shrub with evergreen leaves and reddish twisted branches. Also near the sign, you find some long cones of western white pine, a relatively rare species in the Cascades. The pine suffers from white pine blister rust, an introduced disease that is wiping out most of the mature pine in the West.

The trail to Canyon Creek Meadows takes off to the left and begins to climb up a slope away from the lake. The dry slope features lots of **manzanita**

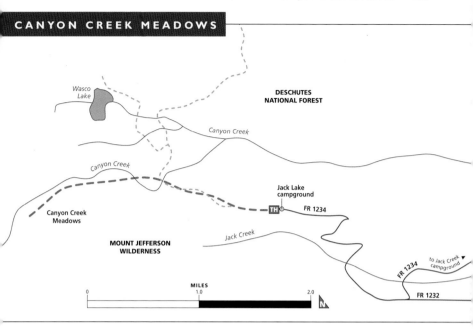

with the lovely **Washington lily** *(Lilium washingtonianum)* mixed in. This lily produces a robust bloom and has a delightful scent. In this section you also encounter blue-flowered clusters of **broadleaf lupine** *(Lupinus latifolius),* **cat's-ear lily** *(Calochortus subalpinus),* **scarlet gilia** *(Ipomopsis aggregata),* **rosy twisted-stalk** *(Streptopus roseus),* and the shrub **serviceberry** *(Amelanchier alnifolia).* Upslope you can see some wind-sheared ponderosa pine, indicating that fierce winds blow across this ridge in winter. Farther along this dry slope grow **snowbush** *(Ceanothus velutinus),* a species that commonly invades slopes after a fire.

The trail continues up through a forest of lodgepole pine dominated by **beargrass** *(Xerophyllum tenax)* understory. You reach a sign for the Canyon Creek Loop, where you should bear left as a clockwise walk is recommended for this trail. The trail climbs up the ridge, passing through dense stands of lodgepole pine with more **beargrass** and **lupine.** You will encounter several sections where an old trail has been covered with sticks and branches for restoration purposes, while a new trail circles off to the right.

Eventually, you pass some rocky outcrops where the white flowered shrub **ocean-spray** *(Holodiscus discolor)* is growing along with more **pinemat manzanita.** In addition, you encounter a few more white pine.

Immediately after passing a diminutive pond, you discover a small, wet meadow covered with yellow **buttercup** *(Ranunculus sp.).* Away from the pond, the trail passes through forest with little understory cover. In some places, there is almost no ground cover.

The trail eventually drops back down through an almost pure stand of mountain hemlock to the valley of Canyon Creek. Both mountain hemlock and its low-elevation cousin, western hemlock, are easy to recognize by their droopy crown leaders.

Along a small drainage you'll find **false hellebore** *(Veratrum viride),* a plant with large-veined, lilylike leaves that sometimes grows up to 4 feet in height. Along this stretch of trail, **five-stamened mitrewort** *(Mitella pentandra)* is just about the only plant growing in the forest.

The trail passes by another small, shallow, meltwater pond (at least in mid-July); take in another glorious mountain view. The path then crosses a small creek, where **yellow violet** *(Viola glabella),* **lupine**, **valerian**, and several **mountain buttercup** *(Ranunculus populago),* **senecio** *(Senecio triangularis),* and **tall mountain shooting star** *(Dodecatheon jeffreyi)* grow.

Just beyond the creek, you enter a meadow that affords a fantastic view of Three Fingered Jack. **Cat's-ear lily** and **lupine** are common in the meadow. About 2.0 miles from the trailhead, you reach a sign and trail junction. To continue the loop to Canyon Creek Falls and proceed back to the Jack Creek trailhead, head to the right. For more of the Canyon Creek Meadows, turn left.

The meadows are full of **lupine**, **senecio**, **false hellebore**, **red Indian-paintbrush** *(Castilleja miniata),* **shooting star**, and **Drummond's cinquefoil** *(Potentilla drummondii).* At peak bloom, the proliferation of **lupine** blossoms fills the air with their fragrant scent. The stream-laced, flower-dotted meadows provide the perfect foreground for a terrific close-up view of Three Fingered Jack—in fact, this is one of the premier vistas in this part of the Cascades! The meadow makes a good picnic spot and turnaround point for day hikers.

WASHINGTON LILY
Lilium Washingtonianum

The **Washington lily**, also known as **Cascade lily**, is one of the most striking flowers you may find in the Cascades. This impressive plant can reach 5–6 feet high, with leaves that are grouped in whorls. The beautiful, trumpet-shaped white blossoms, reminiscent of Easter lilies, fade to purple or pink, and their scent is delightful. The flowers grow in brushfields, meadows, and along the edges of forests from Mount Hood to northern California.

Tidbits Mountain

Old-growth forest and lush understory shrubs adorn the Tidbits Mountain Trail.

This trail leads through an old-growth forest teeming with beautiful forest shrubs such as **Pacific rhododendron** *(Rhododendron macrophyllum)*. You reach at last a rocky pinnacle with exceptional, unobstructed views of the Cascades. Note, however, that no water exists on this hike.

Right at the trailhead, you encounter plenty of **chinquapin** *(Castanopsis chrysophylla)*, a relative of the oak. The plant has leathery, lance-shaped leaves, white flowers, and a spiny, golden-colored burr for fruit. **Chinquapin** is actually more typical of forests to the south in California. You can also discover the sprawling evergreen shrub known as **pinemat manzanita** *(Arctostaphylos nevadensis)* in this area.

More **pinemat manzanita** grow at the trailhead sign along with **pearly-everlasting** *(Anaphalis margaritacea)*. A plant that loves sunshine and open

Nearest Town	Eugene/Springfield
Highlights	Old-growth trail to great views from an old lookout site
Trail Rating	moderate
Trail Length	4.0 miles round-trip
Location	Willamette National Forest
Elevation	4,100–5,184 feet
Contact	Blue River Ranger District, Willamette NF, 541-465-6521
Bloom Season	May to August
Peak Bloom	July
Directions	From Eugene/Springfield, take OR 126 east about 3.0 miles past Blue River. Turn left on FR 15 toward Blue River Lake. Follow this road 4.8 miles to FR 1509, where you will bear left. Wind 8.3 miles uphill on gravel FR 1509 through clear-cuts. When you reach FR 877, turn left. This very steep, one-lane road leads 0.5 mile up a ridge to a parking area on the left. If you have a low-clearance vehicle, park at the turnoff for FR 877 and walk 0.5 mile to the trailhead.

habitat, **pearly-everlasting** retains its white blooms for months, hence its common name. **Pearly-everlasting** is excellent for dried bouquets.

Just after you enter the trail, note the beautiful **Pacific rhododendron**, with pinkish flowers filling the forest in June and early July. In July you can also see **beargrass** *(Xerophyllum tenax)*, which grows in a clump with tough, grasslike leaves and large, plumelike white blossoms. All along the trail you find various species of **huckleberry** *(Vaccinium sp.)*, the most common being **oval-leaf huckleberry** *(Vaccinium ovalifolium)*. **Oregon grape** *(Mahonia nervosa),* easily recognized by their hollylike, evergreen leaves, grow here and there along the entire trail. In the spring, **Oregon grape** sport yellow flowers; later in the fall, the plants produce blue, grapelike fruits.

Douglas fir, with some understory of **Douglas' maple** *(Acer douglasii)*, is the dominant tree along this first part of the trail. You see **beargrass** crowding the trail, more **chinquapin**, and **red huckleberry** *(Vaccinium parvifolium)* with their red berries. **Mountain boxwood** *(Pachistima myrsinites)*, a low-growing evergreen shrub, also thrive here. The plant has toothed, leathery, opposite leaves and very small maroon flowers. In this area you also find **prince's-pine** *(Chimaphila umbellata)*, a flowering evergreen.

After 100 yards or so, the trail enters old-growth forest with more **rhododendron** and scattered clumps of **vine maple** *(Acer circinatum)* beneath. Flowering species found here include **vanillaleaf** *(Achlys triphylla)*, **twinflower**

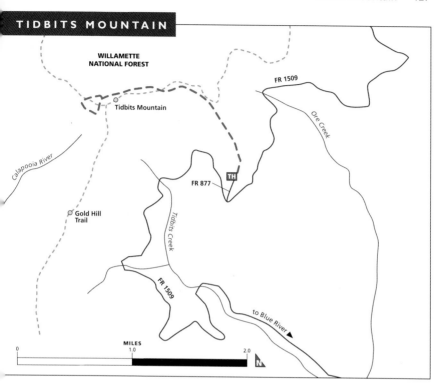

TIDBITS MOUNTAIN

WILLAMETTE
NATIONAL FOREST

FR 1509

Tidbits Mountain

Ore Creek

Calapooia River

FR 877 — TH

Gold Hill
Trail

Tidbits Creek

FR 1509

to Blue River

MILES
0   1.0   2.0
N

(*Linnaea borealis*), **Oregon grape**, **foamflower** (*Tiarella trifoliata*), and **parrot beak** (*Pedicularis racemosa*).

The trail ascends gently upwards, traversing large western hemlock forests. The forest floor houses **queen's cup lily** (*Clintonia uniflora*), **star-flowered false Solomon's seal** (*Smilacina stellata*), **sword-fern** (*Polystichum munitum*), **trail-plant** (*Adenocaulon bicolor*), and **wild ginger** (*Asarum caudatum*). As the trail turns west-northwest, you can spot **vine maple** along with **false Solomon's seal** (*Smilacina racemosa*), **broad-leaved starflower** (*Trientalis latifolia*), **prince's-pine**, **vanillaleaf**, **twinflower**, and **foamflower**.

As you move up the trail, you pass some giant Douglas fir with an understory of **thimbleberry** (*Rubus parviflorus*), characterized by their large, maplelike leaves and lovely white flowers. Just past a large downed log you can see an abundance of **dwarf dogwood** (*Cornus canadensis*), which sport lovely white, cross-shaped flowers in the spring and bright red berries in the fall. Many Douglas fir in this area have curved trunks due to downslope soil movement.

As you continue, you pass on the left a Douglas fir marked with a "4" on a metal sign. You then come to small gully with a wet area and lots of **thimbleberry** and western yew. On an outcrop of rock with thin soils grow more **chinquapin** along with **pinemat manzanita**. Where there is a bit more soil, you'll find lots of **beargrass**.

The trail now begins to climb more steeply. Here and there you can find **serviceberry** *(Amelanchier alnifolia)*, **Douglas' maple** *(Acer douglasii)*, **ocean-spray** *(Holodiscus discolor)*, **snowberry** *(Symphoricarpos albus)*, **yew**, **baneberry** *(Actaea rubra)*, **huckleberry**, **broadleaf lupine** *(Lupinus latifolius)*, **bracken fern** *(Pteridium aquilinum)*, and **trillium** *(Trillium ovatum)*. Western white pine are scattered in the forest, but the species suffers from white pine blister rust, so you seldom see mature trees that aren't half dead or dying.

As you approach the ridgetop, the trail intersects a ridge trail. At this junction a sign on a tree notes "RD 1509 1.2 mile" and other information. **Mountain-ash** *(Sorbus sitchensis)*, **huckleberry**, **rhododendron**, and more **beargrass** all grow at this junction, where the ruins of an old lean-to sit. Go left (west) along the ridge. The trail passes through **salmonberry** *(Rubus spectabilis)* and shifts to the north. From this ridge, you can enjoy views of the surrounding mountains and see nice stands of noble fir on the north slope. The trail passes through more **mountain-ash, foamflower,** and **thimbleberry** and then out into an open talus slope. **Red Indian-paintbrush** *(Castilleja miniata)* grow on the slope, and more **Douglas' maple** live along the base of a rocky pinnacle. On some of the exposed rock outcrop, **gentian** *(Gentiana sceptrum)*, **harebell** *(Campanula rotundifolia)*, and **baneberry** grow.

TWINFLOWER
Linnaea borealis

The common name **twinflower** comes from the white-pink trumpet blossoms that appear in pairs. **Twinflower** grow from trailing, semi-woody runners; the broad, elliptical leaves are dark green on the upper surface and lighter below. The Latin name refers to Linnaeus, the Swedish inventor of taxonomy.

The path crosses another talus slope where more **thimbleberry, huckleberry,** and **fireweed** *(Epilobium angustifolium)* grow among the boulders. When you pass a less-used path rising steeply to the left, ignore it and continue across the slope.

The trail finally switchbacks up the final ridge toward the peak. Alaskan cedar lives here, along with **serviceberry, box-wood, snowbush** *(Ceanothus velutinus)*, **beargrass, stonecrop** *(Sedum oregonense)*, **pinemat manzanita**, and small Douglas fir on this thin, rocky rib of the mountain.

At the next switchback, you see more **prince's-pine**, plus noble fir, mountain hemlock, and Alaskan cedar. The final push to the summit—if you dare to go—requires climbing up an old, half-fallen-apart ladder. From the summit, the views are superb.

Lookout Creek

Stands of old-growth forest along Lookout Creek.

Eugene/Springfield	*Nearest Town*
Pleasant saunter through old-growth forest	*Highlights*
moderate	*Trail Rating*
1.5 miles one way, 3.5 miles if you walk the entire length	*Trail Length*
Willamette National Forest	*Location*
3,000–3,500 feet	*Elevation*
Blue River Ranger District, Willamette NF, 541-465-6521	*Contact*
May to July	*Bloom Season*
June	*Peak Bloom*
From Eugene/Springfield, take OR 126 east about 3.0 miles past Blue River. Turn left on FR 15 toward Blue River Lake. Follow it just past the lake, and then turn right onto FR 1506 and take it 10.0 miles to the trailhead and adjacent, limited parking on the side of the road.	*Directions*

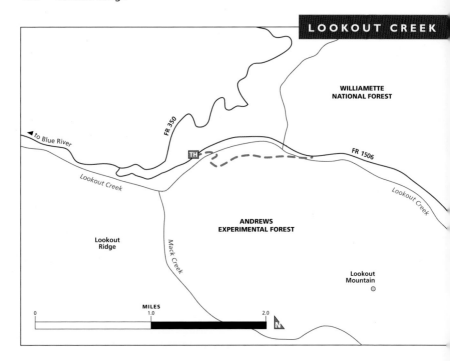

The Andrews Experimental Forest is a U.S. Forest Service research area. Most of the research seems to involve cutting down trees and monitoring the effects. It's unclear why this research can't be done in areas where trees are already being cut down. Fortunately, the Forest Service has spared some old-growth forest growing along Lookout Creek, considered to be one of the largest concentrations of old growth in the Willamette National Forest. The Lookout Creek Trail winds past many large old trees.

The bulk of the larger conifers are Douglas fir intermixed with western red cedar and western hemlock. Right at the trailhead, look for the **Pacific dogwood** *(Cornus nuttallii),* a beautiful understory tree that sports large white blossoms in spring. An introduced exotic disease threatens this native plant.

Growing abundantly about the forest is **oval-leaf huckleberry** *(Vaccinium ovalifolium).* Ground cover consists of **dwarf dogwood** *(Cornus canadensis),* **twinflower** *(Linnaea borealis),* **starflower** *(Trientalis latifolia),* **Oregon grape** *(Mahonia nervosa),* and **vanillaleaf** *(Achlys triphylla).*

Very soon the trail turns east and gradually descends to the stream. Western red cedar and western yew grow along the trail, with ground cover of **Oregon grape, yellow violet** *(Viola glabella),* and **foamflower** *(Tiarella trifoliata).*

At the creekside, note the downed logs in the creek. When large logs fall in the stream, they make a valuable contribution to the aquatic habitat. They provide long-term nutrient sources, serve as cover for fish, and help dissipate the erosive force of water. A good deal of **devil's club** *(Oplopanax horridum)* grow here, and **star-flowered false Solomon's seal** *(Smilacina stellata)*, **trail-plant** *(Adenocaulon bicolor)*, and **foamflower** line the trail.

Western yew and **red alder** *(Alnus rubra)* are abundant along the creek. **Alder** is a colonizer of disturbed habitats, growing on formerly logged sites or along streams where floods create gravel bars. **Red alder** is able to fix atmospheric nitrogen and make it available to other plants.

The trail finally crosses Lookout Creek on a big log serving as a bridge. On the opposite side of the stream you can spot more **devil's club** as well as **baneberry** *(Actaea rubra)*. **Pacific waterleaf** *(Hydrophyllum tenuipes)* grow abundantly along the streambanks. When the trail switches back upslope, you find **trillium** *(Trillium ovatum)* flourishing in profusion along with **maidenhair fern** *(Adiantum pedatum)*.

The route continues to climb the slope above the stream. You'll encounter **devil's club, violet, Pacific bleedingheart** *(Dicentra formosa)*, **star-flowered false Solomon's seal, vanillaleaf, foamflower,** and **lady-fern** *(Athyrium filix-femina)*. Shrubs living here include **huckleberry, Pacific rhododendron** *(Rhododendron macrophyllum)*, and **wild rose** *(Rosa gymnocarpa)*. **Vine maple** *(Acer circinatum)* are also abundant on this slope.

The trail still winds up and away from Lookout Creek. Look for **white-veined wintergreen** *(Pyrola picta)*, **dwarf dogwood, prince's pine** *(Chimaphila umbellata)*, and **evergreen violet** *(Viola sempervirens)* just beyond a small spring.

The route switchbacks up to a ridge above Lookout Creek, passing through more **rhododendron, prince's-pine, salal** *(Gaultheria shallon)*, **queen's cup lily** *(Clintonia uniflora)*, and large Douglas fir. Eventually, you come to a very large rock beside the trail; this makes a good turnaround point as the trail continues to climb up the ridge.

STAR-FLOWERED FALSE SOLOMON'S SEAL
Smilacina stellata

Star-flowered false Solomon's seal, common in moist forests, is a member of the lily family. The large, lance-shaped leaves show the prominent parallel veins common to lilies. This perennial grows from rhizomes and may reach a height of 3–4 feet. Its creamy-white, starlike flowers grow in a terminal cluster. The berries are greenish-yellow with purple stripes, turning dark blue or even blackish at maturity.

Wildflower
Hike 27
Horse Rock Ridge

A hiker taking in the panoramic views from Horse Rock.

Nearest Town	Eugene/Springfield
Highlights	Steep meadows with great views in a BLM natural area
Trail Rating	moderate
Trail Length	minimum of 1.0 mile each way
Location	Coburg Hills
Elevation	1,500–2,000 feet
Contact	Eugene BLM District, 541-683-6600
Bloom Season	April to July
Peak Bloom	June
Directions	From the junction of I-5 and I-105 in Eugene/Springfield (Springfield Exit 194), drive east on I-105 to the Marcola Road Exit. Take Marcola Road for 15.0 miles and turn left onto Shotgun Creek Road. In another 1.6 miles you will pass the Shotgun Creek BLM recreation area. Continue up this road until you reach a gravel pit on the left. Turn right on BLM Road 1615. Turn left at the next junction, keeping on the paved road; you'll pass Owl Creek Road on the left. About 4.8 miles from the fork by the gravel pit, you will be passing a clear-cut on your left. On the opposite side of the road, to your right, is a locked gate and a small sign identifying Road 15-2-113. Park here; if you miss this gate, you'll eventually reach the top of the ridge and know you've gone too far.

The Coburg Hills, easily viewed from the Willamette Valley as you drive I-5 from Salem to Eugene, are the hills you pass just before crossing the McKenzie River as you approach Eugene/Springfield. A checkerboard of BLM and private timberlands, most of the area has been logged at one time or another and is dominated by dense, even-aged trees.

The trail itself is more stroll than hike. Although relatively easy to reach, the meadows are situated on steep sidehills, and you need to hike up an old logging road and hop over a fence to reach the edge of the meadows. Wet seeps exist throughout the area, and the extremely fragile meadows overlay shallow soils on a rocky ridge. Whenever possible, keep to established paths to avoid creating a network of pathways or causing erosion.

The meadows extend down a ridge for 1.0 mile or more, offering outstanding views of the Three Sisters, Mount Jefferson, and Diamond Peak (but you have to overlook the nearly denuded lower hills that make up most of the foreground). This BLM Research Natural Area could easily be overrun by large groups—I suggest that only individuals and small groups explore this area. You can easily spend an entire day wandering the terrain.

The first part of the hike follows an old logging road. Since this road is closed to motorized vehicles except for official business, it's actually quite pleasant for hiking.

Immediately outside the parking area by the gate, you walk through forests of western red cedar and Douglas fir with scattered western hemlock. Common all along the road margin are **candyflower** *(Claytonia sibirica)*, the cloverlike **sorrel** *(Oxalis oregana)*, and **Pacific bleedingheart** *(Dicentra formosa)*. At openings in the forest canopy you can find the bright pink blooms of **salmonberry** *(Rubus spectabilis)*. Under the evergreen forest canopy live the also-evergreen **sword-fern** *(Polystichum munitum)* along with **Oregon grape** *(Mahonia nervosa)*. Scattered here and there are occasional clusters of **red alder** *(Alnus rubra)*, a smooth-barked tree that tends to colonize clear-cuts. The tree is a nitrogen fixer and greatly enriches the soil. **Vine maple** *(Acer circinatum)* is another understory shrub you see here. I saw occasional signs of elk, including an elk trail cutting through the forest about 0.33 mile from the gate.

After 0.33 mile or so, you pass a small culvert under the road. Just around the culvert live **salmonberry, sorrel, candyflower,** and **salal** *(Gaultheria shallon)*, a plant with evergreen, leathery leaves and bell-shaped flowers. In shady areas you find **false lily-of-the-valley** *(Maianthemum dilatatum)*, and you can also spot occasionally some small **wild rose** *(Rosa gymnocarpa)* shrubs.

A hundred yards or so past the culvert, as the road begins to climb a slope, lies a carpet of **twinflower** *(Linnaea borealis)* covering the upslope side of the roadcut. The evergreen leaves of the **twinflower** form a low, vinelike ground cover. **Trillium** *(Trillium ovatum)* are visible here and there, but never

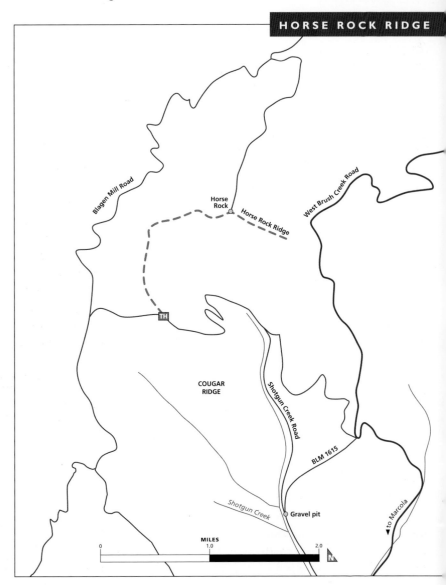

in large quantities. The broad leaves and white, showy flowers of **trillium** are among the earliest blooms in the spring.

Up to this point, the road curved in both directions but remained more or less level. Here, though, it begins a serious uphill climb. Watch for **red flowering currant** *(Ribes sanguineum)*, a lovely shrub with bright red blossoms that is popular for landscaping. You also see **ocean-spray** *(Holodiscus discolor)*, a shrub with drooping clusters of white blooms somewhat reminiscent of the ocean's white spray.

At a fork in the road, stay left on gravel road 15-2-113. **Wild strawberry** *(Fragaria vesca)* grow abundantly along the road margin. You pass an alder swamp on the left where, in the right season, you can see the large, white blossoms of **Pacific dogwood** *(Cornus nuttallii)*. The road eventually starts to go down a hill to yet another road junction—again, stay left. **Ocean-spray** and **Pacific dogwood** thrive in this area. At the next junction, take the right fork—Road 15-2-21. You can find **red huckleberry** *(Vaccinium parvifolium)* along the road. The road climbs up a hill and eventually you reach yet another road junction marked by a green transformer box on the right. Go left at the junction and continue up the hill. You come to a wide former parking area on the right. Through the brush, you can see fences. A small yellow sign announces that the area beyond is a BLM Research Natural Area.

Here you need to climb a metal wire fence to enter the meadows. The fence is designed to keep ORVs out. **Manzanita** *(Arctostaphylos columbiana)*, evergreen shrubs with beautiful, urn-shaped flowers, are scattered about.

The meadow area lies upon a rocky substrate. Since there are no official trails here, you can wander at will over hundreds of acres. One striking feature of the meadows is the lack of weeds. It appears that the area has not suffered the disturbance found in other meadows because of overgrazing or other uses. You will see **western buttercup** *(Ranunculus occidentalis)* dotting the meadows along with **spring gold** *(Lomatium utriculatum)*. In wetter areas look for dainty **yellow monkey-flower** *(Mimulus guttatus)*, **broad-leaved shooting star** *(Dodecatheon hendersonii)*, as well as **western saxifrage** *(Saxifraga occidentalis)*. Pink **plectritis** *(Plectritis congesta)* form almost continuous pinkish carpets in swales. In drier, rocky areas, you see bluish patches of the small-flowered **blue-eyed Mary** *(Collinsia parviflora)*.

The meadow is also home to the **cliff larkspur** *(Delphinium menziesii)*, which is toxic to livestock, and the lovely, white-flowered **meadow death-camas** *(Zigadenus venenosus)*, which is poisonous to humans. Small **common cryptantha** *(Cryptantha*

SLIM-LEAF ONION
Allium amplectens

As the name suggests, **slim-leaf onion** have thin, narrow leaves, and the pink flowers are clustered in a terminal. The Allium family also includes garlic, chives, and our common domesticated onion. You can find **slim-leaf onion** on dry, open slopes from California north to Puget Sound.

intermedia) are scattered about, as are a few **wild cucumber** *(Marah oreganus)* which, in spite of the name, are inedible.

As you amble eastward down the ridge, you are treated to fine views of Mount Jefferson and the Three Sisters. Along the forest/meadow boundary grow the white blossoms of **serviceberry** *(Amelanchier alnifolia)*, sporting dark blue, edible (but mealy) berries in August. In the outlying clumps of Douglas fir that fringe the meadows, you will find white **Oregon fawn-lily** *(Erythronium oregonum)* and a few pink **fairy-slipper orchid** *(Calypso bulbosa)*. Just outside the forest in the meadow, I spotted one clump of **chocolate lily** *(Fritillaria lanceolata)*. A rocky ridge, a relict volcanic intrusion that is more resistant to erosion, sits about halfway down the meadow. From the top of the wall, take in the expansive views of the surrounding mountains, including Diamond Peak. **Stonecrop** *(Sedum oregonense)* and **slim-leaf onion** *(Allium amplectens)* grow along the outcrop; yellow **Oregon iris** *(Iris tenax)* live along the forest margin. Usually iris flowers are blue, but sometimes you can find yellow ones.

Elk tracks were abundant throughout the meadow when I hiked this trail, and I also found mountain lion scat. Lush growth of Idaho fescue cover some parts of the slope along with **deltoid balsamroot** *(Balsamorhiza deltoidea)* mixed with **red Indian-paintbrush** *(Castilleja miniata)*. **Paintbrush** is interesting, because the brilliant color in the flowers actually comes from colored bracts.

Delta Old-Growth Trail Loop

Giant Douglas fir along the interpretive Delta Old-Growth Trail.

Giant red cedar and Douglas fir dominate this lush site along the McKenzie River. This nearly-level trail, which could even be considered wheelchair-accessible, features numbered sites that identify some of the plants and explain some of the basic ecology of the old-growth forest.

Immediately at the trailhead you find **thimbleberry** *(Rubus parviflorus)*, **salal** *(Gaultheria shallon)*, **sword-fern** *(Polystichum munitum)*, and the native shrub **hazelnut** *(Corylus cornuta)*. When cultivated, **hazelnuts** are known as **filberts**. Much of the ground cover along this stretch of trail consists of clover-leaved **sorrel** *(Oxalis oregana)*, which are particularly abundant just before you cross the bridge by the trailhead.

Nearest Town	Eugene/Springfield
Highlights	Beautiful riparian vegetation along the McKenzie River
Trail Rating	easy
Trail Length	1.0-mile loop hike
Location	Willamette National Forest
Elevation	500 feet
Contact	McKenzie Ranger District, Willamette NF, 541-465-6521
Bloom Season	April to July
Peak Bloom	May to June
Directions	From Eugene/Springfield, take OR 126 (McKenzie Highway) east about 4.5 miles past Blue River to FR 19 (Aufderheide Memorial Drive) and turn right (south). Cross the McKenzie River, then immediately take another right onto FR 400 toward Delta campground. Drive 0.75 mile to the end of the campground where you'll find a parking area and a signed nature trail.

After the bridge, you encounter more **sorrel** and **sword-fern.** Other plants growing here in the understory include **snowberry** *(Symphoricarpos albus)*, **Oregon grape** *(Mahonia nervosa)*, **meadowrue** *(Thalictrum occidentale)*, and more **hazelnut. Snowberry** is named for the white berries that grace the plant in the fall.

Douglas fir and western red cedar make up the large trees here. Douglas fir, named for botanist David Douglas who collected plants in western Oregon during the early 1800s, often live to be 500 to 600 years old.

Western red cedars can live even longer than the oldest Douglas firs. Trees this old are unusual, because wildfires burn through these woodlands every few hundred years. It's likely that this old-growth grove survived forest fires because its location on an island in the river has functioned as a natural fire bridge. Here you can also see **wild rose** *(Rosa gymnocarpa)*, **maidenhair fern** *(Adiantum pedatum)*, and **yellow violet** *(Viola glabella).*

As you continue, you come to a bench with a large Douglas fir behind it. More **sword-fern** grow around the post at site number 3. Move on to site number 4, where you find **red huckleberry** *(Vaccinium parvifolium)*, **hazelnut**, and lots of **snowberry**. Slightly farther along the trail, at site number 5, you see **vine maple** *(Acer circinatum)* and plenty of **sword-fern, maidenhair fern,**

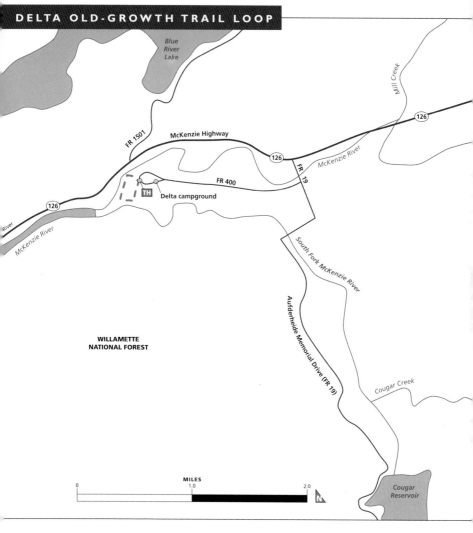

Oregon grape, and **meadowrue. Vine maple**, a common understory shrub
or small tree, grows in wetter old-growth forest stands.

You see more Douglas fir and some **trail-plant** *(Adenocaulon bicolor)*.
Trail-plant is so named because the light undersides of its leaves perk up when
a person or animal passes, thereby marking a trail.

You cross a bridge over the creek and reach a very pretty, calm site with
big Douglas fir. Right after the bridge, you can see lots of **vine maple**, and you
may also spot **baneberry** *(Actaea rubra)*. **Baneberry** sport luscious red berries
that are poisonous to consume. In this same stretch of trail, you can find an
abundance of western hemlock, **oak-fern** *(Gymnocarpium dryopteris)*, **sorrel**,
foamflower *(Tiarella trifoliata)*, and **meadowrue.**

Site number 8 is covered with western hemlock, a shade-loving species that thrives in the understory of other large trees. Just beyond, at site 9, stands a huge Douglas fir by a bench surrounded by **vanillaleaf** *(Achlys triphylla)*. In the mid-elevation level of the forest you can see some very tall bigleaf maple, named appropriately for leaves that are sometimes as long as 10 inches across.

You find yet another enormous Douglas fir at site 10. Just before you reach the parking lot, the final bridge crosses a creek, and you encounter an abundance of **red alder** *(Alnus rubra)* and bigleaf maple.

BANEBERRY
Actaea rubra

Baneberry, with their small, white flowers in dense racemes, resemble clematis in some ways. The flowers are borne on an erect, branched stem that is 1–3 feet tall, and the leaves are incised and toothed. (The Latin name *Actaea* means sharp-toothed.) The most distinctive characteristic of the plants is the bright red, sometimes white, berries that appear late in the summer. As luscious as they seem, berries, foliage, and roots all are highly poisonous—consuming as few as six berries can result in severe reactions. **Baneberry** are common in moist, shady forests.

Castle Rock

Wildflower Hike 29

Lush understory trees border the short trail to Castle Rock.

Eugene/Springfield	*Nearest Town*
Great views and rock gardens at an old lookout site	*Highlights*
moderate	*Trail Rating*
2.0 miles round-trip	*Trail Length*
McKenzie River Corridor	*Location*
3,180–3,808 feet	*Elevation*
Willamette National Forest, 541-465-6521	*Contact*
June to August	*Bloom Season*
July	*Peak Bloom*
From Eugene/Springfield, take OR 126 (McKenzie Highway) east about 4.5 miles past Blue River to FR 19 (Aufderheide Memorial Drive) and turn right (south). Take FR 19 about 0.5 mile, then merge left onto FR 410 and take it for 0.5 mile to King Road W (FR 2639) and turn left. Drive just over a mile, turn right onto FR 460, and drive 5.8 miles (passing several lower trailheads en route) to the end of the road and limited parking.	*Directions*

For a quick leg-stretcher that provides great views for little effort, you can't beat the short trail up to Castle Rock. You pass through quiet forests of large Douglas fir to reach a rocky outcrop, a former lookout site that affords sweeping views of the Cascades, McKenzie River Valley, and the Three Sisters.

From the trailhead, the path heads steadily uphill. The forest is primarily Douglas fir with occasional western red cedar or western hemlock. Ground cover here is made up of hollylike **Oregon grape** *(Mahonia nervosa)*, **trillium** *(Trillium ovatum)*, and **prince's-pine** *(Chimaphila umbellata)*. Other species you encounter include **trail-plant** *(Adenocaulon bicolor)* and **queen's cup lily** *(Clintonia uniflora)*. A bit farther up the trail, you can spot a few **Pacific rhododendron** *(Rhododendron macrophyllum)* along with **red huckleberry** *(Vaccinium parvifolium)*.

After a switchback, the next section of trail features **bracken fern** *(Pteridium aquilinum)*, more **prince's-pine**, **Oregon grape**, **rhododendron**, and **huckleberry**.

You reach another switchback, and the trail continues through an open Douglas fir forest. Scattered in the understory are **rhododendron** and limited amounts of **salal** *(Gaultheria shallon)*, recognizable by their thick, evergreen leaves and white, urn-shaped flowers. Here and there you can spot **ocean-spray** *(Holodiscus discolor)*, **star-flowered false Solomon's seal** *(Smilacina stellata)*, **twinflower** *(Linnaea borealis)*, **maidenhair fern** *(Adiantum pedatum)*, **wild rose** *(Rosa gymnocarpa)*, **thimbleberry** *(Rubus parviflorus)*, **snowberry** *(Symphoricarpos albus)*, **Oregon bedstraw** *(Galium oreganum)*, **whiteveined wintergreen** *(Pyrola picta)*, and some **vanillaleaf** *(Achlys triphylla)*. Along the path grow small trees such as **vine maple** *(Acer circinatum)* and **hazelnut** *(Corylus cornuta)*.

The trail cuts below a cliff, where you see some large Douglas fir on either side. **Sword-fern** *(Polystichum munitum)* are scattered about

CLIFF LARKSPUR
Delphinium menziesii

Although a member of the buttercup family, the dark blue **cliff larkspur** doesn't look anything like a buttercup. The name refers to the flower's "spur," which contains the nectar. Several **larkspur** are found in Oregon. In particular, the plant, sometimes called **Menzies larkspur**, tends to grow on grassy slopes, rocky outcrops, and droughty areas at all elevations. **Cliff larkspur** is toxic to livestock. In some places, government agencies use revenues to kill this lovely plant in order to make public lands safer and pastures more profitable for ranchers.

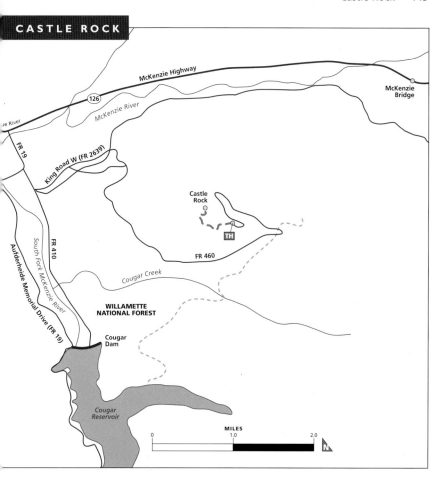

CASTLE ROCK

the slope along with more **Oregon grape,** some **trailing blackberry** *(Rubus ursinus)* and **whiteveined wintergreen.**

You reach another switchback marked by a bunch of **thimbleberry,** with large, maplelike leaves that turn a rich amber-yellow color in the fall. The trail climbs up across shallow soils below outcrops where **wild strawberry** *(Fragaria vesca),* **alpine buckwheat** *(Eriogonum pyrolifolium),* and **ocean-spray** grow.

You encounter one more switchback, and the trail cuts across an open, rocky slope covered with various grasses and flower species such as **cat's-ear lily** *(Calochortus subalpinus),* **cliff larkspur** *(Delphinium menziesii),* **spreading phlox** *(Phlox diffusa),* **yarrow** *(Achillea millefolium),* and **fringecup** *(Tellima grandiflora).* In season, you may find several **penstemon** *(Penstemon sp.)* looming. On rocky outcrops near the summit, Oregon white oak grow in small numbers. A drought-resistant species, the tree is more typical of the Willamette Valley and a little out of place here.

A final switchback brings you up to an old lookout site on top of the peak. **Pacific madrone** *(Arbutus menziesii),* **chinquapin** *(Castanopsis chrysophylla),* **pinemat manzanita** *(Arctostaphylos nevadensis),* and other species typical of dry, arid sites grow here. Despite the heavy rains that fall in this region, the rocky shallow soils on the summit provide little moisture for plant growth—hence the dominance of species such as oak, **madrone,** and **manzanita.**

Despite the numerous nearby clear-cuts, the vista from the top is superb, granting great views of the Three Sisters and the glaciated U-shaped valley of the McKenzie River. This is a good place to eat lunch and enjoy the surrounding landscape before heading back.

The widely distributed cliff larkspur grow in rocky, droughty areas.

Lowder Mountain Trail

Wildflower Hike 30

A flower-studded rock garden by the Lowder Mountain Trail, Three Sisters Wilderness.

The Lowder Mountain Trail follows a hillside that overlooks the unlogged French Pete drainage in the Three Sisters Wilderness. The trail provides fantastic views of the wilderness as you pass through nice old-growth forests and small meadows. The top of Lowder Mountain is blanketed with extensive meadowlands that—if reached during peak blooms—is a wonderland of color.

Several trails leave from the same trailhead; the path to Lowder Mountain (#3329) is on the right and heads uphill. The path switchbacks up the hillside and then levels off, traversing the slope through Pacific silver fir and Douglas fir forest. Right at the trailhead, note the abundant white blossoms of **three-leaved anemone** (*Anemone deltoidea*). The delicate white **foamflower** (*Tiarella trifoliata*) are scattered about the forest floor. **Vanillaleaf** (*Achlys triphylla*),

Nearest Town	Eugene/Springfield
Highlights	Old-growth forest, extensive mountaintop meadows, and great views
Trail Rating	moderate
Trail Length	5.6 miles round-trip
Location	Three Sisters Wilderness
Elevation	4,660–5,500 feet
Contact	Willamette National Forest, 541-465-6521
Bloom Season	May to August
Peak Bloom	July
Directions	From Eugene/Springfield, take OR 126 (McKenzie Highway) east about 4.5 miles past Blue River to FR 19 (Aufderheide Memorial Drive) and turn right (south) toward Cougar Reservoir. Follow FR 19, bearing right at a sharp intersection about 0.5 mile up the road. Continue on FR 19 another 2.5 miles to the reservoir and turn left, crossing the dam. Take FR 1993, 11.0 miles or so to the trailhead and parking lot on the right.

trillium *(Trillium ovatum)*, and **star-flowered false Solomon's seal** *(Smilacina stellata)* also grow here.

As you work up through the second switchback, you see more **anemone, queen's cup lily** *(Clintonia uniflora)*, **vanillaleaf, thimbleberry** *(Rubus parviflorus)*, **western columbine** *(Aquilegia formosa)*, and a few showy **beargrass** *(Xerophyllum tenax)*. You can find **vine maple** *(Acer circinatum)*, a shrub-tree common in the understory of the forest, throughout the route.

As you go up through the third switchback, you encounter **prince's-pine** *(Chimaphila umbellata)*. With its evergreen leaves, it looks like a miniature conifer, hence its common name. You encounter more **vanillaleaf, anemone, star-flowered Solomon's seal**, and the small, white **northern starflower** *(Trientalis arctica)*.

When you pass a sign announcing your entry into the Three Sisters Wilderness, note the large, white terminal cluster of **false Solomon's seal** *(Smilacina racemosa)* and **Pacific bleedingheart** *(Dicentra formosa)*.

On the fourth switchback, look for **wild rose** *(Rosa gymnocarpa)* and **lupine** *(Lupinus sp.)*. Along the fifth switchback, you'll discover more **queen's cup lily** and a few **prickly currant** *(Ribes lacustre)*. The golden prickles along **prickly currant's** stem can cause an allergic reaction in some people.

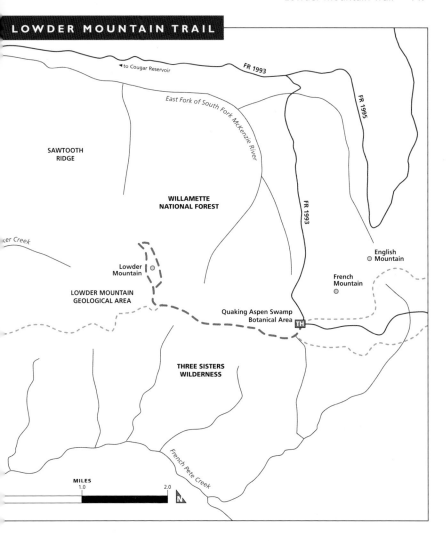

LOWDER MOUNTAIN TRAIL

to Cougar Reservoir

FR 1993

East Fork of South Fork McKenzie River

FR 1995

SAWTOOTH RIDGE

WILLAMETTE NATIONAL FOREST

FR 1993

..er Creek

Lowder Mountain

English Mountain

LOWDER MOUNTAIN GEOLOGICAL AREA

French Mountain

Quaking Aspen Swamp Botanical Area TH

THREE SISTERS WILDERNESS

French Pete Creek

MILES
1.0   2.0

    Along the sixth switchback, you will encounter a few **devil's-club** *(Oplopanax horridum)* with their huge, maplelike leaves. The stems have a dense covering of spines that can cause pain and inflammation on contact. You pass through several more switchbacks before the trail finally levels off.

    As the trail continues, you enter some wonderful old-growth Douglas fir (named for David Douglas, an early botanist who explored much of Oregon during the early 1800s). Along this section you see white-flowered **dwarf dogwood** *(Cornus canadensis)*, which sport bright red, non-edible berries in the autumn. **Trillium, star-flowered false Solomon's seal, thimbleberry,** and **anemone** occur in abundance through here. You also encounter **candyflower** *(Claytonia sibirica)*, which have edible leaves that are high in vitamin C.

The trail enters the first small meadow, where you see **thimbleberry, western columbine,** and **bracken fern** *(Pteridium aquilinum)*, which die each fall and regrow each spring. Here, look for large-leaved **cow-parsnip** *(Heracleum lanatum)*, a member of the carrot family that American Indians peeled and ate like celery. Another beautiful flower living in the meadow is **tiger lily** *(Lilium columbianum)*, with orange blossoms hanging down from the stems. In addition, you see **senecio** *(Senecio triangularis)*, also known as **arrowleaf groundsel,** distinguished by their triangular leaves. In the same meadow, I came upon some bear scat.

Upon leaving the meadow, the trail continues to traverse the slope in a forest rich with **thimbleberry,** a common understory plant. You reach a second meadow full of **thimbleberry, bracken fern,** and **lupine.**

A third meadow features more of the same species and a rocky outcrop near the trail strewn with **sulfur buckwheat** *(Eriogonum umbellatum)*, which you find on drier, rocky sites. You also see large-leaved **avens** *(Geum macrophyllum)* here.

After leaving the meadows, you enter the forest again. The trail comes out on a small ridgetop meadow with more **tiger lily, red Indian-paintbrush** *(Castilleja miniata)*, and **thimbleberry.** When the trail swings up to the ridge, you encounter **spreading stonecrop** *(Sedum divergens)*, a succulent well adapted to arid locations. More **paintbrush, thimbleberry,** and **wild strawberry** *(Fragaria vesca)* grow here as well.

You switchback to a rocky ridge where you find **spreading phlox** *(Phlox diffusa)*, a common plant of rocky areas, plus the white **cat's-ear lily** *(Calochortus subalpinus)*, **wild rose, thimbleberry,** and the blue-flowered **Cardwell's penstemon** *(Penstemon cardwellii)*. I also noted some **snowbush** *(Ceanothus velutinus)*, also known simply as **ceanothus,** which tend to grow on rocky outcrops and have shiny evergreen leaves. **Snowbush,** a common colonizer of burned sites after forest fires, has seeds that remain dormant in the soil for years, then germinate in response to heat.

THREE-LEAVED ANEMONE
Anemone deltoidea

The **three-leaved anemone's** solitary white flowers glow brightly in the subdued light of the moist, shady forests the plant frequents. The leaves are toothed, and the flowers have five sepals. The Latin name *deltoidea* refers to the egg-shaped leaves, which grow in groups of three.

If you take the short side trail leading up to a rocky ridge, you will find more **cat's-ear lily, penstemon, stonecrop, phlox**, and other species common on rocky, dry sites. Back on the main trail, note the presence of Alaskan cedar —as the name suggests, they are more common in (coastal) Alaska. Although this species is rather uncommon in the Cascades, it is relatively common along this trail. You also find **kinnikinnick** *(Arctostaphylos uva-ursi)* growing on this rocky ridge trail.

You pass through some more forest, and then enter a small meadow. This spot offers great views of French Pete Creek below. Forest Service plans to log the French Pete drainage caused a major conservation battle in the early 1970s. Environmentalists in Eugene and elsewhere in Oregon mobilized to garner support for including the drainage in the already-existing Three Sisters Wilderness. This was the first successful campaign to protect Oregon's old-growth forests from the saws of loggers.

A wet seep in the meadow harbors **salmonberry** *(Rubus spectabilis)* and **alder** *(Alnus crispa)*, a shrub common in wet areas. The meadow also hosts **tall bluebell** *(Mertensia paniculata)*, **Queen Anne's lace** *(Daucus carota)*, a member of the carrot family with an umbel of small, white flowers, and even a few **scarlet gilia** *(Ipomopsis aggregata)*, their red flowers a favorite of hummingbirds.

At the far end of the meadow, approximately 2 miles from the trail-head, you encounter a trail junction. To reach Lowder Mountain, take the right fork (otherwise, the trail continues west toward Yankee Mountain). The trail switchbacks 0.5 mile up the mountain slope, passing through stands of Alaskan cedar. Along the way, you'll see **mountain-ash** *(Sorbus sitchensis)*, a shrub-tree with pinnate leaves and white clusters of flowers. **Mountain-ash** sport red berries in the fall.

Eventually you top out on a flat mountain summit with tree islands of Alaskan cedar and mountain hemlock scattered here and there. When I reached the summit, the snow had only recently melted, leaving behind snow gopher tunnels—mounds of soil snaking across the ground. You can see the diggings of pocket gophers everywhere in the meadows. I saw a few blooming **yellow glacier-lily** *(Erythronium grandiflorum)*—one of the earliest species to bloom after snowmelt. **Spreading stonecrop** *(Sedum divergens)* are common across the rocky parts of this meadow.

Trail cairns mark the path across the meadows. At the far end of the meadow complex, you enter the forest again and begin to descend toward Walker Creek. Rather than follow this path, head right and climb up the gentle meadow to the edge of sheer cliffs that affords fine views of the Cascades and two tiny lakes far below. This makes a good turnaround point for the hike; retrace your steps back to the trailhead.

Wildflower Hike 31 Erma Bell Lakes

The falls near Middle Erma Bell Lake, Three Sisters Wilderness.

The Erma Bell Trail is considered wheelchair accessible, which gives you some idea of its grade: nearly level and ideal for families with children. You can enjoy a spectacular waterfall—a worthy destination in its own right —separating Lower Erma Bell and Middle Erma Bell Lakes. Ice Age glaciers scooped out the three Erma Bell Lakes.

At the trailhead, a small campground sits right next to a creek. The Three Sisters Wilderness border lies just beyond the campground. Western hemlock trees, with an understory of **sword-fern** *(Polystichum munitum)* and some **broadleaf lupine** *(Lupinus latifolius)*, shade the area immediately by the campground. Some **mountain boxwood** *(Pachistima myrsinites)*, an evergreen shrub, grow beside the trail.

Nearest Town	Eugene/Springfield
Highlights	Nearly level trail through old-growth forest to lovely lakes
Trail Rating	easy
Trail Length	4.2 miles round-trip
Location	Three Sisters Wilderness
Elevation	4,500 feet
Contact	Willamette National Forest, 541-465-6521
Bloom Season	June to August
Peak Bloom	late June
Directions	From Eugene/Springfield, take OR 126 (McKenzie Highway) east about 4.5 miles past Blue River to FR 19 (Aufderheide Memorial Drive) and turn right (south). Follow FR 19, bearing right at a sharp intersection about 0.5 mile up the road. After 25.6 miles, turn left onto FR 1957, just past the Box Canyon ranger station. Follow this gravel road 3.6 miles to Skookum Creek campground and the trailhead.

To begin the hike, cross a wooden bridge just beyond the campground. According to the trailhead sign, the hike to Otter Lake is 1.25 miles, the hike to Lower Erma Bell Lake 1.75 miles. You will find the trail to Otter Lake branches off from the main trail to Erma Bell Lakes at 0.6 mile, heading toward Irish Mountain.

As you cross over the bridge, stop to admire the riparian vegetation— including **red alder** *(Alnus rubra)* and **thimbleberry** *(Rubus parviflorus)*—along the moss-lined Skookum Creek. Immediately after the bridge, look for **wild ginger** *(Asarum caudatum)*, **bracken fern** *(Pteridium aquilinum)*, **vanillaleaf** *(Achlys triphylla)*, and **sticky currant** *(Ribes viscosissimum)*.

Pacific rhododendron *(Rhododendron macrophyllum)* grow just to the right of the bridge. Well adapted to the Pacific Northwest climate, **rhododendron's** large evergreen leaves allow for photosynthesis throughout the mild winter. The thick, leathery leaves limit water loss, an adaptation to the typical summer drought of the region.

Taller shrubs found along the first parts of this trail include **thimbleberry** with its large, maplelike leaves. **Huckleberry** *(Vaccinium sp.)*, which reach peak ripeness in August, are abundant along this entire path. Earlier in the season, **huckleberry** show small, white, urnlike flowers.

Dwarf dogwood *(Cornus canadensis)* and **twinflower** *(Linnaea borealis)* serve as ground cover along this entire hike. **Dwarf dogwood** have lovely white blossoms in the spring and bright red berries in the autumn. **Twinflower**, as the name implies, produce two small, white blossoms. Their leaves are evergreen, and the plant tends to grow in a sprawling mat.

Another evergreen plant common in the forest here is **prince's-pine** *(Chimaphila umbellata)*. Like **rhododendron**, this plant also has evergreen leaves that permit photosynthesis whenever weather permits while at the same time reducing water losses in summer.

You pass a sign for Three Sisters Wilderness, largest of Oregon's federally designated wilderness areas. You can find more **rhododendron** immediately after the sign. **Queen's cup lily** *(Clintonia uniflora)*, sometimes called **bead lily**, grow here and there. As you amble along this gentle trail, admire more **dwarf dogwood, twinflower,** and **rhododendron.** A few **chinquapin** *(Castanopsis chrysophylla)*, recognizable by the golden, burrlike fruit, also dot the trail.

VANILLALEAF
Achlys triphylla

Vanillaleaf's flowers are white and grow in showy spikes, but the plant's most distinctive feature is its large, fan-shaped leaves. *Triphylla* refers to these leaves, which are divided into three segments. **Vanillaleaf** are common in shady forests. In many places, **vanillaleaf** grow long rhizomes and form a nearly continuous carpet of light green leaves on the forest floor.

The trail curves from its generally western direction to a more southern direction. Along the path here you find **trail-plant** *(Adenocaulon bicolor)*, a species with light-colored undersides that turn when disturbed, marking the trail of someone or something that has gone before. **Oregon grape** *(Mahonia nervosa)* and **wild ginger** also make up the ground cover. The distinctive **white-veined wintergreen** *(Pyrola picta)* also grow low to the ground here.

Through here you see a few Engelmann spruce, which are common in the Rocky Mountains but rather unusual in the Cascades (particularly on their western slope). In the Rockies, the tree is associated

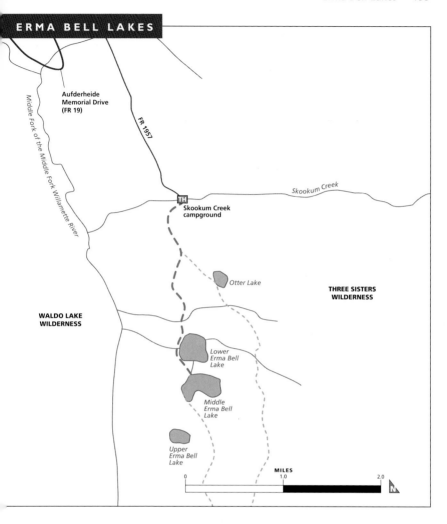

with wet, cool locations, typically along stream drainage bottoms and subalpine cirque basins.

The trail traverses a sidehill through mostly young forest—likely regrowth after a forest fire. Watch for the delicate white blossoms of **foam-flower** *(Tiarella trifoliata)* along with **wild rose** *(Rosa sp.)*, **star-flowered false Solomon's seal** *(Smilacina stellata)*, **trillium** *(Trillium ovatum)*, **baneberry** *(Actaea rubra)*, **broad-leaved starflower** *(Trientalis latifolia)*, **thimbleberry**, **candyflower** *(Claytonia sibirica)*, and **vanillaleaf.**

The trail crosses a small drainage area marked by a drainage pipe. Just downstream from the trail you see a lot of **vine maple** *(Acer circinatum)*, an understory shrub-tree common in west-side forests.

At little more than 0.5 mile from the trailhead, the trail branches. Irish Mountain Trail (#3588) goes to Otter Lake. Bear left to continue on the Erma Bell Trail, heading through an open forest with few plants other than an occasional **thimbleberry, vanillaleaf, dwarf dogwood,** and **bracken fern.**

The route crosses a small dry creek bridged by a metal drainage pipe. While the forest up to this point has been amazingly open, it now becomes denser, with multistory layers. **Vine maple** grow in the understory along with some small hemlock and fir.

A small bridge crosses a creek, where you'll see the small clumps of **beargrass** *(Xerophyllum tenax),* **thimbleberry,** and **lupine** *(Lupinus sp.).* When in bloom in early July, the showy white blossoms of **beargrass** glow. More **rhododendron** live here, along with **huckleberry.** Along the creek you can discover a few cottonwood, and just up from the creek you can also spot several western red cedar.

As the trail rises slightly upslope, it curves to the east and Lower Erma Bell Lake soon comes into view. **Boxwood** abound along this stretch. Walk down to the shore to find tons of blooming **beargrass** (in July) and a nice spot for a picnic. Some dry forest tree species live here, including **Pacific madrone** *(Arbutus menziesii),* **chinquapin,** and even a few lodgepole pine (which, like Engelmann spruce, are somewhat uncommon west of the Cascade crest).

If you wander up the trail another 0.4 mile to Middle Erma Bell Lake, you pass the waterfall just downstream from the outlet of Middle Erma Bell Lake. It's quite a nice falls, set in a small gorge. Along the way in the forest, note the western white pine along with more **rhododendron.** Middle Erma Bell Lake makes an excellent turnaround point to retrace your steps back to the trailhead.

Lone Wolf Shelter

Cow-parsnip flourishes in a meadow near Lone Wolf Shelter.

This hike begins, in less than spectacular fashion, by traversing partially regrown clear-cuts. But stick with it, for it soon enters old-growth primary forest that is gorgeous. During June, **Pacific rhododendron** *(Rhododendron macrophyllum)* in the understory are magnificent. This nearly-level trail, ideal for children, is short enough for most to make it to the Lone Wolf Shelter and meadow. The meadow is rather wet and therefore lush with growth. When I visited in mid-July, it was almost pure white with the blossoms of **cow-parsnip** *(Heracleum lanatum)* along with many other flowers.

Just behind the parking area you may note white blossoms of **red elderberry** *(Sambucus racemosa)*, a shrub-tree that is common in open areas. Along the road you'll see **oxeye daisy** *(Leucanthemum vulgare)*, an exotic from Europe that is a common colonizer of roadsides.

Nearest Town	Oakridge
Highlights	Beautiful old-growth forest and a large, flowery meadow
Trail Rating	easy
Trail Length	2.0 miles round-trip
Location	Willamette National Forest
Elevation	4,000 feet
Contact	Oakridge Ranger District, Willamette NF, 541-465-6521
Bloom Season	May to August
Peak Bloom	late June
Directions	From Eugene/Springfield, take OR 58 (Willamette Highway) southeast. About 5.0 miles before Oakridge, watch for the Shady Dell campground on the right—it's easy to miss—and turn right (south). Follow FR 5847 for 7.8 miles, ignoring all side roads. When you pass a quarry on the right, you're near the end. After you cross a watershed divide, take a right onto FR 555. The road sign is hidden by vegetation, but if you can view the Umpqua drainage from the divide, then you're on the correct road. Drive about 0.25 mile, watching for a small parking area on the right. The trailhead across the road is signed Lone Wolf Trail 3470 (but again, the sign is hard to see).

From the trailhead, which is just beside a clearcut, you walk through trees blown over by the "edge" effect. The removal of trees often leads to a domino effect, causing standing trees outside the clear-cut logged area to fall in high winds. Among the trees found here are western hemlock, Pacific silver fir, and Douglas fir.

At the beginning of the trail, common understory plants include **thimbleberry** *(Rubus parviflorus)*, **foamflower** *(Tiarella trifoliata)*, **parrot beak** *(Pedicularis racemosa)*, and **prickly currant** *(Ribes lacustre)*. Almost immediately you encounter **rhododendron**, which you will find scattered here and there along the entire trail.

As the trail turns north from the clear-cut, you see more **rhododendron** plus a lot of **prickly currant**. **Twinflower** *(Linnaea borealis)* grow low to the ground here, their shiny evergreen leaves and two delicate flowers making the plants easy to identify.

Less than 100 feet or so from the trailhead, you move from scattered, open forest into deep shade. Just at the left of the trail you can find **sorrel** *(Oxalis* *oregana)* surrounding the base of a large, broken-topped snag. You can also spot **prince's-pine** *(Chimaphila umbellata)*, an evergreen plant with nodding flowers, and **Oregon grape** *(Mahonia nervosa)* with evergreen, hollylike leaves.

As the trail turns west and moves slightly uphill, you pass more **sorrel**, plus **star-flowered false Solomon's seal** *(Smilacina stellata)*, **wild rose** *(Rosa gymnocarpa)*, and **trail-plant** *(Adenocaulon bicolor)*.

The trail enters an area with larger old-growth to the left and young regrowth in an old logged area to the right. If you look carefully, you might spot some **striped coral-root orchid** *(Corallorhiza striata)*. The trail passes a very large Douglas fir, more than 6 feet in a diameter. Note the blackened trunk, resulting from a past forest fire. Large Douglas fir are able to survive most fires—the thick bark and lack of lower branches help protect the tree from blazes.

You can see **salmonberry** *(Rubus spectabilis),* with edible berries, in the shaded forest. **Vine maple** *(Acer circinatum),* a common understory shrub-tree, edge the trail. The forest floor hosts **vanillaleaf** *(Achlys triphylla),* **yellow violet** *(Viola glabella),* **candyflower** *(Claytonia sibirica),* and **Pacific bleedingheart** *(Dicentra formosa)*.

Note the occurrence of **bracken fern** *(Pteridium aquilinum)* along the hike, the most common fern in Oregon. The plant is particularly abundant in old clearcuts. Beyond the clearcut and small openings, you enter more old growth. A particularly large, double-trunked Douglas fir stands at left. You can see more large Douglas fir, as tall as 8 feet, along the trail. Under the Douglas fir grow **queen's cup lily** *(Clintonia uniflora),* which bear white blossoms that later become deep metallic-blue berries. **Candyflower,** mixed in with **inside-out flower**

FALSE HELLEBORE
Veratrum viride

False hellebore, despite its lush and attractive appearance, is one of the most poisonous plants in the Northwest: Eating even a small amount of it can be fatal. Common in wet meadows, bogs, and other swampy areas, **false hellebore** ranges from valley floors up to subalpine basins, in which it reaches its greatest abundance. The plant is also known as **corn lily**. Like all members of the lily family, its large broad-to-oblong leaves have prominent, pleated, parallel veins. The small, pale green flowers bloom in drooping terminal clusters and emit a slightly musky odor.

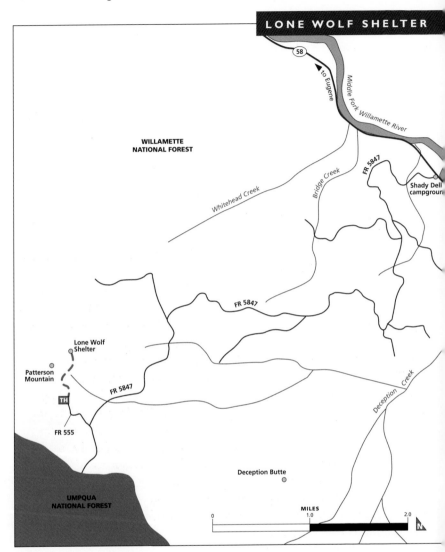

(*Vancouveria hexandra*), are common here. **Inside-out flower's** Latin name refers to Captain George Vancouver, for whom the cities in Washington state and British Columbia were also named.

As the trail begins to descend, it enters a small meadow (an old clearcut with stumps). Sun-loving plants grow here, including **cow-parsnip, senecio** (*Senecio triangularis*), **red Indian-paintbrush** (*Castilleja miniata*), **bleeding-heart,** and **prickly currant. Tiger lily** (*Lilium columbianum*), never common, grow among the other plant species in the meadow. A few **broadleaf lupine** (*Lupinus latifolius*) occur sparingly along the fringes of the opening. **Beargrass** (*Xerophyllum tenax*), a member of the lily family, grow in small groups here.

The trail heads back into unlogged forest and remains in old growth for the rest of the hike. The cloverlike leaves of **sorrel** cover the ground in an almost continuous leafy covering, and **foamflower, vanillaleaf,** and **inside-out flower** thrive here.

The route cuts across a little opening with more **beargrass** and lots of **foamflower.** The trail starts downslope, passing through more **rhododendron.** You reach a switchback and then a trail junction at right with a sign for Road 5840-535. Take a left to reach the Lone Wolf Shelter.

Near the sign, you find more **foamflower, bleedingheart, trail-plant, vanillaleaf, sorrel,** and **inside-out flower.**

Just beyond the junction, an opening features **salmonberry, tiger lily, cow-parsnip,** and **senecio.** Follow the path into forest, and note three giant Douglas fir as the trail climbs gently downhill to a meadow. **Three-leaved anemone** (*Anemone deltoidea*) grow in the shady forest areas; **western columbine** (*Aquilegia formosa*) dot the edge of the meadow with their red flowers.

The trail circles west of a large meadow, which you can see through the trees. When you come to an unsigned trail junction, go right 100 yards to find the Lone Wolf Shelter. The shelter stands in the middle of an old-growth forest, near the wet meadow.

The meadow, entirely surrounded by forest, covers about 3 acres. You could easily spend an hour or more wandering the meadow, looking for new flowering riches. Among the meadow's treasures you can find **white bog-orchid** (*Habenaria dilatata*), **yellow monkey-flower** (*Mimulus guttatus*), **camas lily** (*Camassia quamash*), **American bistort** (*Polygonum bistortoides*), and the pink flowers of **checkerbloom** (*Sidalcea malvaeflora*). The bulk of the meadow, edged with **false hellebore** (*Veratrum viride*) and **beargrass,** is nearly white with **cow-parsnip.** I also found elk beds in the meadows.

If you return to the unsigned trail junction, you can continue walking another 1.5 miles through beautiful old-growth to Patterson Mountain. The hike is relatively easy and grants views of the surrounding mountains.

*Wildflower
Hike 33* # Tire Mountain

*A mountainside
meadow blooms
along the Tire
Mountain Trail.*

Tire Mountain is part of a ridgeline trail system that was spared from the loggers' saws. The trail traverses old-growth forests and several meadows, ending at the summit of Tire Mountain, a former lookout site. On this hike, by far the best views are en route along the trail to the peak; the view from the summit is partially obscured by trees and shrubs.

From the trailhead and parking area, the path enters a young regrowth forest that was previously logged. The trees here are a mixture of western red cedar, Douglas fir, and western hemlock. In the understory you find thick stands of **thimbleberry** *(Rubus parviflorus)*. The large white blossoms and huge, maplelike leaves make this plant easy to identify. Later in the summer, **thimbleberry** are covered with edible red berries.

Nearest Town	Oakridge
Highlights	Numerous meadows spaced along a ridgetop trail
Trail Rating	moderate
Trail Length	7.6 miles round-trip
Location	Willamette National Forest
Elevation	3,728–4,329 feet
Contact	Oakridge Ranger District, Willamette NF, 541-465-6521
Bloom Season	May to July
Peak Bloom	June
Directions	From Eugene/Springfield, take OR 58 (Willamette Highway) southeast toward Oakridge to the Westfir exit. From the covered bridge in Westfir, take Aufderheide Memorial Drive (FR 19) for 4.5 miles, then veer left across the river on gravel FR 1912 and drive 6.6 miles to the junction at Windy Pass. Here, continue straight on FR 1910 for 0.4 mile to another junction, then bear right onto FR 1911, and go another 0.4 mile to the parking area for Trail 3450.

Black huckleberry *(Vaccinium membranaceum)*, boasting some of the best-tasting berries of all the **huckleberry** species, grow here and there beside the trail. Along the trail margin, you find an abundance of **parrot beak** *(Pedicularis racemosa)*, one of the most common **Pedicularis** species growing in the Cascades. The purple blooms of **Cardwell's penstemon** *(Penstemon cardwellii)* line the trail.

You can spot other species typical of the forest floor here, including **wild ginger** *(Asarum caudatum)*, the delicate **foamflower** *(Tiarella trifoliata)*, **Oregon grape** *(Mahonia nervosa)* with their evergreen, hollylike leaves, and **trail-plant** *(Adenocaulon bicolor)*. **Hooker fairy-bell** *(Disporum hookeri)* and **twinflower** *(Linnaea borealis)*, both sporting white flowers in groups of two, frequent the trail margin. A few **red elderberry** *(Sambucus racemosa)*, taller shrubs with white flowers, grow here and there. **Bracken fern** *(Pteridium aquilinum)* and **sword-fern** *(Polystichum munitum)* are abundant.

As you proceed up the trail, other forest-floor plants come into view, including the cloverlike leaves of **sorrel** *(Oxalis oregana)*, **meadowrue** *(Thalictrum occidentale)*, and **yellow violet** *(Viola glabella)*. In places, the **sorrel** make an almost completely green carpet.

About 0.25 mile down the trail, you pass a very large Douglas fir on the right. Large Douglas fir are scattered all along the trail, particularly once you

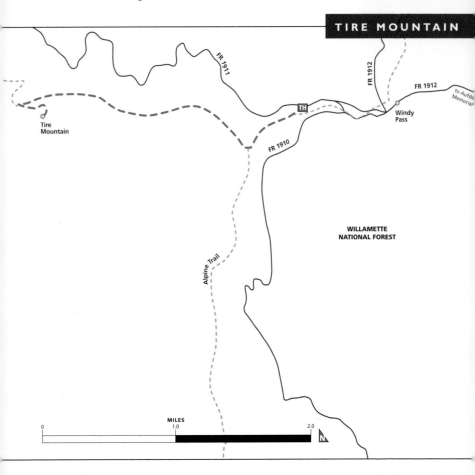

pass beyond the areas previously logged. Almost all the Douglas fir in the western Cascades were established in the aftermath of wildfires, since the trees generally need bare mineral soil and sunshine for successful sprouting. If you enjoy walking in the forests of the Cascades, you are enjoying the benefits of past wildfires.

Just beyond this Douglas fir, you can see the large, maplelike leaves of **vanillaleaf** *(Achlys triphylla)* covering the forest floor. In some areas, **vanillaleaf** form an almost continuous carpet of pale green over the forest floor. Mixed in with the **vanillaleaf** is the curious **inside-out flower** *(Vancouveria hexandra)*. The seeds of this plant contain a fleshy part attractive to ants, which carry the seeds to new locations, thereby assuring seed dispersal. Another fairly common ground cover along this section of trail is **dwarf dogwood** *(Cornus canadensis)*. The pretty, white flowers are followed by bright red berries in late summer. **Ocean-spray** *(Holodiscus discolor)*, a taller shrub that generally rises 3–6 feet high, also grow here.

On the right, you pass a view of a clear-cut. Despite the nearby timber cutting, you can admire some nice Douglas fir and western hemlock along the trail. You also see **trillium** *(Trillium ovatum)*, an early spring bloomer. When the blooming season is past, the plant's three large triangular leaves with drip-tips are still readily apparent. Another common species of the forest floor is **candyflower** *(Claytonia sibirica)*, an edible herb high in vitamin C. In the same area you find **northern starflower** *(Trientalis arctica)*, a small plant whose genus name *Trientalis* means one-third of a foot long. **False Solomon's seal** *(Smilacina racemosa)*, which is nearly 3 feet tall, features longish, elliptical leaves with large veins and a prominent, terminal cluster of small white flowers. Look for another **false Solomon's seal** growing along the trail here—the **star-flowered false Solomon's seal** *(Smilacina stellata)*. This variety produces many fewer flowers and they are less clustered together. Although most were past blooming when I was there, I still encountered a few **Pacific bleedingheart** *(Dicentra formosa)* in bloom.

The trail comes to a "pass" on the ridge before dipping downhill. **Western columbine** *(Aquilegia formosa)*, a favorite flower of hummingbirds, grow in this area. In addition, you can discover a few **Merten's coral-root orchid** *(Corallorhiza mertensiana)*, a plant that lacks chlorophyll and relies entirely upon other plants for its food. The forest floor is rather open at this point, and you're treated to an abundance of **sorrel, foamflower, vanillaleaf,** and **wild ginger.**

The trail shifts to the southeast slope of the ridge, affording views of Oakridge and clear-cuts that span the horizon. A few **fringecup** *(Tellima grandiflora)* occur along with **mountain boxwood** *(Pachistima myrsinites)*, which sport small evergreen leaves and inconspicuous flowers. Another shrub in this area is **sticky currant** *(Ribes viscosissimum)*, a plant with smallish golden thorns on its stems. You also see **maidenhair fern** *(Adiantum pedatum)*, easy to identify by their delicate fronds with leaflets aligned in parallel rows.

At a little more than 1.0 mile, the trail passes through an open meadow, one of several you will see on the hike. In the distance, look for the often-snowy summit of Diamond Peak. Rocky outcrops provide open, dry habitat for a number of rock-garden species such as **spreading stonecrop** *(Sedum divergens)*, a succulent plant. Another species that frequents drier slopes is **Oregon sunshine** *(Eriophyllum lanatum)*, a sunflowerlike plant. You can find the white-flowered floral head of **yarrow** *(Achillea millefolium)* and nearly continuous fields of blue **bluefield gilia** *(Gilia capitata)*. Yellow-flowered **sticky cinquefoil** *(Potentilla glandulosa)* and **virgate phacelia** *(Phacelia heterophylla)* are present also, but less common.

Upon leaving the meadow, you re-enter the forest for a short walk. The understory features **vine maple** *(Acer circinatum)*, **sword-fern, starflower, false Solomon's seal,** and other common forest-floor species.

You quickly enter another open area with a rocky ridge growing more **Oregon sunshine** and **stonecrop**. **Three-toothed mitrewort** *(Mitella trifida)*, a saxifrage, forms a dense stand on one rocky outcrop. You find some incense cedar, far more common farther south in southern Oregon and California. Its occurrence here is an indication of aridity.

After traveling through another short stretch of forest, you enter yet another minor meadow, most of which lies below the trail. From here, you capture views of Oakridge and the Hills Creek Reservoir. This arid meadow has shallow, rocky soils and dries out early. Although the meadow is largely brown by this time of year, some **yarrow, cat's-ear lily** *(Calochortus subalpinus)*, and **wild onion** *(Brodiaea coronaria)* with purple flowers are still blooming. You can recognize **fool's onion** *(Brodiaea hyacinthina)* by the terminal cluster of white flowers. Another flower that seems to bloom after the rocky meadows have dried out is the appropriately named **farewell-to-spring** *(Clarkia amoena)*, a beautiful pink flower with red spots on each petal. Among rocky outcrops and on shallow soils grow pink **plectritis** *(plectritis congesta)*, which boast a cluster of tiny pink blooms.

OCEAN-SPRAY
Holodiscus discolor

Ocean-spray have thick, terminal clusters of small white- or cream-colored flowers; the clusters are similar to lilac groupings. The egg-shaped leaves have coarse lobes or teeth. Also known as **ironwood** because of its strength, the shrub was used by Indians to make arrow shafts, digging sticks, and other implements.

Departing the meadow, you enter the forest again. Look for more **starflower, vanillaleaf, thimbleberry, false Solomon's seal, wild rose** *(Rosa gymnocarpa)*, and **yellow violet**. Walk a little farther and you see another small meadow, most of which lies above the trail. Close to the trail you can find native **thistles** such as **mountain thistle** *(Cirsium callilepis)*, their purple-pink flowers in bloom from June to August.

After admiring this meadow, head back along the trail that takes you into the forest. Again you find the typical forest species plus **three-leaved anemone** *(Anemone deltoidea)*, a pretty white flower with leaves in three segments as its name implies. **Vine maple**, a sprawling shrub-tree, grows all along the trail, but seems particularly abundant in this area. If you look closely, you might also be able to spot the orange-blossomed vine-shrub **honeysuckle** *(Lonicera ciliosa)* here.

In a slightly drier section of this forest trail, you again encounter **twin-flower, parrot beak**, and **wild rose**. For the first time, I spied the evergreen-leaved **prince's-pine** *(Chimaphila umbellata)*. And, glowing in the forest understory, I spotted the large, white clusters of **ocean-spray** blossoms. American Indians valued **ocean-spray's** hard wood, which they fashioned into arrow shafts, digging tools, and other implements.

When you come to a trail junction, the main trail heads up the slope. You are now 1.2 miles from the trailhead. The trail continues in forest, crossing two small meadows in the next 0.5 mile. Very large old-growth Douglas fir live in this stretch, and the forests are magnificent. Understory plants here include **meadowrue, Hooker fairy-bell, thimbleberry**, and **queen's cup lily** *(Clintonia uniflora)*. In the fall, **queen's cup lily** sport gunmetal-blue berries.

One of the small meadows you cross has a wet seep that hosts **yellow monkey-flower** *(Mimulus guttatus)* and **camas lily** *(Camassia quamash)*. **Camas lily**, which has a small, edible bulb, was an important food plant for American Indians. Another **lily** growing in the meadow is the orange-blossomed **tiger lily** *(Lilium columbianum)*. This mountain is rimmed by bigleaf maple, a tree more common at lower elevations.

The second small meadow you reach has more bigleaf maples along the borders. You can't miss the 2-foot-high **wallflower** *(Erysimum asperum)*, the only orange-flowered member of the mustard family in the higher elevations of the Cascades. Once out of the meadows, you pass back into the forest and encounter an extremely large Douglas fir. No doubt it grew rapidly on the edge of this meadow, getting plenty of light and nutrients.

About 0.5 mile from the trail junction, you reach the largest meadow on the entire hike. A rocky rib of the mountain provides shallow soils and steep terrain here. Look for **deltoid balsamroot** *(Balsamorhiza deltoidea)*, a large, sunflowerlike flower with generous, triangular-shaped leaves; "deltoid" means triangular. More **Oregon sunshine, yarrow, gilia, farewell-to-spring, red Indian-paintbrush** *(Castilleja miniata)*, and other flowers found on rocky ledges also grow here. You can discover a previously unseen plant, **barestem buckwheat** *(Eriogonum nudum)*, which has basal leaves and an umbel of tiny, tightly-clustered white flowers. You can spend hours exploring this meadow; the rest of the trail remains primarily in the forest. For those with less energy, this makes a good turnaround point for a total round-trip hike of 4.2 miles.

The remainder of the trail to Tire Mountain dips down into a saddle, working its way on to the top of the ridge. You pass through some open forest with almost no understory aside from **sorrel** carpeting the forest floor. The trail swings back to the left side of the ridge, entering another small meadow that offers nice views. Here you will see some stunted, dwarf Oregon white oak. Normally these trees are tall and have spreading crowns, but under these harsh environmental conditions they grow in a shrubby form. You can also find **pinemat manzanita** *(Arctostaphylos nevadensis)*, a low-growing, twisted shrub with reddish branches and stems, and one of the major components of the chaparral of southern Oregon. **Serviceberry** *(Amelanchier alnifolia)*, another shrub that has white flowers in spring and edible, bluish berries in late summer, grows here along with more **balsamroot, Oregon sunshine, cat's-ear lily,** and another member of the buckwheat family, **sulfur buckwheat** *(Eriogonum umbellatum)*.

The trail swings back to the right side of the ridge, where a substantial bunch of **Pacific rhododendron** *(Rhododendron macrophyllum)* grows. The best blooms are in June, but when I hiked the trail in early July, quite a few of the **rhododendron** were still in bloom. After you pass the **rhododendron,** the forest floor opens up again with tall trees and little understory.

The trail eventually turns back upon itself, traversing a slope to another trail junction. According to a sign, Tire Mountain is another 0.5 mile away. Take the uphill trail and switchback up the slope to the summit. The spacious flattop of the mountain affords only limited views. Look for an old lookout in the top of a sprawling Douglas fir. More dwarf oak grow here along with **serviceberry** and **ocean-spray.** Enjoy the summit, then retrace your steps back to the trailhead.

North Bank Deer Preserve

*Gentle terrain and oak savanna in the North Bank
Deer Preserve near the North Umpqua River.*

The North Bank Deer Preserve, officially known as the North Bank
Habitat Management Area, is cradled in the rolling hills along the
North Umpqua River. The preserve is about three hours from Portland
and about 6.0 miles south of I-5 near Roseburg. This is one of the few
publicly owned low-elevation oak-savanna landscapes in western Oregon
that is open to hiking and closed to motor vehicles. There are a number
of small streams and springs, but it's best to bring your own water. The
gentle lower terrain makes for a good place to explore with children,
while the higher elevations afford more ambitious hikers outstanding
360-degree views. On a good day in spring, walking among the flower-
studded grassy ridges, it's easy to feel like you're in the movie *The Sound
of Music*.

The preserve, a former cattle ranch, was purchased by the BLM in
1994 to protect habitat for the Columbian white-tailed deer, a rare subspecies of white-tailed deer. (Most deer in Oregon are black-tailed or
mule deer). Columbian white-tailed deer once were more widespread,

Nearest Town	Roseburg
Highlights	Oak savanna and the opportunity to see the rare Columbian white-tailed deer
Trail Rating	moderate
Trail Length	3.4 miles round-trip, which can be extended to a 6.7-mile loop
Location	North Umpqua River
Elevation	400–1,480 feet
Contact	Roseburg BLM District, 541-440-4930
Bloom Season	March to July
Peak Bloom	April to May
Directions	From the north, take I-5 south to the Wilbur Exit 135, just south of Sutherlin. Cross the highway, turn right onto OR 99 south and drive 4.0 miles, just past Wilbur. Turn left (east) onto North Bank Road. From the south, take the Winchester Exit 129, 4.0 miles north of Roseburg. Turn left onto OR 99 north and drive 2.0 miles toward Wilbur; turn right onto North Bank Road.

Drive east 5.3 miles on North Bank Road to the preserve's unsigned west gate. You're near when the road comes to a big, looping curve of the North Umpqua River. Parking is limited beside the west gate, but ample a bit farther down the road. |

but habitat loss because of farming and ranching, along with other factors, led to the dramatic decline of this subspecies. By the early 1970s, less than 700 of these deer remained. Today, Columbian white-tailed deer lives in only two places: on an island in the lower Columbia River, and in the Umpqua River Valley, where their numbers have risen so much that hunting is now permitted.

The 10-square-mile North Bank Deer Preserve is open year-round, and the lowest elevations are only 400 feet above sea level. This is a particularly good place to hike in early spring. Wildlife is abundant—in the course of my explorations here, I saw several Columbian white-tailed deer, black vultures, wild turkey, red-tailed hawk, northern harrier, sharp-shinned hawk, meadowlark, and Steller's jay.

One of the joys of the North Bank Deer Preserve is its open, hilly terrain. Much of the area consists of meadows or open oak forests that are easy to hike through without a trail. Cross-country travel is hindered, however, by the abundance of **poison oak** (*Rhus diversiloba*), a shrub with bright, shiny leaves. If you're contemplating off-trail travel, be sure to wear long pants and avoid dense patches of the poisonous plant. Fortunately, you needn't hike off-trail

NORTH BANK DEER PRESERVE

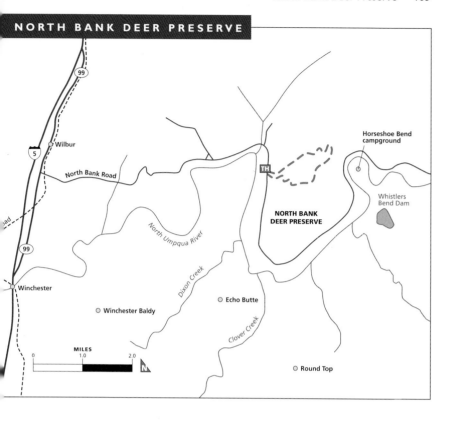

to explore the area, as a number of old ranch roads make for excellent hiking trails. One rewarding trail leaves the west gate entrance.

Park off the road by the west gate or in the nearby parking lot. From the North Bank Road, you immediately pass a locked BLM gate. The main Jackson Creek Road heads east up a slight hill, where there is a toilet on the right just beyond the rise. You, however, want to go right immediately after passing the gate to an old road, now a hiking path. This path takes you up gradually through oak forest to an open ridge with exceptional views. South Knob makes a good turnaround point for the 3.4-mile round-trip hike. You can also extend the hike to a 6.7-mile loop if you wish.

I explored the area in late March, slightly earlier than prime wildflower season. Just beyond the gate, I spotted the pretty white blossoms of **common cryptantha** (*Cryptantha intermedia*). This tiny member of the borage family is usually 4–12 inches tall and grows on dry, open slopes. Mixed in among the **cryptantha** are bright yellow, waxy flowers of **western buttercup** (*Ranunculus occidentalis*), which remain common all along the lower part of the hike. I also saw a few white **baby blue-eyes** (*Nemophila menziesii atomaria*). The trail skirts the lower slope of the hill, intersecting another short feeder trail coming from the parking area. From here, the path turns east up the slope, passing by a **black hawthorn** *(Crataegus douglasii)*. **Hawthorn** is a large shrub or small tree which, as its name suggests, sports thorns on its branches. A member of the rose family, the shrub sprouts clusters of lovely white blossoms in late April and early May.

The trail wanders up the slope and through a lovely savanna of Oregon white oak. Once far more common throughout western Oregon, much of the white oak habitat in the Willamette Valley has been cleared for agriculture. The pink, trumpet-shaped flowers of **broad-leaved shooting star** *(Dodecatheon hendersonii)* are scattered about the meadow openings.

The trail climbs up the north side of a ridge, with small Douglas fir and **sword-fern** *(Polystichum munitum)* mixed in with the oak. Along the trail, I spotted a few **wild rose** *(Rosa gymnocarpa)* not yet in bloom. The trail reaches the ridge line at South Knob (1,480 feet), where you find yellow clumps of **spring gold** *(Lomatium utriculatum)*, a member of the carrot family with highly dissected leaves. Among the ridge grasses you see the delicate white blossoms of **small-flowered prairiestar** *(Lithophragma parviflora)*, a member of the saxifrage family. The ridge affords terrific views of the North Umpqua River Valley and makes a good turnaround point for those not inclined to further exploration.

BABY BLUE-EYES
Nemophila menziesii atomaria

In California, **baby blue-eyes** are actually blue; in Oregon, a white variety is more common. The flower has five rounded petals that radiate outward from the center and sport purple-black spots. The leaves are pinnate and lobed. This annual flower, common in grasslands and meadows, is one of the early bloomers in spring.

As the trail continues up toward Boundary Ridge, the ridge and south-facing slopes tend to be open meadows or scattered stands of Oregon white oak; the north-facing slopes are increasingly forested. The forest mixture here is more California than Pacific Northwest. On the north slope of the ridge grow **Pacific madrone** *(Arbutus menziesii)*, their large evergreen leaves lending a tropical look to the red-barked tree. **Pacific madrone** sprout after fires, favor dry slopes, and become increasingly common farther south in Oregon. Throughout the area you also find stands of incense cedar mixed in with

Douglas fir and a few scattered ponderosa pine. In the forest you can see the drooping blossoms of **Oregon fawn-lily** *(Erythronium oregonum)*, one of a number of varieties of **fawn-lily** in Oregon, all of which have edible bulbs.

The views from the top of Boundary Ridge are superb, ranging east up the North Fork of the Umpqua drainage and southwest toward Roseburg. The ridgeline is open and easy to hike. When you're finished admiring the view from here, you can turn around and head back.

On the other hand, if you're adventurous and comfortable hiking in the woods, you can drop off the ridgeline into the Chasm Creek drainage and loop back. You can follow a number of old logging roads, where selective tree cutting occurred in the past. I followed one to its end near a spring. Then I climbed up to an intervening ridge that runs perpendicular to Boundary Ridge. I hiked on deer trails through open forest of incense cedar, Douglas fir, **Pacific madrone**, and oak until I reached less steep terrain, coming upon a lovely, small wetland full of **false hellebore** *(Veratrum viride)*. The leaves of this 3–6-foot plant are up to 7 inches wide and have prominent veins. In the bottom of Chasm Creek, I found another old road that I followed out to Jackson Creek Road and back to the west gate on North Bank Road. The hike along this section of the lower creek is extremely inviting, with gentle slopes and oak savannas.

Wildflower Hike 35 # Pine Bench

The North Umpqua River, a federally designated Wild and Scenic River, Boulder Creek Wilderness.

Nearest Town	Roseburg
Highlights	Old-growth sugar pine, ponderosa pine, and other unusual botanical species
Trail Rating	moderate
Trail Length	5.0 miles round-trip
Location	Boulder Creek Wilderness
Elevation	1,800–2,600 feet
Contact	Umpqua National Forest, 541-672-6601
Bloom Season	April to August
Peak Bloom	June
Directions	From I-5 in Roseburg, take Exit 124 onto OR 138 (North Umpqua Highway) toward Diamond Lake and drive east about 55.0 miles. Between milepost 54 and 55, turn left and follow Slide Creek Road toward Soda Springs Dam. Drive 1.4 miles to trailhead and park just before the Pacific Power hydro station.

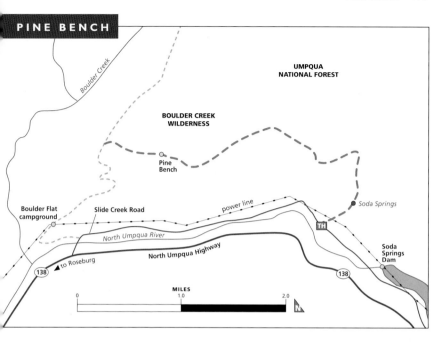

PINE BENCH

UMPQUA
NATIONAL FOREST

Boulder Creek

BOULDER CREEK
WILDERNESS

Pine
Bench

Boulder Flat
campground   Slide Creek Road   power line   Soda Springs

North Umpqua River

North Umpqua Highway   Soda
Springs
Dam

to Roseburg

138   138   TH

MILES
0   1.0   2.0
N

This trail is notable for some unusual botanical features, including huge old-growth sugar pine, a tree more common farther south in California, and ponderosa pine, a species relatively rare west of the Cascade crest. Perhaps the most interesting element of this hike is the opportunity it provides to see the aftermath and regrowth of a 1996 forest fire that burned through most of the Boulder Creek Wilderness.

Finding the trail from the trailhead can be confusing. Just across from the parking area is a huge pipe, which carries most of the flow of the North Umpqua River to the hydro station visible to the west. A small wooden bridge takes you underneath the pipe, where you come to a trail sign. Turn right and follow the Soda Springs Trail/North Umpqua Trail.

Just around the trail sign, note the **scouring-rush** *(Equisetum hyemale),* sign of a seep or spring. The cell walls of this plant contain silicon dioxide, an abrasive. Pacific Northwest Indians used **rush** to scour or smooth wooden objects from spoons to arrow shafts. **Sword-fern** *(Polystichum munitum),* an evergreen, grow here along with **bracken fern** *(Pteridium aquilinum),* which die back each autumn. Trees in this vicinity include Douglas fir, incense cedar, bigleaf maple, and **hazelnut** *(Corylus cornuta).* One of the more abundant ground covers throughout this hike is **trailing blackberry** *(Rubus ursinus),* the only native blackberry in the Pacific Northwest.

The Soda Springs Trail climbs up a hill and almost immediately comes to a junction. The North Umpqua Trail (Deer Leap Segment) goes right, the Soda Springs Trail (#1493) left. As you cross under a power line, you discover lots of **bracken fern**. After crossing two 4–5-foot-long wooden bridges, you enter the Boulder Creek Wilderness, marked by a sign on a tree. Low-growing **snowberry** *(Symphoricarpos albus)* and **wild strawberry** *(Fragaria vesca)* abound along the trail, and you can see a few **broad-leaved starflower** *(Trientalis latifolia)* as well.

As the trail crosses another wooden bridge, note the **Oregon grape** *(Mahonia nervosa)* and scattered **poison oak** *(Rhus diversiloba)*. Just beyond the wilderness boundary, you reach some of the area burned in 1996. The fire killed many of the younger trees, but the older, more mature trees survived the flames. Nearly all the conifer trees common along this hike—Douglas fir, incense cedar, ponderosa pine, and sugar pine—possess a similar strategy for surviving fires: thick bark that protects the tree's living cells from all but the hottest blazes. These species also lose their lower branches through self-pruning, an adaptation that prevents flames from leaping from the ground into the crowns of the trees.

OREGON GRAPE
Mahonia nervosa

The trail starts up a hill, passing some western red cedar, a tree that tends to favor wet habitats. On the right, you soon pass a small meadow that hosts a reddish stream. This is Soda Springs, a favorite lick for elk. Elk trails radiate in all directions from the spring, and the ground is muddy with tracks.

The trail continues up a hill, passing some **whiteveined wintergreen** *(Pyrola picta)*, more **Oregon grape**, and **Oregon bedstraw** *(Galium oreganum)*, which is a rhizomatous perennial that forms an almost matlike covering on the forest floor. When you come to a junction at Pine Bench, turn around and retrace your steps to the trailhead.

Oregon grape, a common plant in the understory of drier, Douglas fir forests, has small yellow flowers and is easy to identify by its compound, hollylike, evergreen leaves. In the fall, the plant produces bluish berries that resemble small grapes. When sweetened, the fruit even tastes like grape juice.

Proxy Falls Loop

*Proxy Falls is an enchanting destination
in the Three Sisters Wilderness.*

Eugene/Springfield	*Nearest Town*
Spectacular waterfalls accessed via a lava field and old-growth forest	*Highlights*
easy	*Trail Rating*
1.2-mile loop hike	*Trail Length*
Three Sisters Wilderness	*Location*
3,150–3,350 feet	*Elevation*
Willamette National Forest, 541-465-6521	*Contact*
May to August	*Bloom Season*
June to July	*Peak Bloom*
From I-5 in Eugene/Springfield, take OR 126 (McKenzie Highway) east. About 5.0 miles past McKenzie Bridge, turn right and continue east on OR 242, the Old McKenzie Highway (closed in winter) for 8.5 miles to the trailhead.	*Directions*

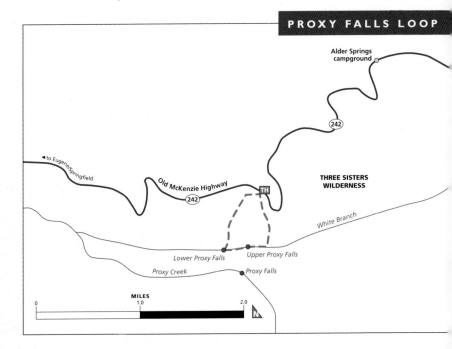

Rushing down a green, mossy cliff face in an old-growth forest, Proxy Falls is one of the most enchanting spots in the Cascades. The trail forms a loop that crosses a lava field and reaches Lower and Upper Proxy Falls before returning to the trailhead.

The trail first climbs close to the road on a rough lava flow strewn with **vine maple** *(Acer circinatum)*. In autumn, **vine maple** produce spectacular red and orange colors. The white flowers of **prince's-pine** *(Chimaphila umbellata),* an evergreen plant, are common in this stretch of trail, along with the double white blooms of **twinflower** *(Linnaea borealis)* and beautiful, pink-flowered **Pacific rhododendron** *(Rhododendron macrophyllum)*. White, three-petaled **trillium** *(Trillium ovatum)* flourish in areas with deeper soils.

The trail meanders through isolated stands of forest, including some old-growth Douglas fir and Pacific yew. Growing within the stands are the hollylike **Oregon grape** *(Mahonia nervosa),* the delicate **foamflower** *(Tiarella trifoliata),* and the relatively rare **Merten's coral-root orchid** *(Corallorhiza mertensiana)*. Moving away from the road, the trail shifts south past many **vine maple** and **rhododendron**. This area is spectacular in late June, when the **rhododendron** are in peak bloom.

As the trail rises up a rocky slope, you will see more **prince's-pine**, the broad, tri-leaved **vanillaleaf** *(Achlys triphylla),* and **chinquapin** *(Castanopsis chrysophylla)*. **Chinquapin**, a small tree more common in California, grows here in dry, rocky locations. Lichens on boulders in the vicinity indicate high winter rainfall; in the dry summers they are largely dormant.

Growing among the lava boulders are several kinds of **huckleberry**, including the deciduous **red huckleberry** *(Vaccinium parvifolium)* and the **evergreen huckleberry** *(Vaccinium ovatum)*. All **huckleberry** produce urn-shaped flowers and delicious edible berries in late summer.

As you leave the lava flow, you find sprawling, low-growing **pinemat manzanita** *(Arctostaphylos nevadensis)* along with more **chinquapin**. The trail switchbacks past large Douglas fir and more **manzanita**, then winds through a western hemlock forest with more **prince's-pine** and **huckleberry** in the understory. A few western red cedar also stand amid the hemlock and fir.

As you enter a small swale, note the fire-blackened trunks of Douglas fir, a testament to past forest fires. Look for **beargrass** *(Xerophyllum tenax)* with clusters of grasslike leaves and large, white, globelike blossoms that brighten the forest in July. More **twinflower, rhododendron,** and **sword-fern** *(Polystichum munitum)* appear as you reach an open cedar forest with small understory trees.

As the trail bears to the east, look for the flat-leaf clusters of **whiteveined wintergreen** *(Pyrola picta),* a flower common in the forest understory. The overhead forest is mostly Douglas fir and western hemlock with some Pacific yew.

Turning southwest, the trail moves into a younger forest stand. The difference in age is another legacy of the past fires that formed most of the Cascade forests. Most fires burn unevenly, creating staggered age classes within a forest. In this younger forest, look for the evergreen shrub **salal** *(Gaultheria shallon).* Though common in the Cascades, **salal** always reminds me of the Oregon Coast, where it is a dominant shrub in coastal forests.

You come to a sign pointing left to return to the trailhead and right to continue to Lower Proxy Falls.

PRINCE'S-PINE
Chimaphila umbellata

Prince's-pine, also known as **pipsissewa**, is a common understory flower of low- and mid-elevation coniferous forests. The plant has bright, shiny evergreen leaves with sharp, toothed margins. Its whitish-pink flowers are waxy and saucer-shaped and tend to hang downward from the stalk. *Chimaphila* is Greek for "winter-loving"—a reference to its evergreen habit. The common name refers to its supposed resemblance to a pine tree—a likeness that requires a little bit of imagination.

Proceeding right, note more **red huckleberry, whiteveined wintergreen, twin-flower**, and an evergreen shrub, **mountain boxwood** *(Pachistima myrsinites)*.

Very shortly you have a view through the trees to the 200-foot falls. To do the falls justice, I recommend hiking down the steep trail to the base of the falls for a grand perspective. Near the bottom you find dense stands of **devil's club** *(Oplopanax horridum)* and **palmate coltsfoot** *(Petasites palmatus)* beneath some western red cedar. **Devil's club,** as its name suggests, is a nasty plant with sharp, slightly toxic spines. The mossy boulders and deep pool at the base of the falls are worth more than a passing moment of reflection.

After enjoying the falls, work your way back up the hill to the main trail and back past the sign to complete the loop. The trail follows the creek for about 0.3 mile to another sign at a level bench. You can observe more **beargrass, dwarf dogwood** *(Cornus canadensis),* **huckleberry, Oregon grape,** and **rhododendron.** At the trail junction, go right first to view Upper Proxy Falls, only 0.1 mile from this point. This waterfall also drops into a lovely pool.

Once back at the trail junction, proceed north (straight ahead at the trail sign) back to Highway 242. You cross a bridge and hike past another large group of **rhododendron** which provide a profusion of pink blooms. You may also encounter more **huckleberry, twinflower, beargrass,** and **vine maple**. The trail descends back to the road and through the lava field. En route you see a huge Douglas fir that has no doubt prospered as a result of the natural firebreak provided by the lava flow.

Hand Lake Trail

Wildflower
Hike 37

Shooting star adorn the shore of Hand Lake.

Eugene/Springfield	**Nearest Town**
A gentle amble to flower-studded meadows bordering a scenic lake	**Highlights**
easy	**Trail Rating**
1.0 mile round-trip	**Trail Length**
Mount Washington Wilderness	**Location**
4,800–5,000 feet	**Elevation**
Willamette National Forest, 541-465-6521	**Contact**
July to August	**Bloom Season**
August	**Peak Bloom**
From I-5 in Eugene/Springfield, take OR 126 (McKenzie Highway) east. About 5.0 miles past McKenzie Bridge, turn right and continue east on OR 242, the Old McKenzie Highway (closed in winter). The trailhead, between mileposts 72 and 73, is easy to miss. Just past the Scott Lake campground turnoff (FR 260) on the left, look for a small sign and forest path on the left.	**Directions**

With frogs, **huckleberry** *(Vaccinium sp.),* and other attractions, the trail to Hand Lake is easy and ideal for children. Mountain vistas and wet meadows frame the lake ecosystem. Near the lake's western edge stands a three-sided wooden trail shelter that is also the junction between Hand Lake Trail and longer loop or day hiking trails.

TALL MOUNTAIN SHOOTING STAR
Dodecatheon jeffreyi

Tall mountain shooting star is one of several species of **shooting star** found in Oregon from sea level to subalpine meadows. All have pink to lavender flowers that appear to hang downward with backward-swept petals; this species has lance-shaped leaves. **Shooting star** are among the earliest to bloom in wet meadows after snowmelt and are known for "buzz pollination": buzzing bees near the blossoms create sound waves that free the pollen. **Tall mountain shooting star** is named for John Jeffrey, who botanized in the mountains of Washington and southern British Columbia in the mid-1800s.

Mountain hemlock and Pacific silver fir dominate the forest at the trailhead. **Grouseberry** *(Vaccinium scoparium),* a tiny member of the **huckleberry** family, thrive in the forest undergrowth. The berries are edible, but the fruit is so small it's difficult to imagine trying to collect it. Also found along the forest floor are the white-flowered **parrot beak** *(Pedicularis racemosa)*—a member of the lousewort family—and runners of **wild strawberry** *(Fragaria vesca).* **Prince's-pine** *(Chimaphila umbellata),* or **pipsissewa,** is common as well, with shiny, toothed evergreen leaves and waxy, whitish flowers sometimes tinged with pink.

About 50 feet from the road, you pass a sign for Mount Washington Wilderness. (As in all wilderness areas, motorized vehicles are not permitted.) You encounter a small meadow on the right, and may see more **grouseberry** growing beneath tall stands of lodgepole pine, a species common east of and near the crest of the Cascades.

The trail dips and rises, passing through more lodgepole pine with some **serviceberry** *(Amelanchier alnifolia)* growing along the trail margins. **Serviceberry** have white blossoms and edible berries. Blue clumps of **lupine** *(Lupinus sp.)* and the yellow flowers of **round-leaved violet** *(Viola orbiculata)* crowd the trail as it turns northwest and slopes down a slight hill. You may also see

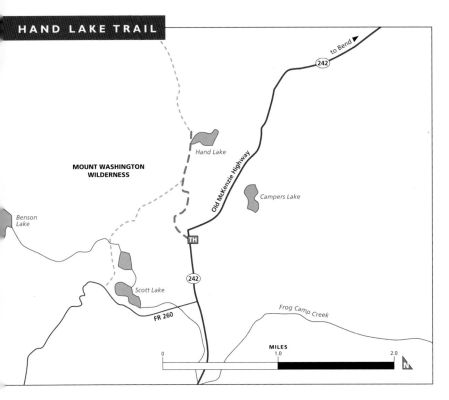

wild strawberry, small-flowered penstemon *(Penstemon procerus)*, and some cat's-ear lily *(Calochortus subalpinus)*.

The trail comes to the lake by way of a meadow of **tall mountain shooting star** *(Dodecatheon jeffreyi)*, whose bright blossoms create a pink pool on the blue border of Hand Lake. Dark **early blue violet** *(Viola adunca)* also grow along the meadow's edge. The trail shelter near the lake's western shore provides a charming view. East of the shelter, a peninsula into the lake is covered with lodgepole pine and **lupine.**

Tadpoles filled the lake margin when I visited in late July; deer tracks dotted the water's edge. A walk around the lake's northern shore affords an outstanding view of the Three Sisters. In the meadows around the lake and west of the shelter, you can find **Sitka valerian** *(Valeriana sitchensis)*, **yarrow** *(Achillea millefolium)*, **senecio** *(Senecio triangularis)*, **penstemon** *(Penstemon sp.)*, **shrubby cinquefoil** *(Dasiphora floribunda)*, **cat's-ear lily,** and **white marsh-marigold** *(Caltha leptosepala)*. After exploring the spacious meadows, retrace your steps back to the trailhead.

Wildflower Hike 38

Maple Ridge Loop

A wild forest trail in the big city of Portland at Tryon Creek State Park.

Nearest Town	In Portland
Highlights	A peaceful hike in forested terrain in the middle of the city
Trail Rating	easy
Trail Length	0.62 mile round-trip
Location	Tryon Creek State Park
Elevation	400 feet
Contact	Tryon Creek State Park, 503-653-3166
Bloom Season	April to July
Peak Bloom	May
Directions	From I-5, take the Terwilliger Blvd. Exit 297. Drive south on Terwilliger past its intersections with Taylors Ferry and Boones Ferry roads. Bear right on Terwilliger past the Lewis & Clark College Law School entrance. The park entrance is 1.0 mile farther south, on the right.

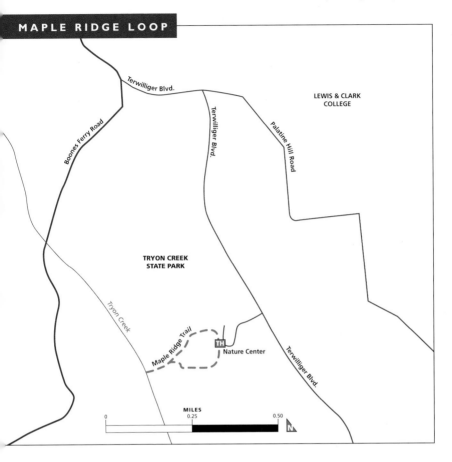

MAPLE RIDGE LOOP

Terwilliger Blvd.

Boones Ferry Road

Terwilliger Blvd.

Palatine Hill Road

LEWIS & CLARK
COLLEGE

TRYON CREEK
STATE PARK

Tryon Creek

Maple Ridge Trail

TH

Nature Center

Terwilliger Blvd.

MILES
0   0.25   0.50

N

The 645-acre Tryon Creek State Park, minutes from downtown Portland, contains 8 miles of hiking trails, 3.5 miles of horse trails, and a 3-mile paved bicycle path. Tryon Creek was logged in the 1880s to provide fuel for an iron smelter in Lake Oswego, but the forest has regrown into a mix of bigleaf maple, **red alder** *(Alnus rubra),* Douglas fir, and western red cedar. Steelhead still swim up the creek to spawn. In the 1960s, the first parcels of land were purchased and in 1970 the state created a new state park on the site. Since the 1970s, the park has grown as adjacent parcels of land have been purchased. A number of different loop trails leave from the nature center at a central location in the park.

The Maple Ridge Loop is just 0.62 mile long and begins just adjacent to the nature center. Right at the trailhead, you can find bigleaf maple, one of the most common trees in the park. Bigleaf maple is a species that recolonizes logged sites. Another tree you see here is western red cedar with its lacy boughs. Ground cover includes **Oregon grape** *(Mahonia nervosa),* **yellow** violet *(Viola glabella),* **trillium** *(Trillium ovatum),* **vanillaleaf** *(Achlys triphylla),* and **Pacific waterleaf** *(Hydrophyllum tenuipes).*

About 100 feet down the trail, the path curves to the west. You discover a big patch of **Oregon grape** on the right and **vine maple** *(Acer circinatum)* on the left. **Vine maple,** a common understory species in coniferous forests, tend to have shrubby, sprawling shapes. **Snowberry** *(Symphoricarpos albus)* grow here too, their white berries giving rise to the common name. You also find **salal** *(Gaultheria shallon),* a shrub with evergreen leaves and urn-shaped white flowers, and **fringecup** *(Tellima grandiflora).*

PACIFIC WATERLEAF
Hydrophyllum tenuipes

Pacific waterleaf have large leaves divided into 5–9 pointed and toothed segments. The lavender to whitish flowers are bell-shaped and form terminal clusters; the stamens and pistils stick out. Deer and elk feed upon these plants, which grow abundantly in moist bottomlands.

Pioneer School/ Willamette River Loop

Cottonwood trees along the Willamette River Trail in the Champoeg State Heritage Area.

Newberg	**Nearest Town**
Cottonwood gallery forest along the Willamette River with numerous spring flowers	**Highlights**
easy	**Trail Rating**
0.75-mile loop	**Trail Length**
Champoeg State Heritage Area	**Location**
300 feet	**Elevation**
Champoeg State Heritage Area, 503-678-1251	**Contact**
late February to July	**Bloom Season**
mid-April to late May	**Peak Bloom**
From OR 219 in Newberg, follow signs 4.0 miles southeast to the park. Or, from I-5, take Exit 278 and drive west 5.0 miles, following signs to the park. The trail begins at a parking lot for the pioneer school in the riverside day-use area.	**Directions**

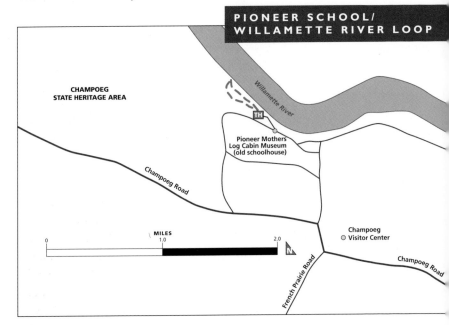

The 615-acre Champoeg State Heritage Area extends along the Willamette River at the north end of French Prairie, named for the original French-Canadian settlers. Primarily a historical park, this site was home to one of the first Euro-American communities in Oregon. In addition, the state's first attempts at self-government took place here. The first order of business in 1843 was enacting a tax to pay for a bounty on wolves.

The park is open year-round and includes a campground, bike paths, and museum. One of the oldest Oregon white oak groves in the state is located within the park. This loop hike is part of a paved, 1.5-mile-long hiking trail that follows the Willamette River—a good bet early in the season, when most trails are still muddy.

The trailhead parking lot is located in a Douglas fir forest. Just to the west of the trail by a garbage dump, you'll find **red flowering currant** *(Ribes sanguineum)*. The Latin name *sanguineum* refers to the blood-red color of the flowers. The shrub was first described and collected by David Douglas for whom the Douglas fir is named. From the sale of **red flowering currant** seeds back in England, Douglas made enough money to pay for his entire two-year excursion to North America. American Indians ate **red flowering currant** berries, although they were not a favorite fruit.

As you enter the forest trail, you immediately pass a sign. To the left of the sign, near the base of some trees and a group picnic area, look for **tall Oregon grape** *(Mahonia aquifolium)*, also known as **berberis**. The bright yellow flowers and hollylike, evergreen leaves make this plant easy to identify;

in late summer, it produces bluish-purple fruit. Growing near the **tall Oregon grape** are **Oregon fawn-lily** *(Erythronium oregonum)*, the white, drooping blossoms and mottled leaves an early harbinger of spring. The edible bulbs of this flower are a favorite spring food of bears.

Here you can also discover the lovely pink blossoms of **broad-leaved shooting star** *(Dodecatheon hendersonii)*. Although a number of **shooting star** species grow in Oregon, this species is the only one in the Willamette Valley that has oval, basal leaves. The plant can be pollinated from the mere vibration of a bee buzzing nearby and is commonly associated with oak forests in the Willamette Valley.

From the picnic area you traverse a low, seasonally flooded swale. Some black cottonwood and Oregon ash grow here, along with a few Oregon white oak on the higher ground. Just as you reach the old pioneer schoolhouse and pavilion, you see an Oregon history sign. Left of the sign, **Pacific bleeding-heart** *(Dicentra formosa)* bloom amid the **sword-fern** *(Polystichum munitum)*.

Just beyond the old schoolhouse, a stairway leads down to the river trail. White blooms of both **Pacific dogwood** *(Cornus nuttallii)* and **red elderberry** *(Sambucus racemosa)* appear immediately adjacent to the stairs. As you descend the stairs toward the river, you pass a lot of **fringecup** *(Tellima grandiflora)*, recognizable by its pale green flowers and broad, heart-shaped but indented leaves. In the general area you can also find **wild rose** *(Rosa gymnocarpa)*, sporting pale pink blooms and the telltale prickles of the rose family, and **yellow violet** *(Viola glabella)*.

Once you reach the river trail, pause for a moment and scan the river for osprey. After watching the sky, head left down the river trail. **Salmonberry** *(Rubus spectabilis)*, **elderberry, snowberry** *(Symphoricarpos albus)*, and **Himalayan blackberry** *(Rubus discolor)* all flourish here. Also look for **star-flowered false Solomon's seal** *(Smilacina stellata)* with its small, white, star-shaped flowers borne on a zigzag raceme.

INDIAN PLUM
Osmaronia cerasiformis

The small shrub-tree **Indian plum** is one of the earliest flowers to bloom—often as early as February. The greenish-white flowers are somewhat bell-shaped and hang in clusters. The alternate, lance-shaped leaves smell like cucumbers when crushed. The common name comes from the ripe bluish-black fruit, which resembles a small plum.

Another member of the lily family, **false Solomon's seal** *(Smilacina racemosa)*, grows along this stretch of trail. The latter variety has larger leaves and small, white, delightfully fragrant flowers.

On the right side of the path, watch for the palmate leaves and small greenish flowers of **Pacific waterleaf** *(Hydrophyllum tenuipes)*. Here you also encounter more **yellow violet** and large white **trillium** *(Trillium ovatum)*, recognizable by their three petals.

The cottonwood gallery forest in this area shades an understory dominated by **thimbleberry** *(Rubus parviflorus)* and **Hooker fairy-bell** *(Disporum hookeri)*. **Thimbleberry** have large, maplelike leaves and white blossoms. You can also discover **Indian plum** *(Osmaronia cerasiformis)* here, one of the first shrubs to bloom in the spring.

As the trail turns a corner, watch out for **stinging nettle** *(Urtica dioica)*. The plant can cause a very irritating rash on contact with skin—hence the "stinging" part of its name. You also encounter **ball head cluster lily** *(Brodiaea congesta)*, another member of the lily family common in the Willamette Valley. The bluish-purple flowers that cluster on the very short stalks give rise to the Latin name, *congesta,* "crowded."

As you move along the trail, you pass more **salmonberry, three-toothed mitrewort** *(Mitella trifida)*, **Indian plum**, **snowberry**, and **Pacific waterleaf**. **Vine maple** *(Acer circinatum)* and **Pacific dogwood** *(Cornus nuttallii)* are two understory trees common in this section.

The trail heads right, sloping uphill and back to the early part of the loop by the pioneer school. **Pacific madrone** *(Arbutus menziesii)*, a tree with reddish bark, also grows by the school. You can end the hike here or explore more of the park's trails.

Mount Baldy

Wild roses frame a gentle hillside in the Baskett Slough National Wildlife Refuge.

Salem	***Nearest Town***
A short hike to a grassy hillside with views of the Willamette Valley	***Highlights***
easy	***Trail Rating***
1.0 mile each way	***Trail Length***
Baskett Slough National Wildlife Refuge	***Location***
400–600 feet	***Elevation***
William L. Finley National Wildlife Refuge, 541-757-7236	***Contact***
April to June	***Bloom Season***
May	***Peak Bloom***
From Salem, drive OR 22 west 10 miles to the Rickreall Exit, then take OR 99W north for 1.8 miles. Turn left onto Coville Road and follow it 1.4 miles to the trailhead.	***Directions***

Baskett Slough National Wildlife Refuge is one of several small refuges in the Willamette Valley providing wetlands for wintering waterfowl. The Baskett Slough refuge's special feature is wintering dusky Canada geese—a subspecies of the familiar Canada goose—that nest in Alaska's Copper River Delta and migrate all the way to Oregon to spend the winter. At one time, the Willamette Valley was rich in wetlands, but most were drained and plowed to grow grass seed. Today, grass-seed farmers bemoan the returning visits of the original population—wintering waterfowl that sometimes descend upon their fields to partake of the grass. Besides wetlands, the refuge includes uplands with native vegetation such as Oregon white oak.

The trail heads north from the parking area on a wide, mowed path and past an old apple tree. Pink-blossomed **wild rose** *(Rosa gymnocarpa)* border the trail; the fruit of the rose, known as rosehip, is rich in vitamin C. You can also spot the shrub **serviceberry** *(Amelanchier alnifolia)* with its white blossoms in spring and edible, bluish-black berries later in the summer.

The ubiquitous **Himalayan blackberry** *(Rubus discolor)* has crowded out many native plant species and wildlife habitat. This plant's thorny thickets produce pretty, white blossoms and luscious black fruit.

Purple **tufted vetch** *(Vicia cracca)*, sometimes known as **bird vetch**, is common here. Easy to identify by the climbing tendril or vine, this introduced exotic plant sports pealike, purple flowers clustered in groups of 20 to 50.

About 50 feet along the path, you pass one of the refuge's Oregon white oak. The tree was once common throughout the Willamette Valley, but clearing the land for farming eliminated most of its habitat. Just beyond this oak on the right side of the path grow a large group of **serviceberry** and some **black hawthorn** *(Crataegus douglasii)*, sporting white blossoms and thorns.

BLACK HAWTHORN
Crataegus douglasii

Black hawthorn, also known as **Pacific hawthorn**, is a flowering shrub or small tree common in low elevations throughout western Oregon. The stout thorns from which it takes its name sprout from the tree's twigs. The white flowers, though beautiful to see, are not as sweet to smell. The nearly-black fruit has a bluish tinge. American Indians of the Pacific Northwest used the thorns for fish hooks, ate the berries, and created weapons and tool handles from the wood.

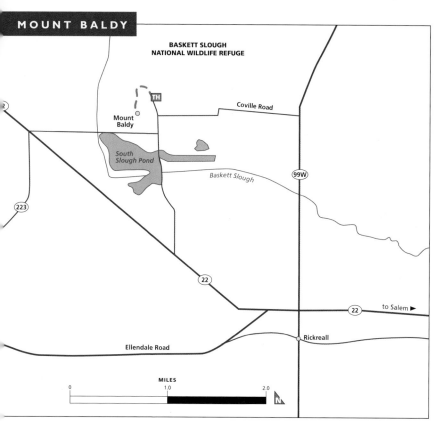

After 200 yards, the trail bears left and begins to ascend a hill. **Wild rose** border the path, and **fool's onion** (*Brodiaea hyacinthina*) appear here and there but never in dense clusters. This wild onion features grasslike, basal leaves and a cluster of white (sometimes blue-tinged) bell-shaped flowers. In disturbed areas along the trail you encounter **yellow parentucellia** (*Parentucellia viscosa*). This member of the figwort family, an exotic introduced from Europe, invades places where the vegetation has been destroyed or removed.

You come to a trail junction at the top of a hill. To loop around Baskett Butte and through more oak woodlands, bear right. The destination of this hike, however, is Mount Baldy to the left. As you head southwest to the grassy summit of the hill, look for **spring gold** (*Lomatium utriculatum*). Also known as **gold star, spring gold** is an annual with multiple stems that often forms carpets of bright yellow. Beware the shiny, oaklike leaves of **poison oak** (*Rhus diversiloba*), which is very common along the path here.

Yarrow (*Achillea millefolium*) edge the path with their fernlike leaves and white flowers. The purple **tufted vetch** remain common as you head through lush meadows toward 3–4-foot-high grass at the summit of the hill. As you

Delicate cat's-ear lily, or mariposa lily, have distinctive, bearded inner petals.

approach the summit, note the small Douglas fir that managed to establish itself. In the past, frequent fires burned these grasslands, preventing the invasion of conifer and other trees.

On the rocky hilltop sections you're treated to **cat's-ear lily** *(Calochortus subalpinus)*, a beautiful white flower also known as **sego lily** and **subalpine mariposa lily**. The flower's furry inner petals inspired the "cat's-ear" moniker. **Spring gold** and **large-leaved lupine** *(Lupinus polyphyllus)* also thrive in this section. **Hairy cat's-ear** *(Hypochaeris radicata)*, a perennial with milky juice, is common in the more disturbed sites along the path.

When you reach the summit of Mount Baldy, the views are tremendous. As you gaze south across the Willamette Valley, east to the Cascades, and west to the Coast Range, note how much of the Willamette Valley's native landscape has been destroyed by farming. In Oregon, land-use laws restrict urbanization to growth boundaries, but farming has no limits. Most of the farmland in the Willamette Valley is dedicated to grass seed, hay, or livestock pasture rather than crops for people.

After enjoying the view, turn around and find your way back to the trailhead.

Mill Hill Loop

*Wildflower
Hike 41*

Willamette Valley native wet prairie preserved at the Finley Refuge.

Corvallis	*Nearest Town*
Meadows, oak savanna, and Douglas fir forest, with rare native prairie and flower species	*Highlights*
easy	*Trail Rating*
2.5-mile loop	*Trail Length*
William L. Finley National Wildlife Refuge	*Location*
400 feet	*Elevation*
William L. Finley National Wildlife Refuge, 541-757-7236	*Contact*
March to July	*Bloom Season*
May	*Peak Bloom*
From Corvallis, take OR 99W south 10 miles to Finley Road and turn right. In 1.3 miles you reach a rest area and kiosk with maps of the refuge. Continue another 1.8 miles to a parking area near a maintenance yard.	*Directions*

The 5,325-acre William L. Finley National Wildlife Refuge is one of three major national wildlife refuges in the Willamette Valley. William Finley, a friend of President Theodore Roosevelt and an early naturalist, lobbied to have refuges set aside as habitats for wildlife. The refuge was established to provide wintering habitat for the dusky Canada goose. This rare subspecies nests in Alaska's Copper River Delta and migrates to Oregon to spend the winter. The draining of the Willamette Valley wetlands and plowing of native grasslands to create farmland significantly reduced wintering habitat for many wildlife species and in particular for waterfowl. Ironically, much of the native grasslands that were lost are now used to grow grass seed.

The refuge is also an important nesting site for the white-tailed kite. In addition, bobcat, elk, black-tailed deer, band-tailed pigeons, varied thrush, orange-crowned and Wilson's warblers, and other birds are common in the refuge. The refuge also protects the largest remaining tract of native wet prairie in the Willamette Valley, plus significant tracts of Oregon white oak savanna, another increasingly rare plant community.

Much of the refuge is closed between November and the end of April to avoid disturbing the wintering wildlife. The Mill Hill Trail, however, is open year-round, and offers one of the best early season wildflower hikes in the Willamette Valley. As you stroll through the meadows and shady, fern-lined forest of this absolutely delightful springtime walk, you are serenaded by warblers and other singing birds. I hiked it on April 1, a bit early since the peak flowering season typically comes in May. Nevertheless, enough flowers were in bloom to keep me happy, especially when combined with the excellent birding and elk-watching opportunities.

Mill Hill isn't much of a hill, rising only 100 feet or so above the slope surrounding it. The trail is an old road, so you can hike several people abreast, and families with small children can easily push baby joggers around the loop. Opposite a fenced lagoon and the maintenance shop, the trail begins as a mowed path across a grassy field. **Wild strawberry** *(Fragaria vesca)* and **western buttercup** *(Ranunculus occidentalis)* frequent the margin of the trail. Within about 100 yards, you enter woods and pass **Indian plum** *(Osmaronia cerasiformis)*, a shrub with 3-inch-long, elliptical leaves and white, hanging blossoms. **Indian plum** is one of the earliest plants to bloom in the spring. In the first 0.25 mile you see other shrubs, including common **snowberry** *(Symphoricarpos albus)*, **sword-fern** *(Polystichum munitum)*, **wild rose** *(Rosa gymnocarpa)*, and **black hawthorn** *(Crataegus douglasii)*. In late April and early May, **black hawthorn** are covered with white blossoms. **Himalayan blackberry** *(Rubus discolor)*, an exotic that grows rampantly over western Oregon, also flourish here.

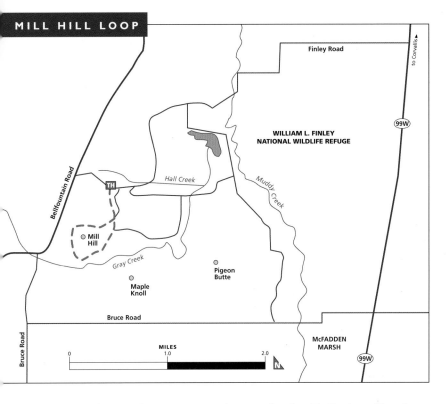

At 0.3 mile, a trail connecting to the Woodpecker Trail takes off to the right. Continue straight ahead on the trail to Mill Hill. Just beyond the trail junction, you pass through a forest of bigleaf maple and Oregon white oak. You then reach a road that leads northeast to the maintenance yard; bear right at this junction. A magnificent specimen of Oregon white oak stands just across the road toward the maintenance shop. **Western buttercup** grow in the grassy areas along the road here. Just beyond the red barn to the east, the trail moves into an oak and bigleaf maple forest with an understory of the ever-abundant **snowberry** shrubs.

The trail comes to another junction, where the road to the left is closed. Continue on the trail to Mill Hill, which heads to the right through a lovely oak savanna. Soon, you reach the Mill Hill Loop trail sign. At this point, you can go either way—I chose to go right.

The trail begins to gently ascend a slope with oaks and increasing numbers of Douglas fir in the understory. Eventually you leave behind the oaks, and Douglas fir dominate the forest with bigleaf maple and **sword-fern** growing beneath. **Yellow violet** (*Viola glabella*), **Oregon fawn-lily** (*Erythronium* *oregonum)*, and **angled bittercress** *(Cardamine angulata)* grow on the shady forest floor. You soon come to a bench, which makes a pleasant place to rest and enjoy the surrounding forest. The trail reaches its high point in a little meadow near Bell Fountain Road. You can't see the road, but you can hear cars traveling on it just beyond the line of screening trees. **Buttercup** and **strawberry** grow in this meadow.

The trail passes through a string of small openings, then enters the forest before coming to a larger meadow of about 2 acres. I encountered elk tracks on the trail by the meadow. As you descend the trail, you come to the Gray Creek swamp. On the slope adjacent to the trail, you can find **candyflower** *(Claytonia sibirica)*, **trillium** *(Trillium ovatum)*, and **Oregon grape** *(Mahonia nervosa)*. A **red flowering currant** *(Ribes sanguineum)* shrub was in bloom, its bright red flowers adding a splash of color to the forest.

Oregon Fawn-lily
Erythronium oregonum

You soon reach another bench and a sign to Gray Creek. About 50 feet beyond the bench, you can find pink **fairy-slipper orchid** *(Calypso bulbosa)* and **Oregon iris** *(Iris tenax)*. **Oregon fawn-lily** and **yellow violet** are also common along this stretch of trail. The trail descends to a low point, then begins to climb again. I found many elk trails, dropping down from the Douglas fir forest heading for Gray Creek. You eventually come to another bench, which offers a nice view of the field. In another 200 yards, you gain the starting point of the loop. From here, make your way back to the trailhead to complete the hike.

The beautiful white blooms of **Oregon fawn-lily** appear in meadows and forests alike, often in dense clusters. The flowers nod down from the end of a thin stem, and the basal leaves are mottled green and dark brown. Northwest Indians consumed both bulb and leaves.

Willow Creek Preserve

Wildflower
Hike 42

Camas lily bloom amid other native prairie species in the Willow Creek Preserve.

Set in wetlands on the west end of Eugene, Willow Creek Preserve boasts the highest concentration of rare and imperiled native prairie species remaining in the Willamette Valley, including **Kincaid's lupine** *(Lupinus sulphureus)*. Prairie once covered more than one million acres of the Willamette Valley and parts of the Coast Range. Today, less than 1 percent of this prairie remains, lost to agricultural development and draining. Typically, the remaining prairie is in small and highly fragmented parcels. The Nature Conservancy owns 394 acres in these wetlands, part of a larger 1,130 acres managed by the BLM. Though it lies entirely within Eugene's urban growth boundary, the preserve provides a surprisingly wild experience.

Nearest Town	In Eugene
Highlights	Rare Willamette Valley native prairie
Trail Rating	easy
Trail Length	1.0 mile round-trip
Location	West Eugene
Elevation	400 feet
Contact	The Nature Conservancy, 503-228-9561
Bloom Season	April to June
Peak Bloom	May
Directions	From central Eugene, drive west on 18th Avenue to about 0.4 mile past Bertelsen Road and look for a parking area along the road's shoulder. If you reach the Hyundai plant, you've gone too far.

Willow Creek's wet prairie, ash woodlands, and streams provide the habitat that sustains more than 200 native wildflowers and grasses. In addition, more than 100 bird species and 25 butterfly species have been documented in the area. Fender's blue butterfly, thought to be extinct, was rediscovered here in 1989. Native tufted hairgrass is the area's dominant cover.

The preserve is home to numerous rare flowering species, including **Kincaid's lupine, white-top aster** *(Aster curtus),* **Willamette daisy** *(Erigeron decumbens),* and **Bradshaw's lomatium** *(Lomatium bradshawii),* a federally listed endangered species. Although the plant is relatively common at the preserve, conversion of prairie lands to agricultural use has reduced its native habitat. Prescribed burns, designed to emulate past Indian ignitions, have been used to keep the prairie open. In burned areas, **Bradshaw's lomatium** has increased by as much as 50 percent.

Without a big sign, the trailhead is not easy to find. But, if you walk just beyond the bridge over the creek, you can see a distinct trail and a small orange-yellow sign marking the TNC preserve. This 1.0-mile loop trail passes through the prairie. The best time to visit is early spring, when the **camas lily** *(Camassia quamash)* is blooming (although not much else will be). It's typically wet here, so wear rubber boots.

The trail heads south, just to the left of Willow Creek. In spring, the open prairie to the left (east) is full of **camas lily**, tinting the landscape blue.

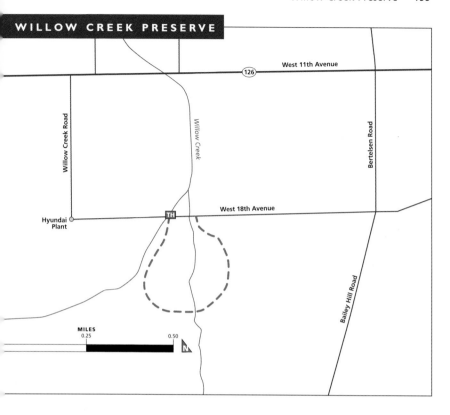

WILLOW CREEK PRESERVE

West 11th Avenue
126
Willow Creek Road
Willow Creek
Bertelsen Road
West 18th Avenue
Hyundai Plant
TH
Bailey Hill Road
MILES
0.25   0.50
N

Once common throughout the Willamette Valley, **camas lily** was a major food source for American Indians. With almost all of the Willamette Valley's native prairies now plowed up for cultivation, **camas lily** are virtually non-existent. You might consider this a good trade if the land were being used to grow food crops for people, but the single-biggest crop in the valley is grass seed. This rich, native ecosystem has been sacrificed to grow rye grass for people's suburban lawns.

In the prairie you can find one of the preserve's special plants, **Bradshaw's lomatium**. Like most **lomatiums**, this plant has finely dissected, carrotlike leaves. **Bradshaw's lomatium**, with yellow flowers clustered in compound umbels, is native to western Oregon's wet prairies.

You see another special species here as well—**Kincaid's lupine**. Fender's blue butterflies require the **lupine** as a food source for its larval stages. Only a handful of areas larger than an acre now support this **lupine**. The situation is further complicated for the butterfly: Other nectar-producing species that it requires for food are relatively rare. Some 300 to 700 Fender's blue butterflies survive at the preserve. **Bicolor lupine** *(Lupinus bicolor),* an annual, also thrive on drier, well-drained sites here.

Another common species on the prairie is **death-camas** *(Zigadenus elegans)*, which sport white blooms and slender narrow leaves. You may spot other members of the lily family that make their home here, **ball head cluster lily** *(Brodiaea congesta)* and **slim-leaf onion** *(Allium amplectens)*, which produce white or pink petals.

BRADSHAW'S LOMATIUM
Lomatium bradshawii

Bradshaw's lomatium, a federally listed endangered species, was once common in the Willamette Valley. The loss of habitat due to farming, livestock grazing, urbanization, and other factors led to its extirpation in most of its former range. The plant now grows in a few isolated populations in Lane, Marion, Benton, and Douglas counties.

The feature that distinguishes this **lomatium** species is the tiny, leafy bracts divided into three bractlets. The leaves are divided into highly dissected segments, the yellow flowers clustered in compact umbels. Leaves and flowers both grow from the plant's base. **Bradshaw's lomatium** bloom typically in April or May.

Oregon iris *(Iris tenax)*, which resemble a lily with long, linear leaves and elegant blue flowers, occur here and there along the edge of the prairie. **Western buttercup** *(Ranunculus occidentalis)*, a perennial with hairy stems and three wedge-shaped leaves, also bloom in spring.

The wet prairie habitat hosts **Oregon saxifrage** *(Saxifraga oregana)*, which bears a single, long, leafless flower stalk and a cluster of white flowers. All the leaves are basal. You also see **grassland saxifrage** *(Saxifraga integrifolia)*, recognizable by wavy, margined leaves and conical, compact white flower groups.

Shrubs growing along the creek include **serviceberry** *(Amelanchier alnifolia)*, **black hawthorn** *(Crataegus douglasii)*, **wild nootka rose** *(Rosa nutkana)*, and various willows. Black cottonwood, a common riparian tree species, appear along the stream with a few wild apple trees.

Himalayan blackberry *(Rubus discolor)* is taking over the preserve—and just about everyplace else. Despite considerable efforts to control the plant, their thorny runners are visible throughout the preserve. **Pennyroyal** *(Mentha pulegium)*, a member of the mint family with square stems, grow near the creek. Introduced from Europe, **pennyroyal** are now widespread in wet prairies and meadows.

The pink spikes of **hardhack spiraea** *(Spiraea douglasii)* thrive along the creek. The flower's Latin name refers to botanist David Douglas, who collected plants up and down the Willamette Valley in the 1820s. A member of the aster family, **apargidium** *(Apargidium sp.),* is common in the wet meadows. Its yellow flowers tend to bloom later in the summer.

The path comes to a fence corner and turns to the west. Look here for **serviceberry** and **black hawthorn** at the fenceline just past the corner. You find plenty of **narrow mule's-ear** *(Wyethia angustifolia),* a showy member of the Willamette Valley prairie community. If you're hiking early in the spring, look for this plant's brown stalks from the previous year. **Narrow mule's ear** have thin, basal leaves and a large disk flower, yellow when in bloom. Near the creek you may find **dead-nettle** *(Lamium amplexicaule),* with branching, leafy stems and purplish flowers in clusters along the leaves' axils.

The path winds past some young Douglas fir invading the meadow. As the path takes you farther from the road, look for **Oregon ash** woodlands. The tree has rough, grayish bark and light green, pinnately compound leaves. Ash woodlands are a prime indicator of wetlands. Among the ash, small amounts of **sword-fern** *(Polystichum munitum)* and **bracken fern** *(Pteridium aquilinum)* grow. **Sword-fern** are evergreen, but **bracken fern** die back each autumn. You also find **snowberry** *(Symphoricarpos albus)* in the ash groves, the white berries that appear in the fall inspiring the common name.

The path passes through the trees and into another meadow. In May, you find plenty of **deltoid balsamroot** *(Balsamorhiza deltoidea).* You continue through more ash woodlands with tons of **blackberry, hawthorn, snowberry,** and other shrubs. Eventually, the path circles along the backside of the meadow, following the edge of the trees, and loops back to the road.

Wildflower Hike 43

Meadow Road/ Water Garden Trail

A lush path near Mount Pisgah in the Howard Buford Recreation Area.

Nearest Town	Eugene/Springfield
Highlights	Camas lily amidst Oregon oak savanna, plus lush riparian forest flora
Trail Rating	easy
Trail Length	1.0 mile each way
Location	Howard Buford Recreation Area/Mount Pisgah Arboretum
Elevation	400 feet
Contact	Mount Pisgah Arboretum, 541-682-6940
Bloom Season	February to June
Peak Bloom	April to May
Directions	From Eugene/Springfield, take I-5 south and exit at 30th Avenue. Turn right (south) at the stop sign. Continue 1.0 mile or so on the frontage road to another light on 30th Avenue. Turn left and cross I-5. At the stop sign, turn left again and proceed north, parallel to the freeway. Take your first right just past the Texaco station, follow this road for 0.4 mile around a curve, then turn left on Seavey Loop Road. Take this road 1.5 miles east to the Coast Fork of the Willamette River, cross the bridge into the park, turn right and drive 0.4 mile to the main Arboretum parking lot.

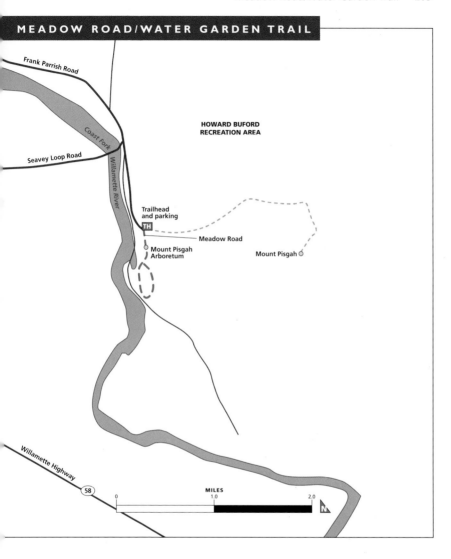

ount Pisgah rises to 1,531 feet above sea level and affords outstanding vistas from its summit. Most of the mountain and its adjacent slopes are part of the 2,363-acre Howard Buford Recreation Area. The largest county park in Lane County, Howard Buford Park features an outstanding example of low-elevation oak savanna grasslands. Once widespread in the Willamette Valley, these grasslands have now largely been converted to agriculture. Sixteen miles of trails provide access to the park's grasslands, which host some of the best early spring wildflower displays in the entire valley.

The 210-acre Mount Pisgah Arboretum at the base of the mountain offers a number of short loop trails and a wildflower garden area with labeled plants. Before undertaking the hike, be sure to take some time to visit the garden. Howard Buford Recreation Area is not only a great place for wild-flower viewing, but it's also home to black-tailed deer, western pond turtle, bald eagle, osprey, mountain lion, coyote, and many other species.

The Meadow Road/Water Garden Trail starts at the arboretum parking lot near the arboretum's caretaker home. Follow the wide, gravel Meadow Road, heading south across a flat of Oregon white oak and meadow. In April, the blue **camas lily** *(Camassia quamash)* and **western buttercup** *(Ranunculus occidentalis)* cover these meadows. Walk through the meadows about a third of a mile to an old barn and silo.

Just beyond the barn, you come to a bench next to the Coast Fork of the Willamette River and a Y in the trail. Turn right and take the second wood-chip path into the woods. Almost instantly, the vegetation becomes more luxuriant. Oak, bigleaf maple, and cottonwood shade a riot of flowers. The dark blossoms of **tall larkspur** *(Delphinium glaucum)*, along with **trillium** *(Trillium ovatum)*, **fringecup** *(Tellima grandiflora)*, **miner's lettuce** *(Claytonia perfoliata)*, **Pacific bleedingheart** *(Dicentra formosa)*, **meadowrue** *(Thalictrum occidentale)*, **false Solomon's seal** *(Smilacina racemosa)*, and **cow-parsnip** *(Heracleum lanatum)* all flourish along this section.

The trail turns east and splits, but both routes converge on a small bridge that crosses a wetland area. As you approach the bridge, look for flowering shrubs such as **Indian plum** *(Osmaronia cerasiformis)* and **wild rose** *(Rosa gymnocarpa)*. **Indian plum**, one of the earliest blooming flowers, typically appears as early as February, while **wild rose** is more likely to bloom in June.

Continue a short way, then cross a second, larger bridge. Under the bridge live **yellow pond lily** *(Nuphar polysepalum)*. At the signed trail junction just after the bridge, go left. Near the sign, you'll see thick pockets of blue **camas lily**. Continue along this trail back to the Vern Adkison Bench, completing the loop. A 0.5-mile walk along Meadow Road takes you back to the parking lot.

TALL LARKSPUR
Delphinium glaucum

Tall larkspur, a common perennial, features deep-blue to purplish flowers with spurs that form loose, terminal clusters. The leaves are palmately divided into wedge-shaped segments. Found in both moist woodlands and meadows, **tall larkspur** are poisonous to livestock. In the past, **larkspur** was sprayed to eliminate it from cattle and sheep grazing areas.

West Summit Trail

*Wildflower
Hike 44*

A view toward Eugene from Mount Pisgah.

Eugene/Springfield	***Nearest Town***
Beautiful oak savanna and spectacular views	***Highlights***
moderate	***Trail Rating***
1.5 miles one way	***Trail Length***
Howard Buford Recreation Area	***Location***
500–1,500 feet	***Elevation***
Lane County Parks, 541-341-6940	***Contact***
February to July	***Bloom Season***
mid-April to June	***Peak Bloom***
From Eugene/Springfield, take I-5 south and exit at 30th Avenue. Turn right (south) at the stop sign. Continue 1.0 mile or so on the frontage road to another light on 30th Avenue. Turn left and cross I-5. At the stop sign, turn left again and proceed north, parallel to the freeway. Take your first right just past the Texaco station, follow this road for 0.4 mile around a curve, then turn left on Seavey Loop Road. Take this road 1.5 miles east to the Coast Fork of the Willamette River, cross the bridge into the park, turn right and drive 0.4 mile to the main Arboretum parking lot.	***Directions***

Mount Pisgah, described in the last hike, looms above Howard Buford Recreation Area, rising to 1,531 feet above sea level. Outstanding oak savanna grasslands with scattered patches of Douglas fir, bigleaf maple, and incense cedar make this a particularly pleasant area for hiking. West Summit Trail is the principal hiking route to the top of Mount Pisgah, mostly through oak grasslands sporting abundant spring flowers. Although the first half of the trail is steep, it tends to be gentler toward the top. This trail is actually an old road, so it's quite wide, making it easy for several people to walk side by side.

Watch for **poison oak** *(Rhus diversiloba)* along the entire hike. Going off-trail is not advisable. The hike begins at the arboretum parking lot, just beyond a closed metal gate. Across the lot from the gate, you find a stand of Oregon white oak with a thick carpet of **camas lily** *(Camassia quamash)* beneath. Lewis and Clark first noted **camas lily** during their 1804–1806 explorations of the West. From a distance, Lewis noted, the prevalent blue flowers took on the appearance of a lake. American Indian tribes in the region collected **camas** bulbs and ate them. Unfortunately, most of the vast acreage housing **camas**, which once cloaked the Pacific Northwest, has been plowed up for agriculture.

Go through the metal gate at the trailhead, then proceed up the slope. Edging the trail are the yellow flowers of **western buttercup** *(Ranunculus occidentalis)*. The three wedge-shaped lobed leaves of this plant, along with the bright shiny yellow flowers, help identify it. The trail quickly enters a tunnel of oak and bigleaf maple. You spot a few **camas** and **buttercup** here, and the beautiful **Oregon iris** *(Iris tenax)* grow on the slope beside the trail. You can find **Indian plum** *(Osmaronia cerasiformis)* grow in the understory along with the exotic **Himalayan blackberry** *(Rubus discolor)*.

CHECKERBLOOM
Sidalcea malvaeflora var. virgata

Checkerbloom, common in meadows, feature pinkish-white blossoms and hairy stems that are 1–2 feet tall. The leaves vary from deeply lobed to divided.

The trail takes you a short way through the trees, and then breaks out into the open. The opening affords great views of the western slope of Mount Pisgah, which is covered with one of the nicer oak woodlands left in Oregon. Just as you cross under some power lines, watch for an abundance of **yellow monkey-flower** *(Mimulus guttatus)* off to the right. **Monkey-flower** prefers seeps, and indeed, these splashes of yellow are primarily found in wet areas.

At this point, you can easily see the effects of the 1999 fire that burned the western slope of Mount

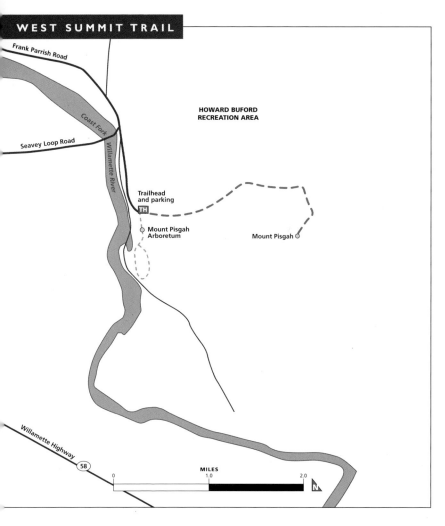

WEST SUMMIT TRAIL

Frank Parrish Road

Coast Fork

Seavey Loop Road

Willamette River

HOWARD BUFORD
RECREATION AREA

Trailhead
and parking
TH

Mount Pisgah
Arboretum

Mount Pisgah

Willamette Highway

58

MILES
1.0
2.0

N

Pisgah. The fire killed some trees, but for the most part the flames consumed only the litter and fine fuels, and new growth in the ground cover has hidden much of the fire's aftermath. This is not surprising—fires are a natural part of these ecosystems, and most western plants and animals tolerate them well. Evidence actually suggests that fires—whether ignited by both lightning or humans—thinned forests, reduced competition, and cleansed the forest. Fires helped keep the Willamette Valley more open than it is presently. Many species, such as the Oregon white oak and bigleaf maple, sprout from their roots when the above-ground bole is killed by flames. Douglas fir has a thick, corky bark that helps it endure low-intensity fires.

At 0.6 mile, you reach a trail junction with the West Slope Trail. From here, you have another 0.9 mile to the summit. As you continue up the ridge, look back for fine views of Springfield and the southern end of the Willamette Valley. A long open stretch heads east up the steep slope, then shifts southeast, traversing the slope past more **buttercup** and **poison oak**. Growing along the trail in rocky areas, you find pretty white **cat's-ear lily** *(Calochortus subalpinus),* with fuzzy petals reminiscent of cat ears. Pink-flowered **checkerbloom** *(Sidalcea malvaeflora var. virgata)* are common here, while a few **death-camas** *(Zigadenus elegans)* appear, recognizable by white, star-shaped blooms.

When you enter the oaks again, you can spot more **iris** and **camas lily.** Just beyond the oaks, another small meadow hosts **buttercup**. Just beyond the meadow, the trail winds back into Douglas fir mixed with oak. You find clumps of white **Oregon fawn-lily** *(Erythronium oregonum),* a plant relatively common in low-elevation forests. The white variety is characterized by drooping, white flowers and mottled leaves. Several kinds of **fawn-lily** grow in Oregon, including a yellow variety, a white variety that inhabits subalpine basins, as well as a pink variety that grows along the coast. Native Americans and bears ate the bulbs of all species of **fawn-lily.**

East of the trail, by the edge of a small oak grove, you encounter white **baby blue-eyes** *(Nemophila menziesii atomaria).* You also can discover along the path some **grand hounds-tongue** *(Cynoglossum grande),* a plant common in oak woodlands. This robust species often rises to more than 2 feet tall and sports large, broad leaves.

The trail curves around to the east again for a short distance, then traverses the slope in a north-south direction. You can discover another lovely oak grove featuring the distinctive pink blossoms of **broad-leaved shooting star** *(Dodecatheon hendersonii)* along with the white blossoms of **small-flowered prairiestar** *(Lithophragma parviflora).* I saw one **western columbine** *(Aquilegia formosa)* with its red, drooping, spurred flowers.

The ubiquitous **poison oak** lines the trail; **wild rose** *(Rosa gymnocarpa)* also begin to appear. When **wild rose** is in bloom, most people recognize the plant easily. When it's not in bloom, the serrated leaves and prickles on the stems give away its identity. Scattered in the trees are evergreen **sword-fern** *(Polystichum munitum),* which grow in clumps up to 3 feet tall.

The trail rises and curves to the east. After a relatively flat stretch, you reach the junction with the Beistal East Trail, a lesser-used alternate route to the summit that begins at the East Trailhead.

Just past the trail junction, **fringecup** *(Tellima grandiflora)* become fairly common. **Ninebark** *(Physocarpus capitatus),* shrubs that may reach more than 10 feet high, appear with shreddy bark on their stems and white flowers. You find one of the shrubs on the east (left) side of the trail, about 50 feet in front of a stump and fallen log (from a giant Douglas fir cut by firefighters). Bigleaf maple shade the trail here. The road created a firebreak that stopped the fire from sweeping over the hill into denser timber on the eastern and northern slopes of the mountain.

You can see **Himalayan blackberry** *(Rubus discolor)*, which was burned off by the fire, sprouting from its root system. The **Himalayan blackberry**, an introduced exotic, has created dense thickets that crowd out most native plants. Nevertheless, the fruit it produces, which ripens in late summer, is delicious.

Just past the stump on the right, **black hawthorn** *(Crataegus douglasii)* grow. This shrub attains a small-tree size and sports beautiful white flowers in the spring. **Black hawthorn** is relatively easy to identify by the presence of its namesake "thorns." To the east, more white **Oregon fawn-lily** and **hounds-tongue** thrive among the trees.

As you approach the summit, delicate pink-white blossoms of **miner's lettuce** *(Claytonia perfoliata)* cover the ground below the oaks and other trees. A few **shooting star** *(Dodecatheon sp.)*, as well as **yellow violet** *(Viola glabella)* and **western buttercup**, are scattered here and there. Just to the west below the summit, you find another patch of white **baby blue-eyes.**

Rest and take in the great vista from the grassy summit, which presents amazing views on clear days. From the top of Mount Pisgah, you can see snow-clad Diamond Peak in the Cascades and most of the upper Coast Fork of the Willamette drainage. To the northwest, views encompass the southern end of the Willamette Valley and the more distant Coast Range. When you've enjoyed the views to your satisfaction, retrace your steps to the trailhead.

OREGON IRIS
Iris tenax

The showy **Oregon iris**, one of the more dazzling spring wildflowers, sports bluish-purple to lavender flowers that are 2–3 inches wide. This **iris** tends to grow in open meadows and woodlands. The species name, *tenax* (Latin for "tenacious"), recognizes the extreme strength of the leaves. David Douglas (for whom the Douglas fir is named) recorded that American Indians would braid **iris** leaves and use these ropes to capture animals as large as elk.

Cape Lookout

The misty trail to Cape Lookout on the Oregon coast, Cape Lookout State Park.

Nearest Town	Tillamook
Highlights	Old-growth forest hike to outstanding ocean views
Trail Rating	moderate
Trail Length	5.0 miles round-trip
Location	Cape Lookout State Park
Elevation	200–800 feet
Contact	Oregon State Parks, 503-378-6305
Bloom Season	May to July
Peak Bloom	June
Directions	From US 101 in Tillamook, take 3rd Street (Netarts Highway) west and follow signs to Cape Lookout State Park, about 13 miles. You can also loop around the Three Capes Scenic Route: take Netarts Highway west and turn right onto Bayocean Road. Again, follow the signs to Cape Lookout State Park and the trailhead.

Cape Lookout is the longest cape on the Three Capes Scenic Route here. John Meares, one of the early explorers of the Oregon Coast, named it. The volcanic basalts that make up Cape Lookout flowed all the way down the Columbia River from sources in eastern Oregon, reaching the sea here and elsewhere along the north coast. Most of this hike is through forest quite some distance above the ocean. Saltwater surrounds the bold headlands. You're granted the best views when you reach the more westerly parts of the cape.

The trail begins in a parking lot at the junction of the Oregon Coast Trail. The path first traverses the southern side of the cape, with occasional views of the ocean. In the center of the cape, the trail undulates through large Sitka spruce and western hemlock. About halfway to the point, you can take in nice views north to Cape Meares, Three Arch Rocks, and Netarts Bay. Finally, the trail shifts back to the south before reaching the tip of the cape.

From the trailhead, you travel through a forest of Sitka spruce, which dominate the forest cover for most of the hike. Sitka spruce has a natural range from northern California to Kodiak Island in Alaska but are found only along the Oregon Coast and inland along some of the coastal rivers. You soon can see understory plants such as **salmonberry** *(Rubus spectabilis)*, a lovely shrub with red flowers and pinkish, edible berries. Another is **red huckleberry** *(Vaccinium parvifolium)*, the most common **huckleberry** in Oregon's Coast Range that sports thin, airy branches and urn-shaped, greenish-yellow flowers that turn into red berries later in the season. **Candyflower** *(Claytonia sibirica)*, with their pinkish-white flowers, **foamflower** *(Tiarella trifoliata)* with their delicate blooms, and **false lily-of-the-valley** *(Maianthemum dilatatum)* with their perfume scent are all abundant as ground cover. The large evergreen fronds of **sword-fern** *(Polystichum munitum)* dot the slopes.

Shortly after leaving the trailhead, you come to a junction with a trail that heads left to the beach. Continue straight here to reach the cape. **Salal** *(Gaultheria shallon)*, another evergreen shrub with

GOATSBEARD
Aruncus dioicus

Goatsbeard, or **spaghetti flower**, thrive in moist forests. A perennial that can reach more than 6 feet tall, the plants spread by rhizomes and tend to form large patches in forest openings. The very large leaves are divided in a compound spray, but the flowers are tiny, growing in dense terminal clusters reminiscent of spaghetti.

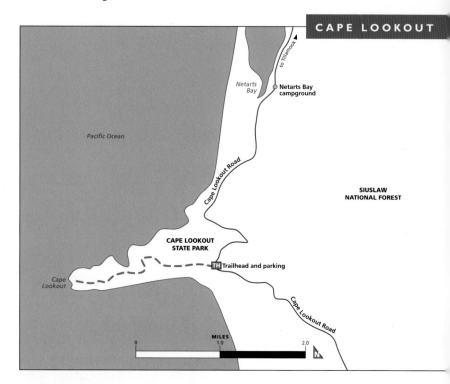

huckleberrylike, urn-shaped leaves, is common as an understory plant here. **Thimbleberry** *(Rubus parviflorus),* with their large, maplelike leaves and white blossoms, also thrive in the ground cover. Here and there you can spot **lady-fern** *(Athyrium filix-femina)* and occasional patches of **Hooker fairy-bell** *(Disporum hookeri),* a member of the lily family.

As the trail rounds a shoulder of the ridge, you see **yellow monkey-flower** *(Mimulus guttatus),* a species common in wet seeps and along streams. Another berry-producing shrub, **red elderberry** *(Sambucus racemosa),* towers up to 20 feet high. The dense clusters of white blossoms and large, divided leaves give away its identity.

Look out for more **candyflower** and **thimbleberry**, plus an occasional **broad-leaved starflower** *(Trientalis latifolia)* and blue **Oregon iris** *(Iris tenax).* You cross another shoulder of the ridge, where western hemlock dominates. Large, white, umbel-shaped flowers of **cow-parsnip** *(Heracleum lanatum)* flourish here, and **false lily-of-the-valley** are particularly abundant.

The trail passes an oddly shaped hemlock, its multiple stems festooned with ferns and lichens. **Red huckleberry, yellow monkey-flower, salal,** and **salmonberry** all flourish in this area.

Just before reaching a wooden bridge, note the cloverlike leaves of **sorrel** *(Oxalis oregana)* along with large, white **trillium** *(Trillium ovatum)* blooms.

Right at the bridge, you can find more **salmonberry, false lily-of-the-valley, elderberry, salal,** and **candyflower.**

After the bridge, the trail swings back to the south side of the ridge with views of the ocean and beaches to the south. You cross an open slope with lots of **salal,** along with **wild strawberry** *(Fragaria vesca)* and some **yarrow** *(Achillea millefolium).* The trail eventually swings back away from the cliff side into a tunnel-like trail that cuts through the dense forest. A large Sitka spruce sits at the entrance to the forest. Opposite the tree grows **single delight** *(Moneses uniflora),* its fragrant, waxy white flowers nodding downward from long stalks. A considerable amount of **sorrel** mixes with the **single delight.**

The trail passes another large spruce, which has a big cavity carved into its base, on the left. You then cross two bridges over wet spots. Just beyond and to the right of the second bridge, look for more **elderberry.** The trail begins to descend, curving to the left and crossing another boardwalk. Here, you're surrounded by **thimbleberry, huckleberry,** and **salmonberry,** and you're treated to another ocean view.

When you encounter a switchback, look for **evergreen huckleberry** *(Vaccinium ovatum)* with their leathery, hollylike leaves. The trail switchbacks several more times, passing through some **Mexican hedge-nettle** *(Stachys mexicana),* a member of the mint family with a telltale square stem.

A wooden post with a "1.0" sign on it indicates the 1.0-mile mark. The trail climbs up a hill and through more **Mexican hedge-nettle** and **vanillaleaf** *(Achlys triphylla).* **Goatsbeard** *(Aruncus dioicus),* a common shrub through here, sport long, stringy, terminal clusters of small white flowers, lending them the alternate name of **spaghetti flower.** You can recognize a member of the saxifrage family, **youth-on-age** *(Tolmiea menziesii),* by its tiny brown flowers.

You come to a fenced viewpoint granting views of the north side of the cape and the ocean. The trail then switches up over boardwalks, passing through lots of **goatsbeard.** On the north side of the cape, the trail traverses an open slope with frequent, unobstructed views of the coast to the north, including Netarts Bay. The path passes a 1.5-mile post and winds back into the forest, crossing the cape to the south side. The trail then descends, crossing three more boardwalks and taking you back to the cliff side for more ocean views.

As the path approaches the tip of the cape, open patches with **red Indian-paintbrush** *(Castilleja miniata),* **wild rose** *(Rosa gymnocarpa),* **honeysuckle** *(Lonicera ciliosa),* **self heal** *(Prunella vulgaris),* and **yarrow** appear on the grassy cliffs. At the end of the trail, you're rewarded with a bench and terrific views of the rocky cape and Cape Kiwanda to the south. The cape is also a good place for spotting whales during the annual migration. After enjoying the cape, head back the way you came.

*Wildflower
Hike 46* # Cascade Head Preserve

*Lupine blooms
with a view of
Cascade Head.*

In the 1960s, the Nature Conservancy purchased some 300 acres of the
scenic slopes of Cascade Head to protect the rare Oregon silverspot butterfly.
(The remaining parts of Cascade Head are in the Siuslaw National Forest.)
Today, this Nature Conservancy preserve is a National Scenic Research Area
and United Nations Biosphere Reserve.

Cascade Head is composed of volcanic basalt, which is resistant to
erosion from the ocean's battering waves. This basalt formation is similar
to other headlands created some 15 million years ago from very fluid lava
eruptions in eastern Oregon and adjacent regions of Idaho. The lava flowed
westward down the Columbia River and through the gorge to spread across
western Oregon. Native species here include red fescue, wild rye, Pacific
reedgrass, **coast paintbrush** *(Castilleja litoralis)*, **goldenrod** *(Solidago sp.)*,

Nearest Town	Lincoln City
Highlights	Scenic coastal headland with native prairie flora and a rare Oregon silverspot butterfly population
Trail Rating	moderate
Trail Length	3.4 miles round-trip, plus 1.0 mile to and from the parking lot
Location	Coast Range north of Lincoln City
Elevation	120–1,300 feet
Contact	Nature Conservancy, 503-228-9561; Siuslaw NF, 541-750-7000
Bloom Season	April to July
Peak Bloom	May to June
Directions	I describe the lower of the two Cascade Head trails here. From Lincoln City, head north about 6 miles on US 101 (Oregon Coast Highway). Just past the Salmon River, turn left (west) on Three Rocks Road. Go 2.0 miles. Just after crossing a bridge over a small stream, you meet a junction. Take the left fork and continue to Knight Park and ample parking—not allowed at the actual trailhead. To get to the trailhead, walk back to the junction, then hike about 0.5 mile up and over Savage Road. At the bottom of the hill, where the road curves sharply toward the ocean, you'll find the signed trailhead on the right.

blue violet *(Viola adunca)*, and **lupine** *(Lupinus sp.)*. The preserve is also home to the **Cascade Head catchfly** *(Silene douglasii var. oraria)* and the **hairy checkermallow** *(Sidalcea hirtipes)*, two rare flowering species. Cascade Head is named for the waterfalls that cascade directly off the landmark's cliffs into the sea.

From Savage Road, the trail zigzags up the mountain, steadily climbing through forest before opening into coastal prairie that affords outstanding views. You have great opportunities in the open meadowlands for spotting raptors hunting in the surrounding headlands and gray whales surfacing in the ocean during their spring migration (beginning in February and continuing through May). You may also see elk grazing in the meadows; elk trails are abundant in the forested areas.

As you begin the walk you will cross a short wooden bridge. Note the presence of **horsetail** *(Equisetum sp.)*, **skunk cabbage** *(Lysichitum americanum)*, **meadowrue** *(Thalictrum occidentale)*, **salmonberry** *(Rubus spectabilis)*, and **red elderberry** *(Sambucus racemosa)*. **Elderberry** and **salmonberry** were both important fruits for American Indians. Wildlife enjoy the fruit as well; bears, in particular, are fond of **elderberry.**

Soon after you cross the bridge, you encounter a huge Sitka spruce. As you hike along this trail, you can admire more spruce, some of which are very large. Sitka spruce is a common coastal species that ranges from northern California to Kodiak Island, Alaska. Sitka's light, strong wood made it an important structural component of early aircraft.

As you begin to ascend the trail, look for the heart-shaped, cloverlike leaves of **sorrel** *(Oxalis oregana)*, its white five-petaled flowers often showing reddish veins. **Candyflower** *(Claytonia sibirica)*, with their opposite egg-shaped blade leaves, flourish here as well.

In the first part of this trail, you rise up numerous wood steps and can see an abundance of **candyflower**, along with **elderberry, salmonberry**, and the chocolate calyx tubes of **youth-on-age** *(Tolmiea menziesii)* with its maplelike leaves. Sitka spruce dominate the overstory, gray-barked **red alder** *(Alnus rubra)* the understory. **Red alder**, the best wood to use for smoking salmon, fixes nitrogen from the atmosphere and contributes to the nitrogen enrichment of the soil.

SALMONBERRY
Rubus spectabilis

Salmonberry, a shrub that grows up to 12 feet tall—though most are half that height—can form dense thickets that sometimes consist of cloned (genetically identical) plants. **Salmonberry** sport leaves with three leaflets, lovely red-pink flowers, and yellow-red, edible fruit that resemble raspberries. The plants are abundant along streams and in other wet areas. American Indians gathered the berries for food.

Near the top of the wood steps you see **yellow violet** *(Viola glabella)* with heart-shaped leaves and **yellow monkey-flower** *(Mimulus guttatus)*, which are common by seeps and streams. At the top of the steep steps, you reach a flat area with large Sitka spruce and an open understory composed primarily of **sword-fern** *(Polystichum munitum)* and **sorrel**. Take a right at the trail junction, marked by a wood post with a "13" on it.

You soon cross a wood boardwalk overshadowed by lots of **elderberry**. Large-leaved, tropical-looking **skunk cabbage** grow in a wet seep area left of the trail. Sometimes black bear eat this plant. And, in times of starvation, American Indians

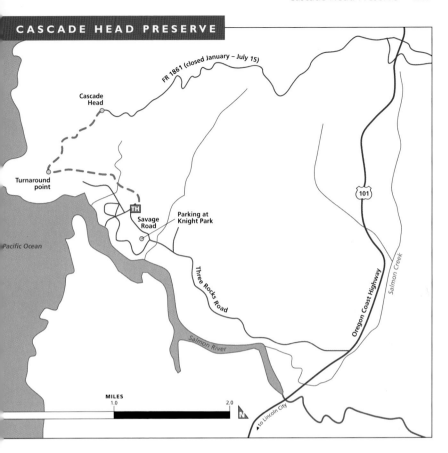

CASCADE HEAD PRESERVE

FR 1861 (closed January – July 15)

Cascade Head

Turnaround point

TH
Savage Road

Parking at Knight Park

Pacific Ocean

101

Three Rocks Road

Salmon River

Oregon Coast Highway

Salmon Creek

MILES
1.0   2.0
N
to Lincoln City

used to consume it—but only after cooking it to destroy the stinking chemical compound in the leaves. As you cross another bridge, look for a nurse log with dozens of small western hemlock on it.

After you cross two more boardwalk bridges, you meet a very large Sitka spruce at least 6 feet across. Loggers probably overlooked it due to its split top. The small meadow, marked with a "12" sign, is thick with **western buttercup** (*Ranunculus occidentalis*) and the inedible **wild cucumber** (*Marah oreganus*). When you re-enter the trees, **False lily-of-the-valley** (*Maianthemum dilatatum*) reign. Northwest tribes used this plant to cure sore eyes and other maladies.

You come to a trail junction marked by a sign that points across a small stream. Almost immediately, you see a sign that says "Leaving National Forest Land." You can hear the ocean from here, but you can't see it. The two round water towers off to the left are presumably for a housing development, just out of sight below the trail. Shrubs of **red huckleberry** (*Vaccinium parvifolium*), an edible fruit important to native people of the Pacific Northwest, are scattered here and there.

After crossing a wooden bridge over a creek, you can find **cow-parsnip** (*Heracleum lanatum*) growing under the **elderberry**. A member of the carrot family, **cow-parsnip** have large, umbrella-shaped clusters of small white flowers rising from huge, palmately lobed leaves. **Cow-parsnip** was sometimes called **Indian celery** because nearly all tribes consumed it (after peeling away the toxic outer skin).

This area offers very robust examples of **red elderberry**, some as much as 1–2 feet in diameter. You soon cross another "Leaving National Forest Land" sign and encounter **maidenhair fern** (*Adiantum pedatum*), **Pacific waterleaf** (*Hydrophyllum tenuipes*), and **yellow monkey-flower**, species all strongly associated with wet seeps and streamsides. You find **thimbleberry** (*Rubus parviflorus*) with their large, maplelike leaves, here as well.

Finally, you reach a sign declaring the entrance to the Nature Conservancy's Cascade Head Natural Area. Almost immediately, you break out of the trees and into the headland's meadows, rewarded with great views of the Salmon River and the ocean.

When I visited, I discovered elk tracks and elk beds amid the grasses. Living along the coast are Roosevelt elk, named after president Theodore Roosevelt, an avid hunter and conservationist. Roosevelt helped establish numerous national monuments, forests, and wildlife refuges during his tenure in office. I also saw quite a number of soaring birds, including several bald eagles, red-tailed hawks, and other raptors. The meadows here are covered with red fescue, wild rye, and Pacific reedgrass. Clumps of blue **lupine** (*Lupinus sp.*) and **buttercup** are scattered among the grasses.

The trail winds along open meadows, then descends into a gully lined by **alder** and **wild strawberry** (*Fragaria vesca*). A small stream flows beneath the gully, where an abundance of **cow-parsnip** and **candyflower** grows.

When you reach a wood post bearing a "7," you've reached a great vantage point overlooking Cascade Head itself. Pause to look for migrating gray whales during migration season, or just relax on the grasses. Wonderful views of Cascade Head are framed by the many **western buttercup**. A few **coast paintbrush**, common on coastal bluffs in Oregon, grow here. Many hikers turn around at this point, completing the first half of this 3.4-mile round-trip hike. You can also continue another 1.6 miles on a steep trail up the ridge to the upper trailhead.

Cooper Ridge

Rhododendron blooms in the understory along the
Cooper Ridge Trail, South Beach State Park.

Newport	**Nearest Town**
Rhododendrons and views of the ocean	**Highlights**
easy	**Trail Rating**
1.5 miles each way	**Trail Length**
South Beach State Park	**Location**
20–50 feet	**Elevation**
South Beach State Park, 503-867-4715	**Contact**
May to June	**Bloom Season**
Late May	**Peak Bloom**
This trail circles the campground at South Beach State Park, just south of Newport off US 101 (Oregon Coast Highway). The trailhead is found just to the right of the campground entrance, although many other access points from various parts of the campground permit shorter loops. Parking is across from the trailhead near the visitor center.	**Directions**

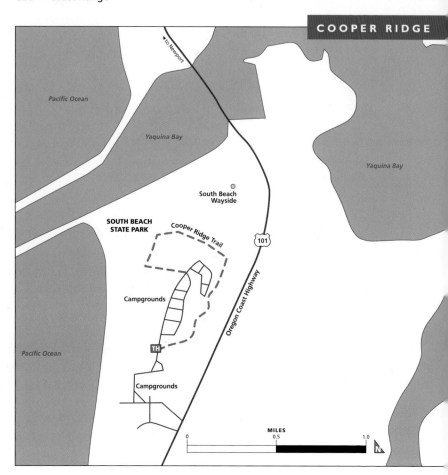

This trail takes you up and down the vegetated sand dune system around the South Beach State Park campground. As you follow the trail into a nearly-impenetrable tunnel of vegetation, you may feel like an elf wandering through a secret forest passageway. When the **rhododendron** *(Rhododendron sp.)* bloom, the hike is one of the more beautiful you'll experience in Oregon.

Just to the right of the entrance station, the hike strikes out, entering a forest of lodgepole pine. A hiker's campground is just off to the left. At this point, the trail is level and passes through **salal** *(Gaultheria shallon)* and **Scotch broom** *(Cytisus scoparius).* A member of the pea family, **Scotch broom** is an exotic from Europe that has invaded many coastal areas from California north to British Columbia.

Amid the ground cover you can find a low, trailing evergreen shrub called **kinnikinnick** *(Arctostaphylos uva-ursi).* Common shrubs on droughty, well-drained soils such as sand dunes, **kinnikinnick** feature small, urnlike, white and pink flowers. In the fall, the shrubs sport red berries, which inspire the other common name, **bearberry.**

A few small, scattered Sitka spruce are mixed in among the lodgepole pine (sometimes known as shore pine). Lodgepole pine needles are 1–2 inches long and grow in groups of two; Sitka spruce needles are sharp and pointed and surround the twig in a thick whorl. **Bracken fern** *(Pteridium aquilinum)* also line the trail.

The trail enters a tunnel of vegetation cut through the dense shrubs. Common here is **evergreen huckleberry** *(Vaccinium ovatum)*, the tallest of the native **huckleberry** species, which occasionally reaches heights of 12 feet or more. The leathery leaves are 1–2 inches long and have sharp, serrated edges that somewhat resemble holly. **Evergreen huckleberry's** sweet, juicy black berries appear in the late summer. You also see more **salal** with its large leathery leaves and small, urnlike flowers.

Soon the trail swings left and you pass through a wall of pink-flowered **Pacific rhododendron** *(Rhododendron macrophyllum)*. The Washington state flower, this shrub is very showy and grows to heights of more than 15 feet. Its waxy, evergreen leaves, which reduce water loss, are a great aid to growing in the sand dunes.

All the species here are adapted to droughty soils, even though they live in a place with an abundance of rain. The overstory consists mostly of lodgepole pine, but a few other species are mixed in. Just at the corner where the trail veers right and up a steep hill, a western hemlock tree stands. Small, soft needles, tiny cones, and drooping crown leaders characterize the tree.

The trail goes to the top of a hill, then jogs left and down. You then curve back to the left, and then back to the right and down again. At left, look for a small, waxy myrtlewood tree with its narrow 3–4 inch evergreen leaves.

PACIFIC RHODODENDRON
Rhododendron macrophyllum

Pacific rhododendron are among the most beautiful flowering shrubs found in Oregon. Their large clusters of pink blossoms brighten up forest stands beginning as early as May along the coast and progressively later in summer as one climbs in elevation in the western Cascades, reaching a peak in early July in the higher elevations. **Rhododendron** have thick, oblong, evergreen leaves often 4–6 inches long. The shrubs often grow in dense stands and may reach heights of nearly 20 feet. Very resilient, **rhododendron** can sprout from their roots if burned or cut.

The trail rolls along, passing a myrtlewood right in the middle of the trail and several Douglas fir. Douglas fir cones have three-prong scales that look something like the two hind legs of a mouse with a short tail.

At the top of a hill, you encounter quite a few **manzanita** *(Arctostaphylos columbiana)*, another evergreen shrub. **Manzanita** have small, urnlike flowers as well, but blood-red crooked stems. As the trail winds around on top of the ancient dunes, you hear the ocean breaking on the shore about 0.5 mile away. You may hear a distant foghorn from Yaquina Lighthouse as well.

You top out on a knoll with a view of the campground and ocean. When you reach a trail junction, you can cut the hike short by taking the short side trail on your left down to the campground. Or, you can continue on the hike by staying to the right, past the G loop of the campground. Several more trails cut back to the campground; at each junction, stay right.

If you continue, the trail winds up and down small hills, and eventually reaches a point where you can see a dirt road to the right. This marks the northern edge of the park. After hiking along the ridge for some distance, the trail descends past a 2-foot-diameter Douglas fir, then spills out into a flat covered with more lodgepole pine. Just opposite a bench on the flat, look for **false lily-of-the-valley** *(Maianthemum dilatatum)*. You will also pass **red alder** *(Alnus rubra)*, a deciduous tree with smooth whitish-gray bark.

About 100 yards beyond the wood bench, the trail curves left and enters a meadow area filled with rye grass, **Scotch broom**, and **kinnikinnick**. You soon find three trail signs that lead you up a hill to another wooden bench surrounded by large Sitka spruce. This area, awash in **false lily-of-the-valley**, affords a great view of the ocean and jetty. From here, the trail winds along the ridge, passing more Sitka spruce. Eventually, you come to the paved Jetty Trail. To get back to the campground, go left. From the campground, walk back to the entrance to return to your vehicle.

Harris Ranch Trail

An old-growth Douglas fir on the Harris Ranch Trail.

Waldport	**Nearest Town**
Forested wilderness setting with lots of old-growth forest	**Highlights**
moderate	**Trail Rating**
6.4 miles round-trip	**Trail Length**
Drift Creek Wilderness	**Location**
140–1,380 feet	**Elevation**
Siuslaw National Forest, 541-750-7000	**Contact**
April to July	**Bloom Season**
May to June	**Peak Bloom**
From Corvallis, take OR 34 (Alsea Highway) west 57 miles (from Waldport, drive east 6.9 miles). Just before crossing a bridge over the Alsea River, turn north on Risley Creek Road (FR 3446). It's narrow but paved. Following the main road, drive 4.1 miles to gravel FR 3464 and turn left (the sign is almost obscured by plants, so watch carefully for this turn). Take this road one mile to a new parking area, some distance from the wilderness boundary and the old parking area.	**Directions**

The Drift Creek Wilderness covers less than 6,000 acres yet represents the largest unlogged tract of mature forest in the Coast Range. In 1984, the Oregon Wilderness Act granted protection to the area. The Harris Ranch Trail takes you down through a beautiful, mature forest to Drift Creek, a medium-size stream in the wilderness. The creek supports runs of chinook, coho, steelhead, and sea-run cutthroat trout. I also saw rough-skinned newts in shallow pools along the creek. If you're interested in camping, several flat, creek-side campsites and a large meadow are adjacent to Drift Creek.

The hike down to the creek isn't bad, but the climb back up does gain more than 1,200 feet. If you're referring to other hiking guides for directions to the Harris Ranch Trail, bear in mind that a new trailhead was constructed in 2000. The directions to the trailhead from the highway remain the same, but the parking area is now farther east on the ridge, adding more than a mile to the total round-trip hiking distance. Large boulders now prevent ORVs from using the old access road. Park in the lot and start down the old road.

(*Note:* For those who have done a shuttle first, you can ford the stream in low water and continue up the Horse Creek Trail to a trailhead on the northern side of the canyon, making for a longer hike. The best old-growth stands are along the Horse Creek Trail.)

Notice, as you walk, the leathery-leaved evergreen **salal** *(Gaultheria shallon)* with its white, urnlike flowers. You find several other fruit producers, **salmonberry** *(Rubus spectabilis),* **red huckleberry** *(Vaccinium parvifolium),* and **thimbleberry** *(Rubus parviflorus)* among them, growing along this trail. American Indians harvested all of these more-or-less edible berries.

The easily recognizable **thimbleberry** has beautiful white flowers, large, maplelike leaves and red, thimble-shaped berries later in summer. Another berry producer here is **trailing blackberry** *(Rubus ursinus),* which is common in the open areas adjacent to the road and the only blackberry native to the Pacific Northwest.

Also watch for evidence of elk, including tracks and trails. The overstory forest includes western hemlock, **red alder** *(Alnus rubra)*, and western red cedar. **Sword-fern** *(Polystichum munitum)* is common under the forest, along with patches of cloverlike **sorrel** *(Oxalis oregana)*. In wetter areas with seeps, you find **yellow monkey-flower** *(Mimulus guttatus).*

As the road begins to descend and bends to the left, look up the slope to find a small patch of **devil's club** *(Oplopanax horridum)*. The plant, which derives its name from the poisonous spines that cover its stalk, has huge maplelike leaves and grows up to 10 feet tall. Along the road and on the adjacent slopes you discover **candyflower** *(Claytonia sibirica)* with its opposite heart-shaped stem leaves and **Pacific bleedingheart** *(Dicentra formosa)*.

Eventually you reach the former parking area. A sign for "Harris Ranch Trail—Drift Creek 2 miles" marks the entrance to the forest. Upon entering

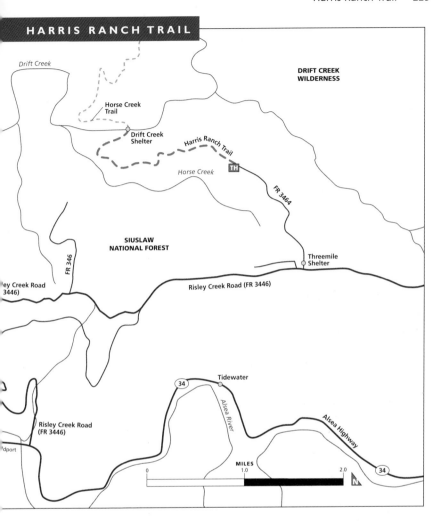

HARRIS RANCH TRAIL

Drift Creek

DRIFT CREEK
WILDERNESS

Horse Creek
Trail

Drift Creek
Shelter

Harris Ranch Trail

TH

FR 3464

Horse Creek

SIUSLAW
NATIONAL FOREST

FR 346

Threemile
Shelter

ey Creek Road
3446)

Risley Creek Road (FR 3446)

Tidewater

34

Alsea River

Alsea Highway

Risley Creek Road
(FR 3446)

dport

MILES
1.0   2.0

0   34

this forest, you will notice a difference from others—this is virgin forest, mostly western hemlock, and the larger-than-average trees tower above you. On the ground is an abundance of old, partially-rotted logs and numerous snags.

You encounter flowering plants such as **red huckleberry** *(Vaccinium parvifolium),* which often grow directly from the top of snags, along with the evergreen, hollylike **Oregon grape** *(Mahonia nervosa),* **evergreen huckleberry** *(Vaccinium ovatum),* **false lily-of-the-valley** *(Maianthemum dilatatum),* **salal**, and **false azalea** *(Menziesia ferruginea).*

As you move down the trail, you can see scattered western red cedar with their characteristic delicate, lacy boughs. Common in the understory are **lady-fern** *(Athyrium filix-femina)* and **deer-fern** *(Blechnum spicant).* Here and there you can spot **red elderberry** *(Sambucus racemosa),* shrubs with creamy-white spikes of flowers that can grow up to 20 feet tall. An **elderberry** is very conspicuous at the first switchback.

As you descend the second switchback, watch for more **elderberry, false azalea, salmonberry, thimbleberry, vine maple** *(Acer circinatum)*, a few small patches of **devil's club,** and other shrubs of the forest understory. **Vine maple** also flourish here. They are especially lovely in early spring when the leaves are lime-green, and in the autumn when the leaves turn a rich, fire-engine red, augmenting the fall color of the forest. American Indians often used **vine maple** for the frames of snowshoes, drum hoops, and other implements.

You cross a spring that fosters a lush growth of **skunk cabbage** *(Lysichitum americanum),* a plant unlike any other you will encounter. **Skunk cabbage's** huge leaves—up to 3 feet long—lend it an almost tropical appearance. In the spring, a bright yellow hood on a thick, fleshy spike surrounds its flower. American Indians of the Northwest occasionally ate **skunk cabbage** roots and leaves, but the plant was considered a food of last resort in times of famine.

As the trail eventually goes back on the ridge, it becomes crowded with **salmonberry.** Moss-draped maple give the entire forest a lime-green light. As you hike, notice that some of the larger snags have fire scars. Surprisingly, prior to the large-scale logging of the Coast Range, fire was the major factor in creating forest stand diversity. Given the wet climate, fires were relatively rare, but every couple hundred years a sufficient summer drought —paired with lightning strikes—caused these woods to burn. Large fires often consumed tens of thousands and sometimes hundreds of thousands of acres.

The fourth switchback cuts down to the creek. Along this stretch of trail, you pass some very large old-growth Douglas fir. Some particularly large fir inhabit a spot just after a small spring. Note the thick, corky bark on these trees,

PACIFIC BLEEDINGHEART
Dicentra formosa

Each **Pacific bleedingheart** stem bears a cluster of 5–15 pink-purple, heart-shaped flowers. The leaves are finely dissected and fernlike. Since it spreads through rhizomes, the plant forms almost unbroken patches in damp forests, stream banks, and other moist sites. The Latin *formosa* means "well formed" or "good looking."

which protects them from the lightning fires that sometimes kill younger trees. Douglas fir don't grow in shade, and nearly all Douglas fir in the Coast Range sprouted in the aftermath of major fires.

As you approach the creek, you encounter a few Sitka spruce. A coastal species, Sitka spruce never grow very far from the ocean. Northern California marks the spruce's southern limits, and the trees become more and more common as you proceed north. In Alaska, Sitka spruce is one of the major coastal tree species.

The trail eventually spills out into a small meadow where the Harris family once homesteaded. A small bridge crosses a wet area where you find **blackberry bramble** *(Rubus sp.)* and **cow-parsnip** *(Heracleum lanatum)*. **Cow-parsnip**, a member of the celery family, has thick, tall shoots (up to 6 feet) that are hollow like those of the vegetable. This meadow also hosts **stinging nettles** *(Urtica dioica),* which can cause a painful rash. When the nettles sting you, tiny hairs inject formic acid into the wounds. Needless to say, it's best to avoid this plant!

After crossing the meadow, you come to a flat area with numerous campsites scattered among the trees adjacent to the creek. Overhung by bigleaf maple, **red alder**, and conifers such as western hemlock, the creek is placid with small runs flowing over smooth ledges. A large, rocky ledge near the campsites makes for a great picnic spot. **Cow-parsnip** and **star-flowered false Solomon's seal** *(Smilacina stellata)* grow along the creek. If you look carefully, you may spot some of the resident cutthroat trout that inhabit the creek. I also observed crayfish crawling among the rocks.

The creek makes a good turnaround point, but be prepared for the uphill climb back to the trailhead.

Wildflower Hike 49 *Mary's Peak Loop*

Penstemon and paintbrush cover the summit of Mary's Peak.

At 4,097 feet, Mary's Peak has the highest summit in the Oregon Coast Range. The peak affords outstanding views of the entire Willamette Valley and the Cascades, plus the surrounding logged-over Coast Range. The summit area boasts a series of meadows and the only noble fir stands in the Coast Range. This part of Siuslaw National Forest is a designated botanical area.

From the large parking lot near the peak's summit, you can choose from several trails. The Summit Trail described here makes for the best wildflower hike. The first part of the trail, an old road, leaves the parking area and climbs uphill through meadows dominated by various grasses. Flowers are scattered in and among the grasses.

Nearest Town	Corvallis
Highlights	High-elevation meadows and old-growth noble fir along with fantastic views
Trail Rating	moderate
Trail Length	1.6-mile loop hike
Location	Siuslaw National Forest
Elevation	4,097 feet
Contact	Alsea Ranger District, Siuslaw National Forest, 541-750-7000
Bloom Season	May to August
Peak Bloom	July
Directions	From Corvallis, take OR 34 (Alsea Highway) west about 15 miles to FR 30 (Mary's Peak Road) and turn right. Drive uphill about 9.6 miles to the turnoff for FR 3010. Turn right and follow FR 3010 to the trailhead.

As soon as you strike out on the trail, you can see the purple-flowered **Cascade penstemon** *(Penstemon serrulatus)*. Several **penstemon** species flourish on the peak; all have blue to purple flowers. Just around the trailhead you also find **field chickweed** *(Cerastium arvense)*, **yarrow** *(Achillea millefolium)*, and lots of **dock** *(Rumex occidentalis)*. **Dock** has a reddish spike and inconspicuous, tiny green flowers. Look closely also for two small violets: **round-leaved violet** *(Viola orbiculata)* and **early blue violet** *(Viola adunca)*.

Oxeye daisy *(Leucanthemum vulgare)*, a white-flowered, introduced species, is scattered along the path. This daisy often invades disturbed areas, hence its abundance along the margin of the path. The meadows have extensive stands of **bracken fern** *(Pteridium aquilinum)*, which spread from rhizomes on their roots. Since the deep roots allow these ferns to survive fires, the species tends to increase in areas where fires are frequent. The orange blooms of **tiger lily** *(Lilium columbianum)* poke up among the grasses. Although **tiger lily** are not common in most places, they thrive on Mary's Peak.

About 0.25 mile from the trailhead, you reach a small tree island of firs. More **early blue violet** grow near the trees, plus **star-flowered false Solomon's seal** *(Smilacina stellata)*, a member of the lily family.

As you follow the old road up the slope, you find **Davidson's penstemon** *(Penstemon davidsonii)* growing in low mats in the roadcut at left. Just before reaching the junction for Meadow Crest Trail, a single **beargrass** *(Xerophyllum* *tenax)* plant grows, sporting a showy, fragrant white cluster of flowers. I found only one **beargrass** plant growing here, although the species is common in higher elevations in the Cascades.

At the trail junction, continue on the old road up to the summit. You can also turn right and take Meadow Edge Trail to the summit, as I did. You immediately see more **star-flowered false Solomon's seal** and then enter an old-growth noble fir forest with magnificent and inspiring trees. Under the fir you can find almost no ground cover save for a few **oak-fern** *(Gymnocarpium dryopteris).* The lower trunks of many of the trees are curved here, because the saturated soils in this high-precipitation area slide downslope, causing the trees to compensate by curving upward.

As you move out of the trees into another meadow, you encounter a lot of **lupine** *(Lupinus sp.).* The many different species of **lupine** all have blue pealike flowers and palmate leaflets. **Senecio** *(Senecio triangularis)* abound in this meadow, their large, triangular, sawtooth-edged leaves making this flower relatively easy to identify.

Moving upslope, the **senecio** give way to **bracken fern, tiger lily,** and **round-leaved violet.** Eventually the trail tops out at the summit and reunites with the old road. You can see **spring gold** *(Lomatium utriculatum),* a member of the carrot family adapted to drier soils, and small **lupine,** which cover the summit in a cloud of blue flowers.

The slope is decorated with a quilt of multicolored blooms, including **red Indian-paintbrush** *(Castilleja miniata),* **Davidson's penstemon,** a couple kinds of **lupine, spreading phlox** *(Phlox diffusa),* and a few **cliff larkspur** *(Delphinium menziesii).* Yellow **wallflower** *(Erysimum asperum)* grow on the meadow above the slope.

TIGER LILY
Lilium columbianum

Tiger lily's bright orange flowers hang downward, and the narrow, lance-shaped leaves are typically arranged in whorls. Purple or reddish spots cover the petals, which curve backwards. The bulbs, since they had a peppery taste, were generally used for seasoning by Indian tribes. **Tiger lily** typically grow here and there in forested meadows, but on Mary's Peak they are especially thick, in patches of orange blossoms.

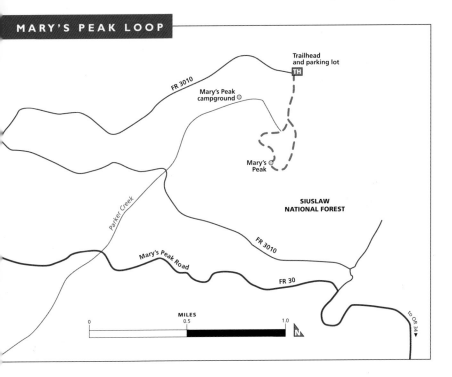

If you follow the old road downhill as it curves around the mountain to the south, you will reach a rock-garden habitat with more **paintbrush, catchfly** *(Silene douglasii),* **chickweed, penstemon,** and other flowers that favor gravelly, rocky soils.

As the road slopes around the east side of the summit, you'll spot a lush growth of **Oregon sunshine** *(Eriophyllum lanatum),* a showy, sunflowerlike plant. Along the roadcut grow more **paintbrush, lupine, yarrow, dock,** and **phlox.** The old road descends past more noble fir and curves back around toward the trailhead.

Wildflower Hike 50 # Sutton Creek Trail

Near the mouth of Sutton Creek with a view of the dunes, Sutton Recreation Area.

Nearest Town	Florence
Highlights	Plenty of rhododendron and coastal forest to ocean views
Trail Rating	moderate
Trail Length	6.0 miles round-trip
Location	Sutton Recreation Area
Elevation	sea level
Contact	Siuslaw National Forest, 541-750-7000
Bloom Season	April to June
Peak Bloom	June
Directions	From Florence, drive north 6.0 miles on US 101 to signs for the Siuslaw National Forest Sutton campground. Turn left onto the road with a sign for Holman Vista and follow signs to the Dune Lake parking area.

A number of potential hikes, including short loop hikes and longer out-and-back hikes, cover the Sutton Creek area. The hike from Dune Lake to the Holman Vista, for one, affords a nice overview of the area. The Sutton Creek Trail gently rolls up and down the terrain as it traverses sand dunes along the coast. The trail passes through a variety of habitats, from old-growth forest to semi-open parks, and the **Pacific rhododendron** *(Rhododendron macrophyllum)* blooms are particularly spectacular in May and early June. Waterproof footwear is advisable for these hikes. The Sutton Creek Trail begins and ends at different parking areas, so with a shuttle it's possible to cut the length of this hike in half. This hike starts from the Dune Lake trailhead.

The trail begins adjacent to the restrooms, and within 0.25 mile you enter a tunnel into a Douglas fir–lodgepole pine forest. **Pacific rhododendron, evergreen huckleberry** *(Vaccinium ovatum)*, and **salal** *(Gaultheria shallon)* shrubs, all evergreens, line the trail. The leathery leaves of these species reduce water loss, an important survival mechanism on the droughty sand soils.

You ascend an old, partially forested dune and follow its ridge for a short ways. The well-drained sand provides ideal habitat for caribou moss lichen and **false lily-of-the-valley** *(Maianthemum dilatatum)*. In 0.25 mile or so, you come off the dune into an open, parklike area of scattered lodgepole pine, also known as shore pine. It's easy to stray off the trail in this area, so watch for the wood posts that mark the main pathway. In April, exotic **Scotch broom** *(Cytisus scoparius)* dominate the area, their pealike flowers turning the shrubs a golden yellow.

On the well-drained sand, you find **kinnikinnick** *(Arctostaphylos uva-ursi)*, a species with evergreen leaves and, in the autumn, bright red berries. Found commonly on well-drained sites from here all the way north to the Arctic, the **kinnikinnick**, mixed with caribou moss, lend an Alaskan feel to the area.

The trail is fairly level for the next 0.25 mile. When I visited in May, I was continuously entertained by the buzzing of hummingbirds. In these sandy soils you can find **manzanita** *(Arctostaphylos columbiana),* which in Spanish means "little apple." **Manzanita** have evergreen leaves; small, white-pink, urnlike flowers; a twisted, shrubby shape; and the bark of mature shrubs is blood red.

Knobcone pine, a very unusual species for the area, are scattered here and there. Knobcone pine's needles grow in groups of three, and the cones are attached in tight clusters to the main trunk of the tree. Known as a closed-cone species, this tree typically sheds its seeds only after a fire has heated the cones. Although knobcone are distributed throughout California's coastal ranges and into southwest Oregon, this location is about as far north as they go.

After passing through the open landscape, you enter dense forest again. Several low points in the trail are often filled with water, difficult to avoid since the coastal forest and understory vegetation is so dense. You almost have to wade through the puddles.

At 0.5 mile, the trail emerges from the forest and passes into an open area at a signed trail junction. If you go left, you can hike back to the Sutton Creek campground. Go right at the sign and follow the trail up an old dune that contains scattered western hemlock and Douglas fir with an understory of **salal** and **evergreen huckleberry**. The trail follows the top of the dune, which affords awesome views of Cape Mountain in the Coast Range. At this point you can sometimes hear the sounds of ocean surf.

The first Sitka spruce of the hike graces this area. A common coastal tree species, Sitka spruce's normal range extends from northern California all the way to Kodiak Island in Alaska. You can identify Sitka spruce by its stiff needles—if it hurts to grab a branchlet, it's probably a spruce.

The dunes in this area are densely covered with the matlike **broadleaf lupine** *(Lupinus latifolius)*. The palmate, compound leaves, finely haired stems, and dense whorl of pealike, blue-white blossoms readily identify this flower. **Lupine** is named after the Latin for "wolf." At one time, these plants were thought to destroy the soil. But like most members of the pea family, **lupine** are nitrogen fixers, which add nitrogen to and actually enrich the soil. Here you also see another member of the pea family, **gorse** *(Ulex europaeus)*. This introduced exotic, which is covered with spines, has green branches and yellow, pealike flowers.

After 0.25 mile, you leave the dunes and enter a forest of lodgepole pine. The understory consists of **salal, evergreen huckleberry, manzanita**, lots of **rhododendron,** and an occasional myrtlewood tree. The trail rolls up and down until you cross a bridge

SALAL
Gaultheria shallon

Salal blossoms, urn-shaped and hanging in one direction, somewhat resemble huckleberry flowers. The evergreen leaves are egg-shaped, thick, and leathery. The black-blue berries that appear in autumn were an important food source for coastal American Indians. One of the most common understory plants in the region, **salal** grow in the Coast Range and on the western slope of the Cascades. David Douglas brought the seeds of this plant back to England and grew it as an ornamental shrub.

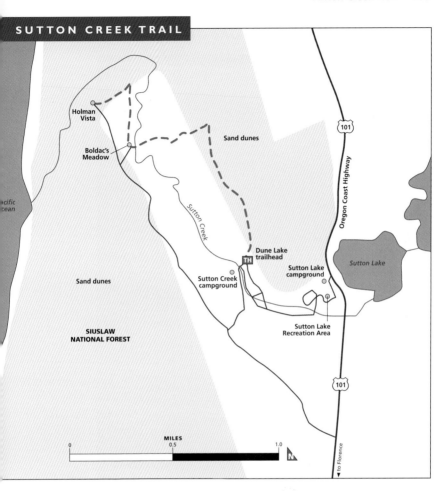

SUTTON CREEK TRAIL

Holman
Vista

Boldac's
Meadow

Sand dunes

Sutton Creek

Pacific
Ocean

Oregon Coast Highway

101

Dune Lake
trailhead
TH

Sutton Lake
campground

Sutton Lake

Sand dunes

Sutton Creek
campground

SIUSLAW
NATIONAL FOREST

Sutton Lake
Recreation Area

101

MILES
0   0.5   1.0   N

▼ to Florence

over Sutton Creek into a small meadow. In the 1930s, this was the home of
Boldac's Meadow resort. No traces of the resort remain, but a historical sign
describes the 14 rooms and nine guest cabins. Sutton Creek boasts runs of
coastal cutthroat trout.

After pondering the resort and its demise, head to the right (north). In
100 yards or so, you come to a trail junction. Both trails take you to the same
location, the Holman Vista; I describe the trail to the left. This trail climbs up
a forested dune to the ridge top and then passes through a forest of Sitka spruce
with a dense understory of **salal, evergreen huckleberry,** and **rhododendron.**
Follow this 0.25 mile or so until you come to the parking lot for Holman Vista.
Hike another 300 yards up the trail for spectacular views of the ocean across
the dunes along Sutton Creek. From this point, retrace your steps back to the
Dune Lake parking lot.

*Wildflower
Hike 51* Sweet Creek

*Upper Sweet
Creek Falls and
pool in Siuslaw
National Forest.*

Sweet Creek tumbles through a mossy, forested valley and down numerous waterfalls. The stream, which hosts steelhead and salmon runs in summer, flows through large, mature forests full of western red cedar, western hemlock, Douglas fir, bigleaf maple, and **red alder** *(Alnus rubra)*. The area was logged selectively about 100 years ago, and although the forest has grown back, you can still find old stumps with their springboard slots.

Departing from the parking lot, you will discover **yellow violet** *(Viola glabella)*, **western bittercress** *(Cardamine occidentalis)*, and **candyflower** *(Claytonia sibirica)*. Also growing in abundance here are **trillium** *(Trillium ovatum)* and **sorrel** *(Oxalis oregana)*, along with **false lily-of-the-valley**

Nearest Town	Mapleton
Highlights	Many waterfalls and an opportunity to see pink fawn-lily, an endemic Coast Range species
Trail Rating	moderate
Trail Length	3.0 miles round-trip
Location	Sweet Creek, Coast Range
Elevation	400 feet
Contact	Siuslaw National Forest, 541-750-7000
Bloom Season	March to June
Peak Bloom	May
Directions	From Eugene/Springfield, take OR 126 west toward Florence. Just past the Siuslaw River Bridge in Mapleton, turn left onto Sweet Creek Road. Travel 11.0 miles to the well-signed trailhead and parking area.

(Maianthemum dilatatum), **red huckleberry** *(Vaccinium parvifolium)*, and **salmonberry** *(Rubus spectabilis).* All along the path, you can encounter small groups of **pink fawn-lily** *(Erythronium revolutum).*

Immediately after the first bridge, look for a **Pacific bleedingheart** *(Dicentra formosa)* among the **false lily-of-the-valley, salmonberry, sword-fern** *(Polystichum munitum),* **salal** *(Gaultheria shallon),* **pink fawn-lily**, and Douglas fir. Just up from the falls, you can also see more **trillium.**

Merten's saxifrage *(Saxifraga mertensiana)* grow by rocks near the falls just before the steel bridge.

PINK FAWN-LILY
Erythronium revolutum

Pink fawn-lily, found only along the coast in Oregon, grow from a corm. The basal green leaves are somewhat mottled with white, and the rose-pink flowers droop from the stem. Northwest Indians sometimes consumed the edible bulbs.

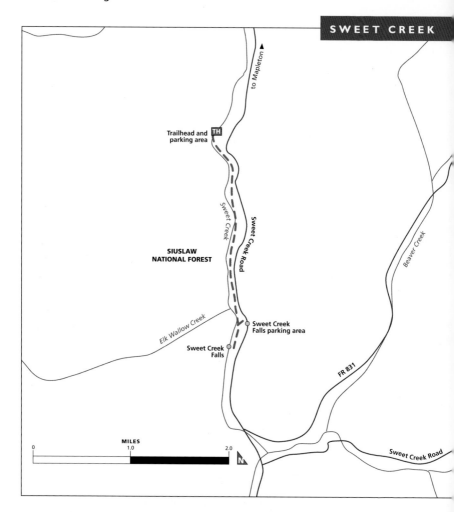

As you cross the steel bridge, watch for both **sorrel** and **youth-on-age** *(Tolmiea menziesii),* sometimes called **piggyback plant.** On the cliff, look for **chickweed monkey-flower** *(Mimulus alsinoides).*

Hemlock trees, **maidenhair fern** *(Adiantum pedatum),* **candyflower, false lily-of-the-valley,** and **false Solomon's seal** *(Smilacina racemosa)* appear just after the bridge. Here also keep an eye out for **Smith's fairybell** *(Disporum smithii),* their smooth stems and leaves distinguishing them from the **Hooker fairy-bell** *(Disporum hookeri).*

Fetid adder's-tongue *(Scoliopus bigelovii)* grow just past a small stream on the left. You can recognize this member of the lily family by its purple, mottled leaves and grayish-yellow flowers. The flower's scent of rotting flesh gave rise to the common name, **fetid adder's tongue**. In this dense forest I heard the call of the varied thrush and the winter wren, both common species in these coastal forests.

As the trail crosses a second metal bridge, you're treated to more **yellow violet** plus a good view of Annice Falls. Note the large leaves of **skunk cabbage** *(Lysichitum americanum)* in the seep just after the bridge. Along the creek, you can spot the whitish-gray bark of **red alder** *(Alnus rubra),* a tree that typically colonizes logged sites and other disturbed habitats. As you move along the trail, you encounter more **false lily-of-the-valley, pink fawn-lily**, and thick stands of **salmonberry.**

When you reach a trail junction with a sign for Sweet Creek Falls, turn right to see the falls. Be sure to read the sign describing springboards: In the days before chain saws, loggers used springboards to save themselves the chore of cutting through the swollen base of larger trees. They cut notches in a tree, inserted boards as a working platform, then stood on the platform and cut the tree above it.

A gorgeous, double cascading falls with a plunge pool below marks the end of the trail. After admiring the pool, retrace your steps back to the parking lot.

APPENDIX A: *Hikes by Elevation*

A hike's elevation can serve as a general guide to both peak bloom season (also see individual hikes for estimated peak bloom times) and to snow-free accessibility. As a rule, flowers at low elevations in Oregon bloom from about March to June; mid-elevation flowers from about May to July; and high-elevation flowers from about mid-July to early September. Bear in mind that these bloom times can vary as much as a month either way from year to year depending upon snowfall, temperatures, proximity to the ocean, location of flowers on north- or south-facing slopes or in milder micro-climates, and other factors. In this list, an asterisk (*) indicates hikes that generally have earlier or later accessibility or peak bloom than others at similar elevations.

Low-Elevation Hikes
(Sea Level to 1,500 Feet)

COLUMBIA GORGE
1. Dalles Mountain Ranch
2. Catherine Creek
3. Hamilton Mountain
4. Dog Mountain
6. Plateau Trail
7. Eagle Creek

CASCADE RANGE
16. Trail of Ten Falls Loop
28. Delta Old-Growth Trail Loop
34. North Bank Deer Preserve

WILLAMETTE VALLEY
38. Maple Ridge Loop
39. Pioneer School/Willamette River Loop
40. Mount Baldy
41. Mill Hill Loop
42. Willow Creek Preserve
43. Meadow Road/Water Garden Trail
44. West Summit Trail

COAST RANGE
45. Cape Lookout
46. Cascade Head Preserve
47. Cooper Ridge
48. Harris Ranch Trail
50. Sutton Creek Trail
51. Sweet Creek

Mid-Elevation Hikes
(1,500 to 4,000 Feet)

COLUMBIA GORGE
5. Silver Star Mountain

CASCADE RANGE
8. Lost Lake Old-Growth Trail
15. Table Rock
17. Elk Lake Creek
18. Middle Santiam
19. House Rock Loop
26. Lookout Creek
27. Horse Rock Ridge
*29. Castle Rock
33. Tire Mountain
35. Pine Bench
36. Proxy Falls Loop

COAST RANGE
*49. Mary's Peak Loop

High-Elevation Hikes
(4,000 Feet to Timberline near 7,000 Feet)

CASCADE RANGE
9. Vista Ridge
10. Cooper Spur
11. Elk Meadows
12. Lookout Mountain
13. Trillium Lake Loop
14. Timberline Trail
20. Iron Mountain/Cone Peak
21. Crescent Mountain
*22. Browder Ridge
23. Patjens Lakes Loop
24. Canyon Creek Meadows
*25. Tidbits Mountain
*30. Lowder Mountain Trail
31. Erma Bell Lakes
*32. Lone Wolf Shelter
37. Hand Lake Trail

APPENDIX B: *Hikes by Difficulty*

This list serves as a quick reference for estimated difficulty levels of the hikes in this book. Please note these are subjective ratings—one person's leisurely hike may be another's marathon trek. Check elevation ranges and trail lengths for particular hikes to help you gauge the effort required, but keep in mind that listed elevations better describe bloom seasons than needed fitness levels. You may like to try a few to assess your own level; most of all, enjoy the experience!

Easy Hikes

COLUMBIA GORGE
2. Catherine Creek
6. Plateau Trail

CASCADE RANGE
8. Lost Lake Old-Growth Trail
13. Trillium Lake Loop
19. House Rock Loop
28. Delta Old-Growth Trail Loop
31. Erma Bell Lakes
32. Lone Wolf Shelter
36. Proxy Falls Loop
37. Hand Lake Trail

WILLAMETTE VALLEY
38. Maple Ridge Loop
39. Pioneer School/Willamette River Loop
40. Mount Baldy
41. Mill Hill Loop
42. Willow Creek Preserve
43. Meadow Road/Water Garden Trail

COAST RANGE
47. Cooper Ridge

Difficult Hikes

COLUMBIA GORGE
4. Dog Mountain

CASCADE RANGE
9. Vista Ridge
20. Iron Mountain/Cone Peak
21. Crescent Mountain

Moderate Hikes

COLUMBIA GORGE
1. Dalles Mountain Ranch
3. Hamilton Mountain
5. Silver Star Mountain
7. Eagle Creek

CASCADE RANGE
10. Cooper Spur
11. Elk Meadows
12. Lookout Mountain
14. Timberline Trail
15. Table Rock
16. Trail of Ten Falls Loop
17. Elk Lake Creek
18. Middle Santiam
22. Browder Ridge
23. Patjens Lakes Loop
24. Canyon Creek Meadows
25. Tidbits Mountain
26. Lookout Creek
27. Horse Rock Ridge
29. Castle Rock
30. Lowder Mountain Trail
33. Tire Mountain
34. North Bank Deer Preserve
35. Pine Bench

WILLAMETTE VALLEY
44. West Summit Trail

COAST RANGE
45. Cape Lookout
46. Cascade Head Preserve
48. Harris Ranch Trail
49. Mary's Peak Loop
50. Sutton Creek Trail
51. Sweet Creek

APPENDIX C: *Contact Phone Numbers*

Please note that phone numbers change frequently. Check with information for the most current number if a number listed is no longer in service. To contact a specific ranger district, first contact the National Forest that it's in.

BLM, Oregon State Office 503-952-6024
   Eugene District Office 541-683-6600
   Roseburg District Office 541-440-4930
   Salmon District Office 503-375-5646

Champoeg State Heritage Area 503-678-1251

Columbia Gorge River National Scenic Area 541-386-2333

Deschutes National Forest 541-388-2715

Gifford Pinchot National Forest, Washington ... 360-891-5000

Horsethief Lake State Park, Washington 509-767-1159

Lane County Parks 541-341-6940

Mount Hood National Forest 503-666-0700

Mount Pisgah Arboretum,
   Howard Buford Recreation Area 541-682-6940

The Nature Conservancy, Oregon State Office ... 503-228-9561

Oregon State Parks 503-378-6305

Silver Falls State Park 503-873-3495

Siuslaw National Forest 541-750-7000

South Beach State Park 503-867-4715

Tryon Creek State Park 503-653-3166

Umpqua National Forest 541-672-6601

U.S. Fish and Wildlife Service 503-231-6828

Washington State Parks 360-753-5755

Willamette National Forest 541-465-6521

William L. Finley National Wildlife Refuge 541-757-7236

Index

NOTE: Citations followed by the letter "p" denote photos.

George Wuerthner

An ecologist, writer, and photographer, George is the author of
24 books, including two previous Westcliffe publications, *California
Wilderness Areas, Volumes 1* and *2,* as well as the forthcoming *Oregon
Wilderness Areas.* He has traveled widely throughout the West and
currently lives in Eugene with his wife and two children.